MW00440113

# Contracting in the New Economy

Norm and Marcia —
Nancy and I greatly value
and cherish our relationship
with you and your family,
serving as an inspiration
in so many ways!

In Him,
Jim

David Frydlinger · Kate Vitasek ·
Jim Bergman · Tim Cummins

# Contracting in the New Economy

## Using Relational Contracts to Boost Trust and Collaboration in Strategic Business Relationships

David Frydlinger
Cirio Law Firm
Stockholm, Sweden

Kate Vitasek
University of Tennessee at Knoxville
Knoxville, TN, USA

Jim Bergman
Commercial Officers Group, Inc
Westminster, CO, USA

Tim Cummins
World Commerce & Contracting
Petersfield, UK

ISBN 978-3-030-65098-8      ISBN 978-3-030-65099-5   (eBook)
https://doi.org/10.1007/978-3-030-65099-5

© The Editor(s) (if applicable) and The Author(s), under exclusive licence to Springer Nature Switzerland AG 2021
This work is subject to copyright. All rights are solely and exclusively licensed by the Publisher, whether the whole or part of the material is concerned, specifically the rights of translation, reprinting, reuse of illustrations, recitation, broadcasting, reproduction on microfilms or in any other physical way, and transmission or information storage and retrieval, electronic adaptation, computer software, or by similar or dissimilar methodology now known or hereafter developed.
The use of general descriptive names, registered names, trademarks, service marks, etc. in this publication does not imply, even in the absence of a specific statement, that such names are exempt from the relevant protective laws and regulations and therefore free for general use.
The publisher, the authors and the editors are safe to assume that the advice and information in this book are believed to be true and accurate at the date of publication. Neither the publisher nor the authors or the editors give a warranty, expressed or implied, with respect to the material contained herein or for any errors or omissions that may have been made. The publisher remains neutral with regard to jurisdictional claims in published maps and institutional affiliations.

Cover designed by Elizabeth Kanna and Kate Vitasek

This Palgrave Macmillan imprint is published by the registered company Springer Nature Switzerland AG
The registered company address is: Gewerbestrasse 11, 6330 Cham, Switzerland

*We would like to dedicate this book
to all of the individuals and organizations that have the courage
to embrace relational contracting in the new economy.*

# Foreword

In December 2016, I was in Stockholm for Nobel Week, an amazing experience, after being lucky enough to receive the Nobel Prize for Economics for my work on contracts. During that week, I was invited to many unofficial as well as official events, too many to accept. But one that piqued my interest was from a Swedish law firm that wanted to hear about my work, and I said yes. My inviter and host was David Frydlinger. We hit it off right away and it soon became apparent that David was particularly taken by my recent work, where I had emphasized the importance of fairness and reasonable behavior in ensuring good contractual outcomes. In turn, I was excited to discover that David was advising clients to embrace similar notions in their contracts. Soon we started working together, combining theory and practice, and later teamed up with Kate Vitasek to write a *Harvard Business Review* article.

I tell this story because I think that it gives some insight into the importance, value and originality of this book. Kate, David, Tim, and Jim have for a long time felt that the traditional approach to contracts, where lawyers try to think of all the possible things that can go wrong in a relationship and include contractual provisions to deal with them, is broken. It never worked that well, and in an increasingly complex and uncertain world it works even worse. The four of them have pioneered an alternative approach. In this approach, the parties write a relatively simple contract, but they combine it with a discussion of shared goals; agree to adopt guiding principles that the parties will apply if and when an uncontracted event occurs; and include structured communication processes to ensure that they are on the same page at all times.

It is rare that theory and practice converge, but this is one occasion where they do. I am an economic theorist who has worked on contracts for nearly forty years. I was initially drawn to the topic via a question of abiding interest to economists: What determines the boundaries of firms? In more prosaic terms, why do companies outsource some goods and services and produce others in-house? Like others before me, I realized that outsourcing involves a detailed contract with an outside provider and that a good contract is difficult to write when the relationship in question is a long-term one carried out under uncertainty—which will almost always be the case. It is hard for the parties to anticipate all the many things that can happen during the course of their relationship and, as a result, any contract they write will be incomplete.

In my initial forays, I focused on the idea that incompleteness makes parties vulnerable to opportunism. Once the buyer and seller are in the middle of their relationship, it is hard for either party to switch partners. If an event occurs that is not covered by the contract, and the good or service traded needs to be modified, each can use the situation to their advantage: the seller can try to raise the price and the buyer can try to lower it. Economists call this the "hold-up problem." Much of my work was about the defensive measures the parties can take to avoid being "held up."

This approach yielded some valuable insights, but at some point I realized that it was inadequate. There were theoretical reasons for this that cannot be adequately explained here, but there were also empirical reasons. Is hold-up behavior that common? Are business people really that opportunistic?

Eventually, while collaborating with John Moore, I was led to a different approach based on the idea that people can get angry if they feel that they are not being well-treated or not getting a fair deal. One of the purposes of a contract is to avoid such feelings. We termed this "contracts as reference points." Anger is to be avoided not just because it is unpleasant but also because it can lead to economic inefficiency. A party who feels badly treated will hit back at the other party with counteractions: they will become less cooperative either because they want to punish the other party or because they want to recoup the gains that they feel are rightfully theirs. This can trigger a tit-for-tat spiral, with consequent large deadweight costs.

Apart from some lab experiments that I carried out with co-authors, my work on contracts as reference points was entirely theoretical. But then I met David and discovered that there is a world out there where the kinds of things I was interested in are real, and where practitioners are figuring out solutions for them. Theory is stronger when it can be linked to practice, but the converse is also true. Many people offer advice on how to write better contracts, or for that matter how to live a better life, run a better business, etc. What makes David, Kate, Tim, and Jim's work stand out in my opinion is that it has a solid scientific basis.

That is what I like so much about this book. It is aimed at practitioners and describes David, Kate, Tim, and Jim's powerful methods for writing better contracts. But it also explains why the practical solutions work. The book offers indispensable knowledge: processes and tools to overcome the challenges of entering into and living through long-term relationships; how to ensure that you and your partner cooperate efficiently and don't resort to blame games; how to build trust; how to avoid bad feelings, and so on. In short how to ensure that the potential gains from a relationship are actually realized.

David, Kate, Tim, and Jim's work is pathbreaking. I have learned an enormous amount from it, and I think that you will too!

September 2020

Oliver Hart
Harvard University
Cambridge, MA, USA

# Acknowledgments

In writing *Contracting in the New Economy*, we stood on the shoulders of many talented individuals. First and foremost, we'd like to honor Stewart Macaulay and Ian Macneil for their work to put the concept of relational contracting on the map. Their work has spurred almost 70 years of research on the topic.

As we pause to formally recognize those who have helped make this book a reality, it is important to point out the spirit of collaboration that was embedded throughout our journey. To say this book is "by David, Kate, Jim and Tim" would be misleading. Without significant insights and contributions made by other people, this book simply would not exist.

We'd first like to start by highlighting the University of Tennessee's Graduate and Executive Education program and the International Association for Contract and Commercial Management. IACCM has changed its name to World Commerce & Contracting (WCC), which we will use as their name throughout the book, except when referencing published works. Without UT's and WCC's continued and steadfast support, much of our continuous progress would not be possible.

Thanks to all of the progressive organizations that provided us with case studies and examples. Your stories bring the vision of this book to reality. You will recognize many of these organizations' names throughout the book such as Island Health/South Island Hospitalists, Inc., Royal Australian Navy, Discovery Health Medical Scheme, and the many others we reference throughout the book. Others must remain unnamed due to corporate rules and competitive advantages, but we could not have achieved progress without them. You know who you are, and you have our deepest gratitude.

We are especially indebted to professor Oliver Hart for his interest, engagement, and valuable input to this book. Also, we would like to thank the following thought leaders who reviewed our work along the way and provided valuable feedback, support, and endorsements that we were on the right track:

| | | |
|---|---|---|
| Lucy Bassli | Craig Conte | Jean Gagnon |
| Robert Gibbons | Jim Groton | René Franz Henschel |
| David Handley | Oliver Hart | Lisa Higgins |
| Philip Hockberger | Rick Hof | Jens Holmberg |
| Greg Laxton | Dan Mahlebashian | Howard Snoyman |
| Mathias Strand | Verlyn Suderman | Dawn Tiura |
| Jeroen Van de Rijt | Jane Winn | |

We would like to recognize the following consulting firms/law firms that have helped us test and deploy our methodology and tools in the field with real companies:

| | |
|---|---|
| Best Value Group | Cirio Law Firm |
| CI Advisory | Commercial Officers Group |
| EY Nordics | Sireas |
| The Forefront Group | |

A special thanks to the professional associations that have been cheerleaders of our work. Thank you for the time you spent reviewing early versions of our work and providing endorsements.

NEVI (Dutch Association for Purchasing Management)
Sourcing Industry Group
World Commerce & Contracting (formerly IACCM)

We must call out a few individuals who helped make his book come to life. Elizabeth Kanna, you offered the vision for what could be and the guidance necessary to make that vision a reality. Marcus Ballenger, you were quick to understand the power of relational contracting. With Palgrave Macmillan, we truly have a great relationship! Bill DiBenedetto and the Palgrave editor,

Srishti Gupta, thanks for paying excruciating attention to detail, reining in our jargon, and adding professional polish to our story.

And last, but certainly not least, to our families, for all your support and patience during this fabulous experience.

Rebecka, Oskar and Klara Frydlinger
Greg and Austin Picinich
Nancy and Sophie Bergman
Sally Guyer

# Praise for *Contracting in the New Economy*

"Many people offer advice on how to write better contracts, or for that matter how to live a better life, run a better business, etc. What makes David, Kate, Tim, and Jim's work stand out in my opinion is that it has a solid scientific basis.

That is what I like so much about this book. It is aimed at practitioners and describes David, Kate, Tim, and Jim's powerful methods for writing better contracts. But it also explains why the practical solutions work. The book offers indispensable knowledge: processes and tools to overcome the challenges of entering into and living through long-term relationships; how to ensure that you and your partner cooperate efficiently and don't resort to blame games; how to build trust; how to avoid bad feelings, and so on. In short how to ensure that the potential gains from a relationship are actually realized.

David, Kate, Tim, and Jim's work is pathbreaking. I have learned an enormous amount from it, and I think that you will too!"

—Oliver Hart, *Lewis P. and Linda L. Geyser University Professor of Economics, Harvard University*

"This book is really a history lesson, a life lesson and a business lesson all in one. The chapter on the psychology of contracting clearly demonstrates the ways in which economic and social motivations can impact how people judge what is "fair." I love how the book is written like an easy to read novel with real stories that make the book come life. Overall, this book is a must read for anyone involved in contracts, negotiations and procurement."

—Dawn Tiura, *President and CEO of Sourcing Industry Group (SIG)*

"As the CEO of APQC, I am always looking for best practices to share with our global member organizations. This latest book on relational contracts should be considered a must-read for today's supply chain and commercial managers who are struggling to try to crack the code on creating more value through their supply chain partners."

—Lisa Higgins, *President & CEO | APQC*

"This is a terrific book—for both academics and practitioners. The theory draws from economics, law, and psychology, yet the five-step process for building a relational contract is not only concrete but also illustrated with many useful case studies. Honestly, this book is ahead of any economic theory I know in suggesting how parties might build and maintain the kind of shared understanding that is of course crucial for many collaborations. The authors have managed a rare feat: not only combining theory and practice, but also getting each to feed the other."

—Robert Gibbons, *Sloan Distinguished Professor of Management, Sloan School of Management, and Professor of Organizational Economics, Department of Economics, MIT*

"A great read for cutting-edge contract professionals both on the in-house as well as outside counsel side of the commercial lawyer spectrum. The concept of relational contracting is both thought-provoking and obvious. *Contracting in the New Economy* is a valuable and inspirational guide for those with ambitions to excel in the New Economy of complex strategic relationships."

—Mathias Strand, *Head of Legal for Microsoft Western Europe*

"This book explains in detail the relevance of relational contracts, a powerful approach to make prosperous and lasting contracts that are beneficial to both parties and focus on the uncertain future. The step by step approach makes it relatively easy to build better and more fruitful business relations. On top of that, it's an easy and accessible book to read."

—Rick Hof, *CPO Alliander (grid operator/the Netherlands)*

"During my 25 years as an outside and in-house attorney, I always felt there had to be a better way to serve my clients who were involved in complex, ongoing relationships and wanted to realize the most possible value from those relationships than either (1) the traditional zero-sum power-based contracting approach that destroys trust and discourages collaboration or (2) the handshake deal that may not be honored by new counterparty leadership and isn't clear enough to drive the desired behaviors and enable its enforceability. This book describes that third and better way—the formal relational contract—which I believe can represent an enormous competitive advantage to those contracting parties who have the courage and vision to give it a try."

—Verlyn Suderman, *Senior Director, Strategic Partnerships at DSC Logistics*

"The Royal Australian Navy had great success with relational contracting in the Navy's FFG Guided Missile Frigate program. However, it has been hard to replicate this success more widely because the relational success factors reside outside of the contract. While it is great to have a relational 'Charter' and associated governance processes—the Navy found that often the performance-based contract itself was not aligned with the intent of the relationship.

As key leadership moves on there is a risk that the relational intent is lost and people revert to asking 'what does the contract say?' I believe that the 'formal' aspect is the missing magic sauce in achieving wider success with relational contracting across more programs. Integrating the relational constructs with the formal contract is a brilliant concept. I consider it a 'must do' for any large, complex contract."

—Captain Greg Laxton, *Former Executive Director Fleet Support Unit for the Royal Australian Navy*

"If you manage strategic business relationships and are looking for an alternative to traditional "transactional" contracts, then this is the book for you. The authors successfully combine both critical research and application of relational contracts in a compelling writing style that is clear, informative, and insightful. Each chapter is important and necessary to assess why, how and when to create a "relational" contract."

—Philip Hockberger, Ph.D., *Associate Vice President for Research, Northwestern University*

"In this remarkable book, the authors provide a clear and practical step-by-step answer: the formal relational agreement. This innovative way should be taught to all law and management students as long-term collaboration relationships will continue to be more and more frequent, and more and more important."

—Jean H. Gagnon, Ad.E., *Of Counsel | Mediator | Arbitrator, FASKEN (Montreal, Canada)*

"This book examines the science of why relational contracting is preferable to ordinary transactional contracting, the psychology and economic rationale that drives contracting behaviour, and provides practical guidance on how to optimize contracting environments so as to maximize opportunities for relational contracting. A must-read for lead-negotiators and C-Suite Executives."

—Howard Snoyman, *Head of Legal and Ethics, Discovery Health Medical Scheme*

"Transactional Lawyers have a professional obligation to help their clients create sustainable business relationships. This book is an essential tool for accomplishing that important professional goal in today's diverse economy."

—Jim Groton, *Retired Partner, Eversheds-Sutherland*

"In these dynamic times we need, more than ever, to transform strategic buyer-supplier relationships into win-win situations. This book provides practical tools and tips on how to do this, all based on solid theoretical frameworks. A must read for all contract managers and procurement professionals."

—Jeroen Van de Rijt, *Co-Founder, Best Value Group*

"For those of us that need our complex contracts to be high performing, this book is a must read. The importance of the relationship in working together for mutual benefit is a prevalent theme that inspires the reader to act boldly. Follow the framework and tools within to achieve success with Relational Contracts."

—David Handley, *VP Business Partnerships PHSA, Provincial Health Services Authority*

"The careful balance of academic analysis with practical insights is truly remarkable. Dragging outdated contracting practices into the new world is no small task, and this book creates a useful platform for understanding WHY this shift is so necessary. The old ways of doing contracts are starting to experience pressure cracks. Rather than allowing a chaotic explosion, companies should take practical steps to own and manage their own shift in how they contract by embracing and learning from books like this."

—Lucy Bassli, *Founder, InnoLegal Services, PLLC*

"American lawyers influenced by the Legal Realist tradition think in terms of 'law in action' versus 'law in the books.' The authors have written a practical guide to business relationships in action in the 21st Century while many lawyers and legal academics remain mired in anachronistic conventions of law in the books."

—Jane K. Winn, *Professor, University of Washington Law School*

"This book is a must-read for all professionals working with relational contracts and looking to increase value creation through collaborative contracting. The book stirs one's curiosity about the future of contracting and the authors are truly at the forefront of introducing new thoughts and ideas to the marketplace. This thinking is a driving force in ISS's ambition to create and grow strategic business partnerships with our large international customers and suppliers based on collaborative contracting–and I have recommended the book to several of my colleagues working with international contracts."

—Jens Holmberg, *Global Commercial Legal Counsel, ISS World Services A/S*

"This book as a must-read for everyone that wants to know more about why, when and how to move from traditional transactional contract models to relational contract models. The authors demonstrate deep insight and experience into the theory and practice of relational contracting and have created a truly original and ready-to-go approach on how to understand and create more efficient, flexible and value-adding contracts and relationships in strategic business partnerships. The book is a perfect example of how practitioners and academics must work together to explore, create and manage new contracting models that will be able to better meet the challenges of our modern, ever-changing and disruptive economic landscape. The book can be recommended for both contracting professionals, business people, lawyers etc., as well as academics and students in business schools, universities, etc."

—René Franz Henschel, *Professor, Ph.D., Aarhus Universitet, School of Business and Social Sciences, Juridisk Institut*

"Commoditized contracts are what they are and should be fair and quick. But for real, long term, mutually beneficial and mutually dependent contracts it is essential that there is a model of contracting that accepts an approach of "how do we solve" vs. "who do we punish." Let's get real with the relationships between suppliers and customers and use what we know. This book gives tools, strategies and ideas on how companies can better focus on collaboration. A path for the future."

—Craig Conte, *Partner, Deloitte Legal*

"A clear and concise guide, from a practitioner's perspective of the why, what, when and how to craft, implement and maintain a Relational Contract that dispels this deeply entrenched contracting notion that there has to be a winner and a loser in order to deliver an effective commercial agreement. This easy-to-read and highly actionable book on Relational Contracts is a very effective example of how simplicity is the ultimate sophistication. A must-read for all commerce, commercial and contract management professionals worldwide!"

—Daniel Mahlebashian, *Retired General Motors Senior Global Executive, Executive Director Global Business Services, Chief Sourcing and Contracting Officer, Global Information Technology*

# Introduction

The metaphor of dwarfs standing on the shoulders of giants expresses the meaning of discovering the truth by building on previous discoveries. Although it is originally attributed to Bernard of Chartres in the twelfth century, Isaac Newton popularized the concept in 1676.

The concept is just as relevant for us today as it was for Newton in the seventeenth century. Since the early 1960s, pioneering legal scholars such as Stewart Macaulay and Ian Macneil began promoting the value of the softer "relational" side of contracts. Macaulay's original 1963 article on the topic would go on to be the most cited in contract law. No one would debate these pioneers set a spark in the legal and economic fields which have fostered hundreds—if not thousands—of articles debating the merits and pitfalls of relational contracts.

But why hasn't the concept of using relational contracting practices and relational contracts taken off despite the debate?

One reason is that relational contracts are most widely associated with the informal "non-contractual" relational side of business transactions. Perhaps unsurprisingly, most organizations—and their legal counsels in particular—are uncomfortable with informal handshake deals, especially when the stakes are high. One Fortune 500 lawyer even used the term "hairy-fairy" to describe relational contracts. The result? While Macaulay and Macneil were espousing the benefits of the relational aspects of business, the vast majority of the legal profession was headed in the other direction in search of more complete contracts to stave off even the most opportunistic of business professionals who might pose a risk to an organization entering into a contract. The result? Today's contracts are longer, more rigid, and full of more risk-averse language than ever before.

But are they better?

Harvard University's Oliver Hart thinks not—calling the quest for the complete contract a fool's errand. Why? Today's environment is more dynamic and is filled with greater uncertainty than ever before. The tried and true tools and tactics adopted over the last 30 years for creating transactional contracts are not effective for complex and interdependent relationships that are fraught with the risk of unknowns and evolving business needs long after the contract is signed.

Simply put, the world has changed. But contracts have not changed.

Many academics and practitioners refer to the subtle shifts that have taken place since the turn of the century as "the new economy." Today's business environment is driven by the following:

- Globalization is accelerating market interconnectedness. Globalization includes the increased mobility of human resources creating a marketplace made up of a network of highly integrated organizations.
- A business environment challenged with increasing volatility and risk, including international terrorism, sovereign debt defaults, natural disasters, and port slowdowns caused by labor disputes and inadequate transportation infrastructure.
- An increasingly fast consumer-driven society that demands agile and more flexible supply chains.
- The continued evolution of a service economy that is shifting to strategic, not just tactical, outsourcing.
- A shift in purchasing skills and processes to create value, not simply procure goods and services.
- The expansion and introduction of capabilities of cloud computing cloud-collaborationcollaborative in procurement activities.

These foundational economic shifts in how business is done demand that contracting professionals view contracting through a different lens. Research has proven and continues to validate the power of collaborative partnerships. The business battles of this century will be fought by harnessing the power of strong strategic alliances where organizations combine core competencies to create value beyond what each organization can do alone. It also means embracing the hard fact that business is risky; rather than shifting risk through market power and contractual clauses, partners can create more value with a strong foundation of transparency and trust, working together to mitigate risk much better than merely shifting risk to the weaker party.

The path to harnessing relational contracts differs from the road now traveled with rigid, risk-averse transactional contracts. However, the road less traveled can bring significant benefits. We believe that road means incorporating *formal relational contracts* for complex and interdependent relationships that demand innovation and risk mitigation.

Just what is a formal relational contract? We define a formal relational contract as:

> *A legally enforceable written contract*
> *establishing a commercial partnership*
> *within a flexible contractual framework*
> *based on social norms and jointly defined objectives,*
> *prioritizing a relationship with the continuous alignment of interests*
> *before the commercial transactions.*[1]

We want to stress there is a difference between a *formal relational contract* and *relational contracting*. In this book, when we talk about relational contracting, we refer to *the process* through which two or more parties establish a commercial relationship based on relational elements such as shared visions and values and collaborative ways of working. These elements are not necessarily incorporated into a formal, enforceable contract. If not incorporated into a contract, the relationship will still be a relational contract, but more of the informal kind MacaulayStewart and Macneil studied. For example, in Chapter 1 we share how McDonald's uses relational contracting to create informal "handshake" deals regarding how they work with their most strategic supply chain suppliers. Virtually none of the secret sauce to supply chain success is codified in a formal relational contract.

The focus of this book provides a proven relational contracting process to help organizations develop a formal relational contract. We want to emphasize that there can be many paths to deeper collaboration in commercial relationships.

# Evolution of the Formal Relational Contract Concept

Many wonder how we came to think in terms of formal relational contracts. We cannot attribute the concept to any one individual; rather, it has evolved from the ideas and diverse experiences of the four of us, the authors, and many, many others.

In 2003, the University of Tennessee (UT) began what would become over a decade of research to study strategic relationships. Kate Vitasek led a small team of researchers. The initial research was conducted over several phases between 2003 and 2009, and the study is ongoing. The analysis included in-depth case reviews from some of the world's most successful buyer-supplier relationships.

Vitasek and her research team codified their research into a methodology and sourcing model they called Vested®. Vested is a business model in which buyers and suppliers carefully craft highly collaborative relationships supported by a true win-win outcome-based economic model. A win for the buyer is a win for the supplier. Buyers and suppliers are *vested* in each other's success. The work led to the books *Vested Outsourcing: Five Rules That Will Transform Outsourcing* and *Vested: How P&G, McDonald's and Microsoft are Redefining Winning in Business Relationships*.

In 2012, David Frydlinger became intrigued with the work the University of Tennessee was doing. Frydlinger—a practicing Swedish attorney with a Masters in sociology—liked how UT was incorporating the relational aspects of contracting into their Vested model. Having a background in social science the concepts immediately resonated with the teachings of Eleanor Ostrom, Douglas North, Robert Ellickson, and others who had done extensive research on social norms. Frydlinger joined the UT faculty as an adjunct faculty teaching UT's Collaborative Contracting Executive Education course. Frydlinger and Vitasek overhauled the curriculum to incorporate their expanded research on applying social norms into contracts. The work led to the book *Getting to We: Negotiating Agreements for Highly Collaborative Relationships* (with Jeanette Nyden).

At the same time as the University of Tennessee was looking at how to apply relational contracting into practice, Professor Oliver Hart (Harvard University) and Professor John Moore (University of Edinburgh and London School of Economics) were looking at the contracting problem from an economics perspective. In 2016, Frydlinger met Professor Oliver Hart when he came to Stockholm to receive the Nobel Prize in Economic Sciences for his work on Contract Theory. The two hit it off and immediately began to collaborate, ultimately leading to the Harvard Business Review article titled *A New Approach to Contracts: How to Build Better Long-Term Strategic Partnerships.*

In a separate but parallel timeframe, the International Association for Contract and Commercial Management (IACCM), now World Commerce & Contracting (WCC), began to experiment with a relational contracting process where parties came together in a series of workshops to develop a relationship "charter" and establish guidelines around nine relational "tenets." Vitasek and Frydlinger began to collaborate with Tim Cummins (then CEO of IACCM) and Jim Bergman  (CEO of Commercial Officers Group) to write the white paper titled *Unpacking Relational Contracts: The Practitioner's Go-To Guide for Understanding Relational Contracts.*[2] It was in this white paper that the authors proposed the definition of a formal relational contract referenced earlier.

Ultimately, the four collaborators came together to create this book. This book brings together over four years of curiosity and a lot of hard work to come up with a powerful yet simple way to help organizations understand and apply the concept of formal relational contracts.

## Relational Contracting on the Rise

Relational contracting has been on the rise in recent years. Specifically, some of the larger advisory firms and the Corporate Executive Board have become staunch advocates of incorporating relational governance practices in large sourcing relationships—especially outsourcing deals.[3] More recently, the Australian Navy has had success with relational contracting practices by developing a one-page "charter" and adopting nine relational "tenets." Their success gained notoriety in 2016 when they won the International Association for Contract and Commercial Management (IACCM) Innovation award for operational improvement.[4] And in 2020 a Harvard Business Review article "A New Approach to Contracts" shared the success story of how Dell/FedEx and the Canadian government are effectively using formal relational contracts.[5]

In this book, we describe and recommend an approach for using relational contracting for getting to a formal relational contract. We want to point out that while getting to a formal relational contract is desired, it is not mandatory to achieve success in commercial partnerships. However, we believe that after you have read this book you will understand and agree that the likelihood of success will increase significantly for those organizations who take the step to create a formal relational contract.

## Our Vision for This Book

Most people quickly grasp the concept of relational contracts, but many get stuck when trying to digest the why, what, and how to put the theory into practice. This is where this book comes in.

Our vision for this book is simple: help contracting professionals navigate their most complex, interdependent, and risky strategic partnerships in the new economy.

As you read this book, we have two specific goals. We start with the WHY, showing how reliance on conventional transactional contracts is limited. We show extensive research and scenarios on how conventional contracting approaches can backfire—especially in complex contracts where there is high interdependency between the contracting parties. Likewise, we share extensive research and examples proving beyond a doubt the benefits of relational contracting.

Second, we challenge contracting professionals to adopt formal relational contracts for strategic relationships. By strategic, we mean those relationships that are complex, interdependent, and risky in that they are fraught with changes and where the future is hard to predict. It also means those that demand investment and innovation where the future outcome is hard to predict. To help organizations make the leap we provide a simple five-step approach for creating a formal relational contract and share powerful examples of how organizations have transformed theory into practice, yielding significant tangible and intangible benefits. For organizations not ready to take the step to formal relational contracts, this five-step relational contracting process can still be used and will bring significant value.

## A Note on Terminology

As you read this book, it is helpful to understand a few key terms we use throughout. We often use the term *contracting professionals*. So just who are "contracting professionals"? We offer a broad definition, being anyone with an interest in delivering more successful trading relationships. This includes lawyers, procurement and sales professionals, and business professionals who manage their organization's strategic relationships.

Second, we use the term *organization* because it is a more generic term than *company* and can refer to a public or private institution.

Third, because many types of contracts deal with buying goods and services or developing distribution partnerships, we use the term *buyers* and *suppliers* to refer to the individuals chartered to lead their organization in buying and selling goods and services. We primarily use the term *suppliers* but occasionally also use the term *providers* or *service providers*. We use the terms *procure*, *source*, *purchase*, *buy*, and *acquisition* interchangeably. In all cases, we use these terms in the context of an organization buying goods and services.

Last, we use several terms to refer to business partners coming together. Although we primarily use the term *relationship*, we also use *partnership*, *agreement*, *arrangement*, *deal*, and *contract* to reduce redundancy.

## Getting Ready for a Shift in Thinking

Why read this book?

Contracting in the new economy demands a new approach. Using conventional transactional contracts does not work in complex strategic relationships where the parties depend highly on each other, future events cannot be predicted, and flexibility and trust are required. Instead of promoting the partnership-like relationships needed to cope with uncertainty, conventional contracts undermine them.

Simply put, you should read this book because *contracts matter*. And getting contracts right can create (or, if done poorly, cost) millions if not billions of dollars of value. Think about it. Billions of dollars, euros, yen, and other currencies change hands every day under contracts. It matters whether the events anticipated by contracts succeed or are not successful in the sense they assist people and organizations in pursuing their business and daily lives. If you find yourself in an adversarialrelationship with a strategic partnership—or you are simply frustrated by the lack of collaboration and innovation from your business partner—this book is for you.

This is not an academic book; rather it is a practitioner's guide to help individuals and organizations better understand, create, and manage relational contracts. While we start with the theoretical underpinnings of why relational contracts are essential in today's economy, the bulk of this book is about what, when, and how.

Maybe the better question to ask is whether you are ready for this book. Are you ready to reconsider how you work with strategic business partners? Are you willing to consider sharing more—and expecting more— from these partners? Are you willing to rethink how you approach risk with these partners—and rewards? And are you willing to challenge your conventional contracting processes and contract structures? If not, put the book back and save your money.

To understand the power of a paradigm shift, you must start with an open mind. Keep it open, and you will surely see new opportunities around you.

We wish you well as you take the road less traveled and learn how to harness the power of formal relational contracts.

## Notes

1. Frydlinger et. al. "Unpacking Relational Contracts: The Practioner's Guide for Understanding Relational Contracts," *University of Tennessee, IACCM, CIRIO* (White Paper, 2019). Available at: http://www.vestedway.com/wp-content/upl oads/2016/10/Unpacking-Relational-Contracting_v19.pdf.
2. Ibid.
3. See "Framing the future of corporate governance: Deloitte Governance Framework," *Deloitte Center for Board Effectiveness* (2016). Available at https://www2.deloitte.com/us/en/pages/risk/articles/framing-the-fut ure-of-corporate-governance-deloitte-governance-framework.html. See also the *University of Tennessee, IACCM and Corporate Executive Board*, "Unpacking Outsourcing Governance: How to Build a Sound Governance Structure to Drive Insight Versus Oversight" (White Paper, 2011). Available for download at http://www.vestedway.com/vested-library/.
4. Kate Vitasek, "Relational Contracting On The Rise With The Success Of The Australian Navy," *Forbes*, Nov. 30, 2016. Available at https://www.forbes. com/sites/katevitasek/2016/11/30/relational-contracting-on-the-rise-with-the-success-of-the-australian-navy/#40867f43303a.
5. David Frydlinger, Oliver Hart and Kate Vitasek, "A New Approach to Contracts," *Harvard Business Review*, September-October 2019. Available at https://hbr.org/2019/09/a-new-approach-to-contracts.

# Contents

# List of Figures

# Part I

## Contracting in the New Economy

# 1

# Welcome to the Contracting Paradox

More and more organizations are facing a *contracting paradox*. Contracting is about planning for future exchanges of goods, services, and other valuables for money and how to deal with the risks and opportunities entailed in such exchanges. Yet today—more than ever—the search for the perfect plan is painful, if not impossible. Today's market is faster, more global, and more complex than ever. Change is the new constant, making accurate planning and forecasting almost an illusion. The search for the complete contract through the lens of a conventional contract is often far from effective if not down-right disabling.

Psychological research has revealed the troublesome fact that evolution has made us ill-equipped to make good plans *and* at the same time well-equipped to believe we are good planners.[1] The result is a planning fallacy, leading to the *contracting paradox*.

So, what is the contracting paradox? It is the delusion we write contracts to make plans, but we cannot accurately plan. And, as a nice twist, we trick ourselves into believing we can plan.

The contracting paradox is a recent phenomenon. Never has it been so important to enter into strategic contractual relationships in complex commercial deals requiring planning. But never has it been harder to plan for the future.

The formal relational contract promoted in this book shows a way out of the contracting paradox, enabling organizations to cope with the challenges of planning for the future in a highly complex environment.

© The Author(s), under exclusive license to Springer Nature
Switzerland AG 2021
D. Frydlinger et al., *Contracting in the New Economy*,
https://doi.org/10.1007/978-3-030-65099-5_1

Relational contracts are not new. They have existed as long as humans have been carrying out commercial exchanges. But then, these were *informal* relational contracts, not documented in written agreements.

A small number of organizations such as McDonald's have kept with this tradition, choosing to forge long-term trusting relationships with strategic business partners without a formal contract. But many—especially those in the legal profession—eschew informal relational contracts as extra-contractual and something that cannot be upheld in court.[2] Simply put, the informal contract is seen as risky. This is one of many reasons to promote *formal* relational contracts. But let's first look at how McDonald's and the Royal Australian Navy have succeeded in using informal relational contracts.

## Relational Contracting in Practice: The McDonald's Story

McDonald's has used informal "handshake" deals with their most strategic suppliers since Ray Kroc founded the company in 1955.[3] Take for example the McDonald's and Coca-Cola relationship. The parties have been operating together for nearly seventy years with no contract. That's right. McDonald's does business with its most strategic suppliers based on the commitment of an "old-fashioned handshake" grounded in trust and loyalty. An added benefit of a handshake deal? McDonald's and its suppliers can flexibly address dynamic changes in the market and business needs as they occur. Case in point: who ran out of chicken during the Avian Flu crisis? *Not McDonald's.*

Francesca DeBiase, McDonald's Vice President, Strategic Sourcing, World-wide Supply Chain Management, explains the rationale for handshake deals. "Many of our strategic suppliers have been working with McDonald's for years, even decades. They know that we base our partnerships on mutual trust, respect, and financial success. Over the years, our actions and behaviors have shown our suppliers we conduct business with a high level of integrity. This allows us to operate with a handshake agreement."[4]

Many have credited McDonald's with transforming the food industry, bringing unparalleled innovations around food safety and efficiencies in their supply chain. USA Today proclaims McDonald's to have the safest supply chain in the world—serving over 63 million people every day without an E. coli incident since 1987. Gartner ranks McDonald's as consistently having one of the world's best supply chains.

Ask any of McDonald's key strategic suppliers and they will tell you the long-term trust they have with McDonald's regularly inspires collaboration that drives process and product innovations. Pete Richter, President, Global McDonald's Business Unit for Cargill, explains how a long-term relationship founded on high degrees of trust impacts Cargill's interaction with McDonald's. "The difference between McDonald's and the rest of the world is that, as a supplier, we generally spend 50% of our time and effort worrying about what our future business looks like. Will consultants come in and shake things up? Will some new procurement person come in and demand RFPs every year or a 20% price cut simply to help them get their bonus? At McDonald's, we feel comfortable. So, all of our energy can be directed to improvements, working together, and innovations that create a competitive advantage for both McDonald's and Cargill."[5]

Ask most contracting professionals, however, and they are stunned to learn that McDonald's still uses a handshake deal for some of their largest and most strategic supplier relationships. However, McDonald's is not alone in its pursuit of relational contracting practices. Japanese keiretsu, an arrangement in which buyers form close associations with (and often own stakes in) suppliers, is a type of relational contract. Organizations such as Chrysler also began adopting informal relational contracting practices in 1989 as profiled in a 1996 *Harvard Business Review* article.[6] And more recently the Royal Australian Navy has adopted relational contracting.

## Relational Contracting in Practice: The Australian Navy FFG Story

Bruce McLennan understood the contracting paradox was very real.[7] He sat at his desk, his head swimming on a warm and sunny Australian summer day during Christmas break in 2007. McLennan—the Chief of Staff for the Major Surface Ships Branch—had been tasked to draft a letter summarizing supplier performance issues to the CEO of the Defence Materiel Organisation (DMO). The list was long: suppliers offered unrealistic schedules; they bid low and then found profit in growing the scope of work and change orders; they captured niche monopolies and used them to leverage prices charged for supplies by up to 300%. Distrust ran high.

McLennan found himself in a dilemma. "Initially I was tasked to write a letter to the CEO of the Defence Materiel Organisation that would basically chastise these naughty suppliers." But as McLennan began to dig deeper, he pondered the classic master-slave mentality the Navy had created with suppliers. "Industry is nothing but a mirror of us. We pay the cheques. If we use sticks, the contractors have to modify their behavior to mitigate against the stick. We have to change first."

The Navy's strategy for change included a two-prong approach. The first included making the shift to a performance-based "Group Maintenance Contract," which focused on improved asset management practices that leveraged the strengths of both the Navy and strategic industry partners. But changing the commercial nature of the contract to a performance-based contract was only half the battle. McLennan also knew the Navy needed to change the mindset of how they treated suppliers. It is here they turned to the International Association for Contracts and Commercial Management (IACCM), now World Commerce & Contracting (WCC), for support in how to apply relational contracting practices for what is now known as the FFG Enterprise program.

The FFG Enterprise is a term that describes the collaborative relationship between the Navy and two suppliers—BAE Systems and Thales. The FFG Enterprise exists to provide the Royal Australian Navy with materially seaworthy FFG guided missile warships—*on time, every time*—until they are withdrawn from service. There are four frigates (vessels) supported by the FFG Enterprise.

A key part of the WCC relational contracting process is to develop a one-page formal Charter. A key feature of the FFG Enterprise Charter is the documented agreement concerning relational ideals. However, the Charter itself—as well as much of the other relational aspects of how the parties work—is not formally included in the contract. In the case of the FFG, the Charter is a simple one-page PowerPoint slide signed by the senior leadership of the Navy, BAE, and Thales.

Success was enhanced by three leaders consciously deciding to demonstrate to the entire FFG Enterprise it was essential to live the behaviors agreed to in the Charter. The three men included Captain Brad Smith as the Royal Australian Navy FFG System Program Officer (SPO), Tony Mills, as the FFG GMC Program Manager Maritime/Asset Management—of Thales Australia, and Andrew Laing, as the Project Manager FFG Integrated Materiel Support Maritime & Integrated Systems—of BAE Systems Australia. The three men, with Charter in hand, set out to lead their organizations by living the principles of the Charter designed to foster trust and collaboration between the Navy, BAE, and Thales.

Rear Admiral Adam Grunsell—head of Maritime Systems Division—is full of praise for what the FFG Enterprise team has done, stating "BAE and Thales would normally be competitors. But they came together under the FFG Enterprise and made this an award-winning project. The Charter was a single piece of paper which committed the parties to missions and values, and to work to outcomes rather than hide behind what was in the contract." He adds, "It's been an incredible success."[10]

## Benefits of Relational Contracting

The benefits of relational contracting practices have been studied for almost seventy years. Legal scholars Stewart Macaulay and Ian Macneil were early advocates in the 1960s (Macneil coined the term "relational contract" in a 1968 book.)[8] Their work has inspired dozens (if not hundreds) of research studies from some of the most influential legal, economic, social, and psychology thinkers around the world—including six Nobel Prize winners. We profile many of them in Part 2 of this book, The Science of Contracting.

More recent research by the University of Tennessee, WCC, and others provides applied case-based research supporting the fact that the benefits of relational contracting are real.[9] Hard numbers back up Rear Admiral Adam Grunsell's previous statement. Some of the results include:

- The number of days an FFG is available for service increased from a low of 210 days to more than 300 days.
- A significant improvement in the quality from 67 Significant Defects in 2015 to 16 in 2017.
- Over 20% realized cost savings, in the order of AUD$28 million per year.
- 45% savings on a like-for-like scope of work.
- 46% reduction in costs per task.
- 43% reduction in labor hours per task.
- 44% reduction in labor costs per hour.
- 8+ labor hour reduction per Technical Repair Specification (TRS), a document which informs the costing and conduct of maintenance, as a result of process improvements identified through Lean Six Sigma (LSS) activities.
- 100% on-time or ahead of schedule delivery of the FFG capability out of maintenance.
- 25% increase in the achievement of Material Ready Days (MRDs).

Some argue if McDonald's can create world dominance in the fast-food industry with handshake deals, then *why do we write contracts?* And if the Royal Australian Navy can have success by using a relational contracting process without the creation of a formal relational contract, why bother to go the extra step?

The question deserves careful reflection and consideration and stems from the very pragmatic question of "*why are contracts written?*"

## Why Are Contracts Written?

Contracts are written not for theoretical reasons but *practical* reasons. Contracts affect the lives of billions of people every day. Billions of dollars, euros, yen, and other currencies change hands every day under contracts.

*Contracts matter.* It matters whether the events anticipated by contracts succeed or not. Contracts play a key role in assisting people and organizations in pursuing their business and daily lives.

An Internet search shows multiple definitions for a contract. While they vary slightly, almost all view a contract as a promise or set of promises that are legally enforceable which, if violated, allow the injured party access to legal remedies. This is the classical view of a contract, where the critical element is *enforceability*. If the contract is breached, one can go to court and get remedies from the other party. The contract's enforceability holds part of the answer to why contracts are needed.

Consider a contract between two organizations in a megadeal. The organizations may agree on a set of services and a price. But what if the seller wants to maximize profit by providing services of low quality, using unskilled staff and old computers? Without an enforceable contract specifying quality standards, the seller may very well do that when the time comes for the services to be provided. And what if the buyer regrets the choice of buying the services, and wants to spend the money on something else? Without an enforceable contract specifying the price and payment terms, the buyer may very well choose not to pay.

It points to the sad fact that humans are *opportunistic*. By opportunistic, we mean humans are often inclined to do what is best for themselves and disregard the interests of others. As such, contracts are used as a mechanism to protect against the other party's opportunistic choices. An economist would say that the contract is entered to safeguard the investments in time, work, money, etc. The contract is, from this perspective, a risk mitigation instrument. And the fact that you can take someone to court for breach of contract serves as the enforcement mechanism. However, it is vital to understand the simple act of contracting brings risks such as the risk of hold-up and shading, as identified by Oliver Hart.

## Hold-Ups, Incomplete Contracts, and Shading

Oliver Hart (2016 Nobel laureate in Economic Science for his work on contract theory)[10] offers compelling evidence of why contracts are written. Organizations traditionally use contracts as protection against the possibility that one party will abuse its power to extract benefits at the expense of the other—for example, by unilaterally raising or lowering prices, changing delivery dates, or requiring more onerous employment terms. Economists call this the hold-up problem: the fear that one party will be held up by the other. The fact that virtually all contracts contain gaps, omissions, and ambiguities—despite an organization's best efforts to anticipate every scenario—only exacerbates hold-up behavior.

Contracting practitioners employ a range of tactics to ensure that they are not victims of hold-up behavior. These include contracting with multiple suppliers, forcing suppliers to lock in prices, using termination of convenience clauses, or obligating suppliers to cover activities that might arise after the initial contracting phase.

Early research by Hart predicted that in response to the combined problems of hold-ups and incomplete contracts, organizations are likely to make distorted investments that produce poor outcomes. Using multiple suppliers instead of only one, for example, increases costs; so too does operating a shadow organization to micromanage a supplier one does not trust. While adding deadweight costs is not good, author Steven M.R. Covey, Jr. suggests the less visible transaction costs stemming from lack of trust in an unproductive relationship often adds the most cost. Covey cites the following seven "taxes" arising from distrust[11]:

1. Redundancy is unnecessary duplication. It stems from the mindset that people cannot be trusted unless they are closely watched.
2. Bureaucracy is when too many rules and regulations are in place, or when too many people have to "sign off" on something.
3. Politics is when one uses a misaligned strategy to gain power. Too much time is spent in interpreting other people's motives and trying to read hidden agendas.
4. Disengagement is when people are still getting paid even though they "clocked-out" years ago. They will put in the minimal effort required to get their paycheck.

5. Turnover results when the best performers in an organization leave an organization in pursuit of jobs where they are seen as trusted and a contributor adding value.
6. Churn is the effort and costs associated with constantly having to find new customers, suppliers, distributors, and investors because there is a lack of loyalty.
7. Fraud is flat-out dishonesty. Fraud is a circular tax; when companies tighten the reigns to prevent fraud they reduce their fraud-related losses, but they inevitably see an increase in the other six areas.

Contract clauses themselves can cause deadweight costs, especially when a clause is ill-suited for a more strategic partnership and creates an inherent perverse incentive. Consider how the common contractual clause—the "termination for convenience"—can backfire in a strategic business relationship. A termination for convenience clause grants one party total freedom to end the contract after a specified period. The clause is used to protect that party—typically the party with the most power—from getting trapped in a relationship. While a termination for convenience clause is designed to protect a party, it actually confers a false sense of security. Take for example a complex and dependent outsourcing relationship such as Dell and FedEx.

In 2005, Dell outsourced its return-and-repair process to FedEx under a traditional supplier contract. The 100-page-plus document was filled with "supplier shall" statements that detailed FedEx's obligations and outlined dozens of metrics for how Dell would measure success. For nearly a decade, FedEx met all its contractual obligations—but neither party was happy in the relationship. Dell felt that FedEx was not proactive in driving continuous improvement and innovative solutions; FedEx was frustrated by onerous requirements that wasted resources and forced it to operate within a restrictive statement of work. Dell's attempts to lower costs, including bidding out the work three times during the eight-year relationship, ate into FedEx's profits.

By the eighth year, the parties were at the breaking point. Each lacked trust and confidence in the other, yet neither could afford to end the relationship. Dell's cost of switching to another organization would be high, and FedEx would have trouble replacing the revenue and profits the contract generated. It was a lose-lose scenario—despite a termination for convenience clause.

More interesting is that a simple and standard clause, such as a termination for convenience clause, can create an inherent perverse incentive in complex and dependent relationships as seen in how FedEx never seemed to drive proactive continuous improvement and innovation for Dell despite working together for nearly ten years.[12]

One CFO of a Fortune 100 supplier explains the logic. "A 60-day termination of convenience translates to a 60-day contract. It would be against our fiduciary responsibility to our shareholders to invest in any program for a client with a 60-day termination clause that required longer than two months to generate a return." The implications for innovation are apparent. "Buyers are crazy to expect us to invest in innovation if they do the math." This example proves Hart's point: when trying to find protection from being held-up by the other party, a lot of inefficiencies are typically created.

In 2008, Hart together with economic theorist John Moore revisited his work on contracts.[13] They realized that—equally important to the hold-up problem—organizations suffer from a post-contract signing problem they coined as *shading*. Shading is a retaliatory behavior in which one party stops cooperating, ceases to be proactive, or makes countermoves. Shading happens when a party is not getting the outcome it expects from the deal and feels the other party is to blame or has not acted reasonably to mitigate the losses. The aggrieved party often cuts back on performance in subtle ways, sometimes even unconsciously, to compensate for the perceived imbalance between the parties.

Shading often launches a negative cycle of tit-for-tat behaviors where the parties pursue power-play games during a contract—often rationalizing their behavior.

A real-world example of shading comes from Canada's Island Health Authority and South Island Hospitalists Inc (SIHI).[14] Island Health and SIHI had operated under a labor services contract since 2000 when Island Health pioneered Hospitalist services in Canada. At first, the parties were excited, proud to be the country's first to bring progressive Hospitalist services to Canada, which focuses on specialty care to the sickest and most complex patients in a hospital setting. The contract included provisions on how volume changes would affect the hours allocated for Hospitalist services. All worked well until 2010. It was then Island Health—on short notice—decided to halt the use of allowing community physicians to perform work in a hospital setting. This created a significant workload increase for the Hospitalists left to pick up the slack and put them under a great deal of pressure. Since they could not respond quickly by hiring additional staff, their workloads soared and they could not devote adequate time to patients to provide safe, high-quality care.

Physicians became fatigued. Fear of mistakes led to disengagement with promoting efficiency in the systems of hospital patient flow. With time pressures, discharges became slower and admissions lasted longer (both from conscious and unconscious action), slowing throughput of patients through an overburdened hospital system.

The Hospitalists eventually responded by refusing to accept the responsibility for admitting some patients from the emergency room, which was a requirement to facilitate flow through the emergency department and the hospital. This led to a heavy strain on the relationship. The administration grew increasingly frustrated, eventually revoked the privileges of three Hospitalists, claiming that they refused to provide patient care.

Although the contract did not preclude Island Health's decision to cut back on the use of community doctors, the Hospitalists felt that the decision was unilateral and unanticipated, and resulted in unreasonable expectations, costs, and burdens of the Hospitalists. The Hospitalists responded with a shading/shirking action: by not agreeing to take patients from the emergency room they relieved their stress. They also avoided ethical issues arising from not being able to devote adequate time to patients (a doctor can ethically decline new patients if they cannot reasonably be assured of providing an expected and consistent standard of care both to any new patients and to their existing patient load). On the other hand, Island Health expected the Hospitalists to take care of the patients and at the same time deal with volume changes, even significant ones, despite insufficient manpower, and they were aggrieved by the Hospitalists' actions. Both sides reacted in ways they would not have done if everything were going well. Simply put, shading diminished the overall value being created by the contract and relationship, resulting in dead weight losses.

## Contracts as an Expectation Management Instrument

Considering post-contract shading, Hart and Moore's expanded theory focuses on contracts as reference points, a new perspective emphasizing the need for mechanisms to continually align expectations—or updated reference points—as unanticipated events occur and require change. The contract is therefore not only an instrument of risk mitigation but also an *expectations management instrument*.

## The Rise of Lawyers and Formal Contracts

Not everyone can succeed without contracts in the way McDonald's has. The majority of today's organizations do not even try. Rather they turn to formal contracts to manage risk and set expectations. Let's look at how this has come about.

The post-World War II era fostered significant growth for businesses. As organizations like McDonald's mastered the art of specialization and growth, so too did law firms. The 1970s ushered in significant growth in legal and regulatory expansion, with law firms specializing in corporate business law—particularly in the United States.

The cottage industry of law itself became more factory-like. Gillian Hadfield profiled the morphing of the legal industry into a bureaucratic behemoth in her book *Rules for the Flat World*.[15] For example, in 1968 there were only twenty law firms in the country that had over 100 lawyers; the largest had 169. By 1979, the largest law firm in Chicago was over ten times larger than the largest Chicago law firm in 1950, with 500 lawyers, and grew to 700 by 1984. By 2008, 23 American law firms employed over 1000 lawyers each. At the same time, corporations also grew their in-house legal staff.

Demand for the sheer number of lawyers also grew. The 1970s saw the number of lawyers grow by 75% and lawyers per 100,000 people jumped over 250—a 60% increase in just ten years. The 1980s saw the number of lawyers per 100,000 people pushed up another 20% to over 300. By the end of the twentieth century, there were almost 400 lawyers per 100,000 Americans.

As America entered the 21st century, the corporate law profession was a booming business, with many lawyers and firms specializing in niche roles as experts. One such specialty amounted to negotiating and structuring complex deals that complied with regulations while maximizing tax and jurisdictional advantages. Some firms micro-specialized into areas ranging from cloud-based software licenses to facilities management outsourcing agreements.

As the legal industry grew, so too did the philosophy of how to write contracts. Gone was the day of handshake deals, replaced by more formal and "complete" contracts designed to document the underlying business agreements. As the decades have passed, contracts have generally grown longer, containing detailed and futile plans on how to deal with an endless list of "what-if?" questions. Informal moral norms were replaced with formal contractual obligations resulting in the currently dominant form of contract—the *transactional* contract. The concept of business as a "transaction" has become so dominant in today's business lexicon that deal makers the world over often refer to "the transaction" rather than "the relationship" that will stem from papering the deal. A case in point is a mega-million dollar "strategic partnership" between a large university health system and an urgent care service provider who created an alliance with the intent of dominating regional health care in the northeast United States. While the grand plans discussed in board rooms and over expensive wine made great sense, the lawyers manifesting the agreement whittled down the intent of the partnership in the preamble of the agreement as follows:[16]

> WHEREAS, simultaneously with the closing of the Transactions, the parties are entering into a Trademark License Agreement in the form set forth as Exhibit A and a Clinical Affiliation Agreement in the form set forth as Exhibit B.

A closer look at the details of the contract revealed the true nature of what the parties legally manifested. The vast majority of the contract was about how to allocate shares of stock in lieu of the urgent care clinics using the university's logo. The Trademark License Agreement exhibit was a classic cut and paste licensing agreement. And the Clinical Affiliation Agreement—with over 100 pages peppered with "shall" statements—had no more than a mere reference to the lofty thinking left behind in the boardroom—with only two short paragraphs on how the urgent care service provider would collaborate on key initiatives to improve cost and patient flow between the organizations. Not surprisingly, the so-called partnership did not fulfill expectations.

Today, it is common for complex "transactions" to be hundreds, if not thousands, of pages long. We have seen one government supplier contract that was eight and one-half feet tall when printed on standard-sized paper! Many argue a need to hammer out every detail in black and white because they do not trust their partner. After all, today's business partners are no longer your neighbor; they are frequently an organization based halfway around the world, with a significantly different culture.

But is it realistic to believe you can address every commercial scenario in a contract? This is a question many scholars have studied over the years—including Nobel laureates Oliver Williamson and Oliver Hart. In the words of Oliver Williamson, "All complex contracts will be incomplete; there will be errors, omissions and the like."[17] Both Olivers strongly advocate that chasing the perfect contract is a fool's errand. Why? We live in a dynamic world. Writing a contract for a dynamic and complex relationship "today" will often not help us "tomorrow." Simply put, business happens. Things change, including the underlying deal covered by the contract.

# A New Approach—Putting the "Formal" into Relational Contracts

At the same time Hart and Moore were looking at traditional contracting approaches from an economic theory perspective, University of Tennessee researchers were studying relational contracting practices. How does healthy "give-and-take" manifest itself in practice and keep the relationship healthy? The University of Tennessee's work profiled some of the world's most successful relational contracts in the book *Vested: How P&G, McDonald's and Microsoft are Redefining Winning in Business Relationships.*[18] Researchers took their learnings and codified them into a methodology they coined "Vested," intending to create a repeatable process that would produce healthier and more sustainable relationships—and perhaps even get parties such as Island Health and the Hospitalists over their impasse in contract negotiations. This innovative approach is called Vested because the parties have a vested interest in each other's success.

One aspect that fascinated UT researchers was how informal relational contracting practices could be wildly successful—but are often eschewed and rarely embedded into a formal contract. Worse—the "goodness" from these informal relational practices outside of the contract were often abandoned when new stakeholders or leadership entered the picture. Take for example the widely touted Chrysler supplier relationships profiled in the July/August 1996 issue of *Harvard Business Review.*[19] The article profiles how Chrysler adopted relational contracting practices in 1989 to foster more collaboration and innovation from many of its key suppliers. The results were nothing short of an HBR-worthy article.

In the article professor Jeffrey Dyer explained how Chrysler adopted supplier management practices—including involving suppliers in product development and process improvement—thereby "radically changing the nature of the relationship" to one of a strategic partnership with shared risk and shared reward.

Here is the primary reason why we have become advocates for formal relational contracts rather than allowing informal relational contracts to suffice. Much of the commitments and collaborative relationship building and supplier management practices Chrysler adopted with their suppliers were never formally documented in their supply contracts. For example, the HBR article states, "Chrysler has given oral guarantees to more than 90% of its suppliers that they will have the business for the life of the model they are supplying and beyond."

After the DaimlerChrysler merger in 1998, Daimler's stronger command and control culture for managing suppliers overtook the softer and more collaborative approach Chrysler had built during the early 1990s. By 2000, many of the senior Chrysler leaders who had led the transformation of the firm during the previous decade had left DaimlerChrysler, either voluntarily or through outright firings, and had been replaced by Daimler personnel. The "new" Chrysler executives re-established the conventional adversarial approaches and suppliers did not have a contractual leg to stand on, as many of Chrysler's commitments were simple oral "handshake" deals and management practices. Suppliers quickly learned that handshake deals were not worth the paper they were (or were not) written upon! Shading started to replace collaboration and value quickly diminished.

"Sorry, nothing personal. It's business." This mantra is often a harbinger of informal relational contracts like Chrysler's hitting a contracting wall with relationships unraveling. What is the ROI for the supplier who made significant asset investments, benefiting Chrysler, on an oral commitment—only to be disappointed after the "New Sheriffs" have rolled into town? Without the *formal contractual* aspect, relationships like those with Chrysler are prone to shading.

UT researchers found while informal relational contracting practices, such as those implemented by Chrysler, can yield significant short-term results, they often are unsustainable due to New Sheriffs. Greg Laxton, Executive Director Fleet Support Unit for Australia's Royal Navy agrees. "Relational contracting practices can yield significant benefit such as what we found with the FFG. However, the strength of the FFG Enterprise is in the Charter that is simply one piece of paper sitting atop everything else. One person could do a lot of damage."[20]

John Henke's compelling research on Chrysler confirms Laxton's fears about how hard it is to sustain informal relational contracts. Henke has spent over twenty years studying the impact of supplier trust in the automotive industry. His 2014 article "Lost Supplier Trust, Lost Profits" tells the rest of the Chrysler story, showing how Chrysler missed out on $24 billion in profits between 2002 and 2014 due to Chrysler's reversion to adversarial contracting models—which drove suppliers to shading and abandoning their informal handshake commitments and eventually diminishing their drive toward continuous improvement and innovation.[21]

UT researcher's observations have led them to advocate creating *formal* relational contracts—in which the "fluffy" aspects of the parties' relationship that has proven to create value would be formally documented into a legally enforceable contract. Such a formal, well-structured relational contract includes many components of a traditional contract but also contains relationship-building elements such as a shared vision, guiding principles, and robust governance structures—designed to keep the parties' expectations and interests aligned.

The UT researchers' premise is simple. The contracting parties co-create a flexible contract framework purposefully designed to meet the dynamic nature of business. The driving purpose of the contract shifts from documenting the deal to guiding the parties toward continuous alignment over the life of the relationship. To do this, the parties first negotiate the rules of the relationship, including establishing guiding principles that will help the parties work through tough and often conflicting goals when business happens. Then, and only then, do parties move on to agree on the specific deal points.

UT researchers were curious if they were on to something. To test the concept, the researchers piloted the idea with willing organizations around the world such as Island Health.

A key contribution of this book is Part 4, which goes into the "how-to" through a proven five-step approach for creating a formal relational contract. Equally important as showing the how-to, we profile real-world examples of how progressive organizations and their commercial partners, such as Island Health and the Hospitalists, are putting formal relational contracting into practice.

## Harnessing the Potential

After spending ten years with over 50 organizations piloting the relational contracting concepts, one thing is clear—most contracting and legal professionals also view formal relational contracts as "fluffy." But should they?

Glenn Gallins, the attorney representing South Island Hospitalists, and a law professor at the University of Victoria, offers the following advice for embracing formal relational contracts: "The focus on negotiating the foundation of the relationship first is brilliant. But the real power is it threads all the way down to core decisions on how the parties would work ultimately into the contract clauses." Turning proven relational contracting practices into a formal contract ensures trust is built not just between individuals— but creates *organizational trust*—preventing the backsliding and shading that slipped into Chrysler's supplier relationships, ultimately limiting Chrysler's success through lost trust.

Could a formal relational contract have curbed shading and prevented the erosion of trust for Daimler Chrysler? In this book, we present compelling scientific research (see Part 2) why the answer to this question is YES. We also share real examples of how real organizations are using formal relational contracts to optimize value in their strategic business relationships.

## A Look Ahead

In a business world where strategic, long-term relationships are crucial to creating competitive advantage, contracting professionals have no choice but to overturn the status quo. In Chapter 2, we share a compelling case study of how Vancouver Island Health Authority and their Hospitalists challenged the status quo to view their labor services agreement through a different lens which led to a dramatic turnaround in the relationship. Read on to learn *why, what, when, and how* to apply the proven research into real-world relational contracts, which will benefit your strategic relationships and create a commercial competitive advantage.

## Notes

1. Daniel Kahneman, *Thinking, Fast and Slow* (New York: Farrar, Straus and Giroux, 2011).
2. For example, the discussion was debated at the *Stanford—IACCM Academic Symposium on Contract and Commercial Management* (a collaboration of WCC and the Arthur and Toni Rembe Rock Center for Corporate Governance at Stanford University on November 8, 2019).
3. Kate Vitasek and Karl Manrodt, with Jeanne Kling, *Vested: How P&G, McDonald's, and Microsoft are Redefining Winning in Business Relationships* (New York: Palgrave Macmillan, 2012).
4. Ibid.
5. Ibid.
6. Jeffrey H. Dyer, "How Chrysler Created an American Keiretsu," *Harvard Business Review*, July–August 1996.
7. The FFG example has been well-documented in several articles as well as comprehensive case study authored by University of Tennessee researchers. See Kate Vitasek, Andrew Downard and Jeanne Kling, "The Royal Australian Navy FFG Enterprise," University of Tennessee case study (2018). Available at https://www.vestedway.com/wp-content/uploads/2018/05/The-Royal-Austra lian-Navy-FFG-Enterprise-April-27-2018.pdf.

8. Ian R. Macneil, *Contracts: Instruments for Social Cooperation* (Hackensack, NJ: F. B. Rothman, 1968). Also see The Relational Theory of Contract: Selected Works of Ian Macneil (Modern Legal Studies), 2001.

9. Kate Vitasek and Karl Manrodt, with Jeanne Kling, *Vested: How P&G, McDonald's, and Microsoft Are Redefining Winning in Business Relationships* (New York: Palgrave Macmillan, 2012).

10. See "The Long and the Short of Contracts," *The Royal Swedish Academy of Sciences*, 10 October 2016 press release. Available at https://www.nobelprize.org/prizes/economic-sciences/2016/press-release/.

11. See Stephen M. Covey, et al., *The Speed of Trust: The One Thing That Changes Everything* (New York: Free Press, 2006).

12. Kate Vitasek, Mike Ledyard, and Karl Manrodt, *Vested Outsourcing: Five Rules That Will Transform Outsourcing*, Second Edition (New York: Palgrave Macmillan, 2013). Chapter 12.

13. Oliver Hart, John Moore, Contracts as Reference Points, NBER Working Paper No. 12706, Issued November 2006, revised 2007.

14. David Frydlinger and Oliver D. Hart, "Overcoming Contractual Incompleteness: The Role of Guiding Principles," National Bureau of Economic Research Working Paper No. 26245 (September 2019). Available at https://www.nber.org/papers/w26245.

15. Gillian Hadfield, *Rules for a Flat World: Why Humans Invented Law and How to Reinvent It for a Complex Global Economy* (Oxford University Press, 2016).

16. Companies wish to remain anonymous. Contract Reviewed by Kate Vitasek September 2019.

17. Oliver E. Williamson, "Outsourcing: Transaction Cost Economics and Supply Chain Management," *Journal of Supply Chain Management,* Vol. 44, No. 2 (April 3, 2008). Available at https://onlinelibrary.wiley.com/doi/full/10.1111/j.1745-493X.2008.00051.x.

18. *Vested*, Ibid.

19. Dyer, Ibid.

20. FFG case study, Ibid.

21. John W. Henke Jr., Thomas T. Stallkamp, and Sengun Veniyurt, "Lost Supplier, Lost Profits," *Supply Chain Management Review*, May/June 2014.

# 2

# Viewing Contracting Through a Different Lens

When Kim Kerrone joined Vancouver Island Health Authority (Island Health) in September 2012 as the Vice-President, Chief Financial Officer, Legal Services & Risk, she was excited about the prospects of bringing her business and contracting acumen to Island Health. However, she was not excited about inheriting what many referred to as "the troubles" with South Island Hospitalists Inc. (SIHI)—a collective bargaining group comprised of family physician Hospitalists who cared for some of the sickest patients in Victoria, British Columbia.

Between 2000 and 2012, Island Health and SIHI had negotiated their contract three times.[1] Kerrone did not want to go through the historically grueling SIHI contract negotiations on her watch. Despite multiple attempts at negotiation, the contract expired in July 2014, with the parties continuing to operate under the terms of the expired contract. The environment to achieve a new contract was challenging. Deep-seated distrust led to a negative tit-for-tat negotiations cycle. Each side argued that the contract talks were not about money, but about how to perform the job and by how many doctors. The Hospitalists felt they were being mismanaged and monetarily squeezed. They wanted a more flexible workload-based contract and argued Island Health's plan included cutbacks that would jeopardize physician safety and the ability to deliver an excellent and consistent service to patients in Victoria. SIHI argued more Hospitalists were needed to maintain quality of care levels safely.

© The Author(s), under exclusive license to Springer Nature Switzerland AG 2021
D. Frydlinger et al., *Contracting in the New Economy*,
https://doi.org/10.1007/978-3-030-65099-5_2

For their part, Island Health Administrators were concerned about the transparency of SIHI's scheduling and hourly billing practices. The Hospitalists' inefficient reporting procedures caused Island Health Administrators to distrust the Hospitalists' census number calculations, as well as how they managed scheduling. Limited data and poor communications, coupled with a longstanding lack of trust, exacerbated the situation.

Dr. Manjeet Mann, MD, FRCP, a cardiologist who had been promoted to Island Health's Executive Medical Director, describes the relationship: "It became toxic and the lack of trust and transparency led to a tit-for-tat cycle of actions on each side."

Contract negotiations came to an abrupt halt with the notice to cease the contract at midnight on February 28, 2015. Headlines from local papers added fuel to the fire:

- "Doctors suspended for refusing patients, health authority says." *Times Colonist*, March 10, 2015
- "One year later, no sign of deal for Greater Victoria hospitalists." *Times Colonist*, April 8, 2015

Kim Kerrone's enthusiasm for bringing contracting excellence to Island Health waned.

Kerrone reflects, "We had made no progress on getting a contract because of the deep-seated feelings of distrust and animosity between the two sides. Patient care was happening, but we didn't have a contract; it was just a really bad environment – there was no trust, no trust whatsoever."

## Making the Shift

Call it serendipitous, a coincidence, fate—or all three—but Kerrone attended a presentation on February 1, 2016, that would be marked as a seminal turning point in how Island Health and the Hospitalists would approach contract negotiations. Kate Vitasek, a University of Tennessee (UT) faculty member for graduate and executive education, was presenting the Vested business model for the British Columbia (BC) health authorities where she shared a highly collaborative methodology in which buyers and suppliers co-created a relational contract.[2] As part of the presentation, a Vancouver Coastal Health Authority (VCH) representative shared how they used the Vested model to transform the way VCH worked with an environmental services provider, Compass.[3]

Kerrone noted that listening to Vitasek made her think, "Wow, this is what we need for the Hospitalists. I thought that the approach would be just perfect for resolving the standoff."

She went to other Island Health Administrators to get their feedback, including Courtney Peereboom, Director, Special Projects and In-Facility Care at Island Health, and Dr. Brendan Carr, MD, CCFP(EM), MBA, and Island Health's President and CEO at the time.

Peereboom reviewed UT's website on Vested and downloaded the open-source material to learn more about Vested. She commented, "A Vested partnership approach made sense given that the Hospitalists care for the majority of our adult inpatients in South Island. If we wanted to move the dial on strategic priorities such as improving patient flow and system access, we had to work with this group differently than we had in the past. We had really run out of options using traditional negotiation methods. Vested seemed like the only way forward that we had and we had to try it."

Kerrone got the green light to arrange an initial meeting with Hospitalist leaders. Of course, there was still distrust and suspicion and the meeting was tense. But Dr. Jean Maskey, MD, CCFP, FCFP, remembers thinking, "The Vested methodology sounded incredible. We were, of course, skeptical. But we had nothing to lose; nowhere else to go."

Dr. Patrick Slobodian, MD, CCFP, was one of the skeptics. He was one of the original Hospitalists in Victoria who helped to develop the Hospitalist program. He remembers feeling "disenfranchised and disempowered." Dr. Slobodian described the overall sentiment of the Hospitalists: "As a group, the Hospitalists really felt trapped by obligations to our patients through the College of Physicians and Surgeons to stay at work. It was a hard time and we were all very cynical about anything suggested by the Administrators. However, there was little other choice but to tentatively give the Vested method a try."

Ultimately Island Health and the Hospitalists engaged with The Forefront Group—a Vested Center of Excellence—to facilitate a three-day "Alignment workshop." If that went well Island Health and SIHI would then make a "go/no go" decision to proceed with the Vested methodology to help them shift to a formal relational contract. The Forefront Group had helped Vancouver Coastal Health and Compass co-create a Vested agreement for environmental services and had experience in creating Vested agreements in the healthcare sector. Both parties liked the idea of The Forefront Group playing the role of a neutral third-party facilitator. They also liked the fact they did not have to formally commit to the Vested methodology out of the gate.

The result? Both parties set the three-day workshop[4] to begin on May 30, 2016.

Part 4 shares how Island Health and SIHI used a proven five-step methodology to help them transform their troubled relationship and traditional transactional contract into a healthy and productive relationship founded on a formal and flexible relational contract.

## Success with the Shift

Do formal relational contracts really work? If you ask Kim Kerrone and Dr. Jean Maskey, they will echo a resounding, "YES!". The parties used the UT Vested methodology to help them ink a highly collaborative win-win deal in 2016—something which many believed was impossible. Dr. Maskey—the lead negotiator for SIHI—calls it "fairytale-ish." She adds, "The approach was not our usual way of thinking – but it was wildly successful at getting us unstuck. We were no longer simply interested in developing 'a' contract, but in developing an excellent contract with excellent relationships that would allow all of us to be leaders in Canadian health care, whether as Administrators or Hospitalists."

Dr. Ken Smith, MD, CCFP, reflects, "The contract really did mark a profound fundamental change that has persisted in our relationship with the administration and our group. We now work together on what our goals are. We are actually helping each other get past the hurdles as opposed to putting up barriers. The change is quite profound."

The before and after descriptions of the relationship are nothing short of transformational—*with a shift from 84.5% negative words to 86.2% positive in just over two years* (Figs. 2.1 and 2.2).

Dr. Smith believes the improved relationship is the number-one success factor stemming from the Vested process, "because I think you can't work together unless there's a relationship." And true to a formal relational contract, the Island Health-SIHI contract puts the parties' relationship front and center in the actual contract.

But having happy physicians is only one aspect. True success comes from delivering on the shared vision and desired outcomes formalized in the contract. Some of the tangible benefits arising from the improved relationship include:

- A stabilized Hospitalist program with reduced turnover
- Improved scheduling, dramatically improving working hours and resulting in the Hospitalists beating the budget target the first year of the agreement

**Fig. 2.1** The VCH/Hospitalist relationship description 2016–2018—Wordle™ Before Vested (May 2016)

**Fig. 2.2** The VCH/Hospitalist relationship description 2016–2018—Wordle™ After Vested (October 2018)

- Shared savings generating incentives that were reinvested for the Hospitalists to use on Quality of Care initiatives
- Proactive hiring—enabling the Hospitalists to have the manpower they need and reducing physician burnout
- Formalized governance structures enabling collaborative discussions—with the level of interest and participation increasing beyond the original Deal Architect team
- Improved reporting and data accuracy across many aspects of the business (e.g., scheduling, billing)
- Improved communications and transparency
- Streamlined information flow between the Hospitalists and Administrators
- Joint working on initiatives—creating improved patient outcomes

Kim Kerrone points to a success story where occupational therapists, clinical nurse leaders, and physician leaders came together and worked on increasing efficiency in patient discharges and developing support structures for improved access and flow. This occurs daily on all of the wards where Hospitalists work with the interdisciplinary teams in "Structured Team Reports".

Kerrone believes the parties are just scratching the surface. "Both sides want to work together and do great work. It's truly transformational."

The COVID-19 pandemic hit the healthcare industry particularly hard and one could expect tensions to run high in the face of uncertainties and change. We interviewed them to see how they fared in the wake of the pandemic. Specifically, were they living into the intentions and guiding principles they put in place as part of their formal relational contract? And did the relational mechanisms they established in their contract help them work through the many issues raised by the pandemic fairly and flexibly?

Kerrone explains the situation. "When the pandemic hit, we were suddenly faced with a 60% reduction in overall patient census on the one hand - yet on the other hand physicians needed to manage higher-risk COVID-19 patients. The impact on budget and workload was drastic: physicians treated far fewer yet higher risk patients. Questions such as who would get to work what hours and who would have to work in the new high-risk COVID-19 ward were front and center."

Dr. Maskey explains how the parties' formal relational contract helped them be ready to address the changes fairly and flexibly. "Our Vested relational contract uses Guiding Principles such as autonomy and equity. Using these Guiding Principles as the backdrop for decisions, we found an effective way to rethink schedule allocations to reduce Hospitalist hours while keeping all physicians employed. Part of the process also 'banked' hours which can be used for future surges. Without our Vested relational contract, this would have been arduous under the old contract."

## Why Change? Why Now?

In Chapter 1, we profiled how McDonald's and the Royal Australian Navy use informal relational contracts to drive collaborative behaviors and generate value. In this chapter, we shared how Island Health and SIHI took a path to create a formal relational contract. If McDonald's and the Australian Navy have had so much success with informal relational contracts why bother to have a formal relational contract?

The simple answer to this question is that business has changed and continues to evolve, but contracts have not. As a result of businesses changing, those organizations have started to face the contracting paradox.

Most of the twentieth century was dominated by the *vertically integrated enterprise*, incorporating complex supply and distribution chains in one organization or group of organizations. Harvard Business School's Michael Porter wrote the manuals for creating a competitive strategy in a vertically integrated enterprise in his best-selling books, *Competitive Strategy*,[5] and *Competitive Advantage*.[6] For Porter, the enterprise was a combat unit on a battlefield forged by five market forces creating a threat of rivalry among existing firms, the threat of new entrants, the threat of substitute products or services, the bargaining power of buyers, and the bargaining power of suppliers.[7]

Ironically Porter wrote the rulebook at a time when vertically integrated organizations were already beginning to shift to more decentralized and networked structures. The shift was brought to the forefront in 1989 when management guru Peter Drucker eloquently argued in his *Wall Street Journal* article that organizations should "Sell the Mailroom."[8] A year later, Prahalad and Hamel argued that corporations should focus on their core competencies in their influential *Harvard Business Review* article.[9] CEOs around the world mandated, "Do what we do best and outsource the rest."

A new economy emerged. The result is that organizations today have a virtual network of suppliers and business partners around the globe that supply not just commodities that feed the industrial engine of the past, but also highly strategic and essential services. While many organizations chose growth through strategic supplier relationships and outsourcing agreements, others were choosing franchise or distribution agreements to gain access to new markets around the world. In these new models, the organization no longer relies solely on employees, employment agreements, and human resource strategies. Instead, a hybrid model that also includes commercial partners, commercial contracts, and commercial strategies has been established.

Let's look at some of the key attributes of today's market.

Today's markets are more **global.** In the past, markets were smaller and more confined by national boundaries. Globalization has either lowered or removed these boundaries. While national market segmentations do still exist, today's markets are geographically much more diverse.

Today's markets are more **complex.** In the mass-market economy, with large vertically integrated corporations as the main players, demand was easier to predict. Orders were managed through a backlog and demand was largely driven by the corporations themselves. This approach was proclaimed by Henry Ford, "My customer can have a car painted any color that he wants so long as it is black."[10] Today, *the* customer no longer exists; rather, the economy includes a multitude of customers with different expectations that rapidly and constantly change in unpredictable ways. Entire organizations, such as Amazon, have succeeded in serving the "long tail" of customer demand to an extent previously deemed as unprofitable.[11]

Today's markets are *faster.* The speed of the market and market changes is astonishing. New products and services can become obsolete in a matter of months. While innovation has always been important, innovation is now an imperative, requiring that organizations be flexible and responsive to change. Contracting must address VUCA—a term borrowed from the defense sector.[12] VUCA stands for Volatility, Uncertainty, Complexity, and Ambiguity—realities that today's organizations and supply chains continually face. Contracts are not the only arrow in the quiver. Relationships and social norms are part of the solution.

To summarize, markets are more global, more complex, and faster. Successful organizations rely on partner networks through more strategic commercial relationships to navigate the new economy. Whatever the contract vehicle, the combat unit is an organization's network, not the discrete organization entity itself. Commercial contracting success depends on how the commercial partners manage VUCA.

As organizations transitioned into the new economy, trading practices and behaviors were disrupted. Long-term relationships were discarded in the search for competitive advantage, whether in the name of innovation or cost reduction. The mantra "Nothing personal, it's just business" emerged as a common excuse in the quest for opportunistic behavior. Commercial culture became more adversarial, as "partners" battled over minimum prices, onerous terms, and allocating risks and responsibility for performance to the other party. The contracting paradox was rearing its ugly head.

Unfortunately, stories like Island Health (prior to their relational contracting journey) are not unique. A quick review of newspaper headlines highlights the same story. A sobering example is a very public debacle involving Apple's $578 million "strategic" partnership with GT Advanced Technologies (GTAT) for production of the sapphire glass for Apple's much anticipated Apple Watch.[13] Apple claimed GTAT failed to reach performance targets in their contract. GTAT then claimed they could no longer afford to service Apple because Apple kept changing the specifications for the glass for its new Apple Watch. The constant pressures and variations in volume commitments put a severe strain on GTAT as they spent their time and money adjusting to Apple's every whim. Apple eventually withheld payment, which led to GTAT declaring bankruptcy. Ultimately, the case went to court.

To quote GTAT's legal team, "Our management foolishly accepted oppressive and burdensome terms and obligations - so now we are trying the Chapter 11 route to escape the noose we placed around our own necks."

While no one will ever know if this was preventable, the Apple-GTAT story is one depicted by organizations operating in today's new economy. Apple needed to have the flexibility to tweak the design for the glass for its newly designed Apple Watch. And volumes for a new product are hard to predict. While shifting risk to GTAT through contract terms might have sounded like a way to reduce risk, the risk was still present. The bottom line: Apple and GTAT fell victim to human nature in a downward spiral of negative tit-for-tat behavior that ultimately ended up in court.

Some skeptics might be thinking, "yeah, yeah – but how many contract disputes go to court? All this fuss is over such a small minority of deals that go bad. My organization can navigate to keep us out of court."

It's a good argument when you consider only a small fraction of contracts appear in court. But have you considered the opportunity costs associated with having friction with trading partner relationships? Research by World Commerce & Contracting (WCC) suggests the lost potential can be staggering, showing that poor contracting costs the average organization an equivalent of 9.15% of its annual revenue.[14] This loss—often called *value leakage*—takes the form of increased costs, missed savings, and lost revenues.

WCC is not the only body researching this topic. The Corporate Executive Board found that, in a typical outsourcing deal, the parties might erode up to 90% of anticipated value due to poor contract governance.[15] London School of Economics professor Leslie Wilcox studied 1200 outsourcing agreements and found that "power-based agreements" (those where the more powerful party imposes the terms) generate up to 40% higher costs than trust-based agreements.[16] And of course, there is John Henke's research linking the lack of supplier trust to lost profits.[17]

Perhaps the most illustrative example is General Motors, which was once regarded as one of the best managed and most successful firms in the world. But between 1980 and 2009 its market share in the United States fell from 62.6% to 19.8%, and in 2009 the firm went bankrupt.

GM's plight has been well researched—including being profiled in a Harvard Business School case study titled "Management Practices, Relational Contracts, and the Decline of General Motors."[18] Leading researchers suggest GM's issues stem from problems in developing contractual relationships essential to modern design and manufacturing. Researchers also suggest

GM's troubles can be linked to GM's arms-length approach and transactional contracting strategy, which include: (1) GM's historical practice of treating its suppliers as homogeneous, interchangeable entities; (2) GM's view that expertise could be partitioned; and (3) that holistic decisions could be made by solely using financial criteria. Dr. Ignacio Lopez—GM's worldwide head of purchasing—was known for saying, "I do not want to hear any more that prices are already down too far and you are making no profits. We have to change our attitudes. No more excuses."

GM's approach led to one major supplier observing: "When is a contract not a contract? The answer – when it is with GM." When GM entered bankruptcy, many parts suppliers silently rejoiced. They knew that their parts would still be needed, as GM's production and sales would be diverted to other automobile manufacturers who were more collaborative, more relationship-based, and less like GM.

Simply put—there has to be a better way to keep business partners in continual alignment ensuring—to use the legal scholar's terminology—the real deal and the paper deal are aligned. We contend that a better way is a *formal relational contract* grounded in transparency, mutual goals, and a commitment to guiding principles to keep the relationship and economics in harmony throughout the life of a business relationship.

## Contracting in the New Economy

Oliver Hart offers compelling research validating why a formal relational contract is essential for contracting in highly dependent and complex scenarios such as purchasing arrangements, strategic alliances, joint ventures, franchises, public-private partnerships, major construction projects, and collective bargaining agreements—such as that between Island Health and the Hospitalists.

Recall in Chapter 1 Hart and Moore's expanded theory focusing on contracts as reference points?[19] This perspective emphasizes the need for mechanisms to continually align expectations—or updated reference points—as unanticipated events occur and require change. The logic is simple yet profound. If a contract sets the reference point for expectations, the contract should also set out the mechanism to keep the parties aligned when "business happens" and evolves, or when one (or both) of the parties are not meeting their expectations. Non-alignment will undermine the relationship, especially as the parties shade "to get even." The contract is, therefore, not only an instrument of risk mitigation but also an *expectations management instrument.*

In practice, alignment typically arises outside of the formal contract, via reciprocal daily interactions between the parties. The prevailing logic is these informal "relational" practices cannot be fully incorporated into a contract. Others argue a contract change control procedure is sufficient to keep the parties aligned.

*But is that enough?*

The answer is "it depends." Not all contracts or relationships are created equal. There is a spectrum of contracts and relationships, with small and simple transactions on one end and large and complex relationships on the opposite end. One can easily argue in a one-time $1000 transaction the relationship does not matter more than the deal itself. However, the more complex, dependent, and uncertain the future is, one can easily argue the justification to make the shift to formal relational contracts. In these most strategic deals, social norms—such as equity, reciprocity, and honesty—are an essential foundation for continual alignment of interests and expectations.

## The Rise of Formal Relational Contracts

As we have seen in this and the previous chapter, in today's complex markets, neither the informal relational contracting practice nor the formal transactional contract typically in use today enables the contracting parties to face the challenges represented in the contracting paradox. A new approach is needed. A growing number of organizations are adopting such a new approach.

Increasingly, value is emerging from a different kind of arrangement: a *formal relational contract* designed from the outset to foster trust and collaboration. The heart and soul of the relationship are formally documented by a commitment to mutual goals, guiding principles, and governance structures to keep the parties' expectations and interests aligned over the long term.

A growing number of large organizations—such as the Canadian government, AstraZeneca, Discovery Health, EY, Stedin, and the Swedish telecommunications firm Telia—are successfully using this approach to help build strategic partnerships. Or—with Island Health and SIHI—formal relational contracts are being used to help overcome contracting and relationship troubles.

Formal relational contracts are especially useful for highly complex relationships in which it is impossible to predict every what-if scenario. These include complicated outsourcing and purchasing arrangements, strategic alliances, joint ventures, franchises, public-private partnerships, major construction projects, and collective bargaining agreements—such as the one between Island Health and SIHI.

A key reason for the rise of formal relational contracts is that organizations increasingly understand that their business partners, suppliers, or labor unions play a critical role in generating value—through lowering costs, increasing quality, and driving innovation. Leaders routinely talk about the need for strategic relationships with shared goals and risks. However, when contract negotiations begin the parties frequently default to a transactional mindset. And when lawyers get involved, they often agonize over every conceivable adverse scenario, trying to put everything in black-and-white—most often reverting to tried and true contract clauses that aim to shift risk to the other party. Outside counsel often exacerbates the issue, as they must protect clients from these risks. Savvy contracting professionals recognize they have fallen victim to the contracting paradox and they need a shift in thinking to get them unstuck. As the saying goes, the significant problems you face cannot be solved with the same level of thinking when you created them. However, many are still skeptics.

## A Look Ahead

We discuss the skepticism head-on in four chapters in Part 2—The Science of Contracting. Read on where we share over seventy years of science supporting the concepts behind why a formal relational contract is perhaps the best defense in today's new economy.

## Notes

1. "The Island Health – Hospitalist Journey to Vested: A New Day, New Way," University of Tennessee (Case Study, 2018). Note all subsequent quotes from Administrators and Hospitalists are from the case study available at https://www.vestedway.com/wp-content/uploads/2018/11/Island-Health-TEACHING-case-study-2018.pdf.
2. See Kate Vitasek, Mike Ledyard, and Karl Manrodt, *Vested Outsourcing: Five Rules That Will Transform Outsourcing*, Second Edition (New York: Palgrave Macmillan, 2013).

3. Information and subsequent quotes are in the UT/Vested case study "Vested for Success: How Vancouver Coastal Health Harnessed the Potential of Supplier Collaboration." Available at http://www.vestedway.com/vested-library/.

4. For information on Vested workshops, see the UT/Vested website at http://www.vestedway.com/3-day-open-enrollment-course/ for details about the 3-Day Open Enrollment Course.

5. Michael Porter, *Competitive Strategy: Techniques for Analyzing Industries and Competitors* (New York: The Free Press, 1980).

6. Michael Porter, *Competitive Advantage: Creating and Sustaining Superior Performance* (New York: The Free Press, 1985).

7. Porter, Competitive Strategy, p. 3.

8. Peter Drucker, "Sell the Mailroom," *Harvard Business Review*, July 25, 1989. Available at http://www.wsj.com/articles/SB113202230063197204.

9. C. K. Prahalad and Gary Hamel, "The Core Competencies of the Corporation," *Harvard Business Review* Vol. 68, No. 3 (1990), pp. 79–91.

10. Henry Ford, *My Life and Work*, in collaboration with Samuel Crowther, 1922, p. 72.

11. Chris Anderson, *The Long Tail: Why the Future of Business Is Selling Less of More* (New York: Hyperion, 2006).

12. See the Wikipedia definition at https://en.wikipedia.org/wiki/Volatility,_uncert ainty,_complexity_and_ambiguity.

13. Eric Sherman, "An unsightly peek into Apple business practices," CBS News MoneyWatch, October 14, 2014. Available at https://www.cbsnews.com/news/ gt-advanced-technologies-blames-apple-agreement-for-its-failure/.

14. "The Value of Contract Management: Return on Investment-Survey Results," *International Association for Contract and Commercial Management* (September, 2013).

15. Ibid.

16. L. Willcocks, S. Cullen, "The Outsourcing Enterprise 2: The Power of Relationships" (London: LogicaCMG, 2005).

17. John W. Henke Jr., Thomas T. Stallkamp, Sengun Veniyurt, "Lost Supplier, Lost Profits," *Supply Chain Management Review*, May/June 2014.

18. Susan Helper and Rebecca Henderson, "Management Practices, Relational Contracts and the Decline of General Motors," *The Journal of Economic Perspectives*, Vol. 28, No. 1 (Winter 2014), pp. 49–72(24).

19. Oliver Hart, John Moore, "Contracts as Reference Points," NBER Working Paper No. 12706 ? (November 2006), revised 2007.

# Part II

## The Science of Contracting

There is an old saying the only one who likes change is a wet baby. Change is never easy and seldom welcome; it has always been the case and will always be. This is especially true with relational contracts—it has met and will continue to meet resistance since legal scholars first introduced the concept in the 1960s.

For many, the shift to a new way of thinking starts with the WHY? *Why are contracts written and entered into? What purposes does the contract fulfill?* The answers can, to a large extent, be found as we address *the science of contracting in* Part 2.

It is important to remember that knowledge and reason have always been staunch allies of change in human history. In the 2018 best-seller *Enlightenment Now*,[1] professor Steven Pinker of Harvard University describes how the movement towards science and reason–started in the eighteenth century and called the Enlightenment—has brought about unprecedented progress for mankind in health, prosperity, safety, peace, and happiness.[2] While we don't want to compare the current state of the contracting world to the Dark Ages, we do believe a good portion of scientific knowledge and sound reasoning will enable and bring about the shift towards relational contracts and, as a consequence, the many benefits that typically come with such contracts.

Part 2 provides an aerial view of the science of contracting to help you connect the dots on the WHY. Some may find Part 2 controversial, as we openly look at contracting not just from the legal perspective, but also from the social science, economic science, and psychological aspects. Others will think it is eye-opening.

We start with a short chapter revisiting Stewart Macaulay's iconic 1963 article "Non-Contractual Relations in Business: a Preliminary Study."[3] We say *revisit* because Macaulay's article is the most cited article on contracting of the last fifty years, and sets the scene with his premise that while businesses want contracts, business people do not—or at least, not in their current form.

Chapters 3–6 are devoted to sharing the science of contracting. We draw upon the research from some leading thinkers whose work challenges the conventions that have driven how much of the Western world has approached contracting for the last century. These thinkers include mostly non-legal professionals who explore significant social, economic, and psychological factors that cannot be ignored by today's contracting professionals. There is a chapter devoted to each discipline.

Chapter 3 explores why businesses want contracts, yet business people do not.

Chapter 4 explains the social science of contracting and lays the foundation for why organizations need to make the shift to relational contracts that embed social norms in the very fabric of their contracts.

Chapter 5 introduces Nobel Prize-winning economic research that cannot be ignored in today's dynamic and risky contracting environment and goes to the heart of the economic rationale that underpins every contract.

Chapter 6 brings in the often overlooked and ignored psychological research that proves that we must think about how people think—and act—when it comes to contracting. In this chapter, we also discuss the important insights from behavioral economics.

When viewed in combination, the chapters in Part 2 provide an enlightening view of the science behind contracting—much of which challenges the conventional dogmas and approaches to how organizations contract. Those who do not recognize the need to change and attempt to cling to the old ways will steadily lose relevance, especially as research increasingly reveals the cost associated with outdated contracting practices leftover from a by gone century.

We encourage you to spend time digesting Part 2 to challenge your thinking of how you contract. We will frequently refer back to these chapters throughout the book, since the relational contract—its structure, the process for entering into it, as well as much of its content, is based on much of the science discussed in this part.

For those wanting to lead the change effort, you will likely find yourself coming back to the science of contracting time and again, not least when you need to arm yourself with arguments for change.

# Notes

1. Steven Pinker, *Enlightenment Now*, (New York: Penguin Random House, 2018).
2. Ibid.
3. Stewart Macaulay, Non-Contractual Relations in Business: A Preliminary Study, American Sociological Review, Vol. 28, No. 1, February 1963, pp. 55–67.

# 3

# Businesses Want Contracts; Business People Do Not

In 1963, Stewart Macaulay likely did not know that he would become one of the most influential legal scholars of the 20th century. And he certainly never imagined his work would spur vast research in the scientific and scholarly side of contracts well into the 21st century.

Macaulay began his academic career at the University of Wisconsin Law School in 1957 where he dutifully taught bright young law school students about contracts.[1] But Macaulay, now a professor emeritus, was doing more than just teaching. He was busy researching what would become the most cited article in contract law.[2] His research involved studying the contracting practices of 43 businesses including General Electric, S.C. Johnson, and Harley Davidson. Macaulay collected and analyzed standard contract forms.[3] He also conducted surveys and interviews with businesspeople and reviewed 15 years of court cases involving the 500 largest manufacturing firms in the United States at the time.[4]

The work culminated with an article titled "Non-Contractual Relations in Business: A Preliminary Study" in 1963,[5] which would become one of the most influential—and controversial—cited works on contract law of the twentieth century. Ironically, the article itself had little to say about contract law. Rather, the article starts with a challenge to contract law—"What good is contract law? Who uses it, when and how?"

A seminal conclusion of Macaulay's study was that contract law and contracts matter much less than many think, not least lawyers.[6]

Macaulay defined the term "contract" as involving two elements:

© The Author(s), under exclusive license to Springer Nature Switzerland AG 2021
D. Frydlinger et al., *Contracting in the New Economy*,
https://doi.org/10.1007/978-3-030-65099-5_3

(a) Rational planning of the transaction with careful provision for as many future contingencies as can be foreseen, and

(b) the existence or use of actual or potential legal sanctions to induce performance of the exchange or to compensate for non-performance.[7]

Many, if not most, contracting professionals would agree with Macaulay's definition. Some would also argue, at least based on the contract theory and research of Nobel laureate Oliver Hart, that the definition is incomplete. Chapter 6 will suggest that a contract also is a reference point for the parties' expectations of their future exchanges. But Macaulay's definition is of course partly true. Contract drafting involves a certain degree of planning for the future—some goods or services will be delivered; some money will be paid. Also, certain things can go wrong and must be dealt with. Simply put, contracts would probably not be written if there were no legal sanctions or informal ways to resolve disputes while keeping the parties aligned to the intent of their agreement.

So why did Macaulay's research spark such debate and become the most cited work on contract law of the twentieth century? Primarily because many found Macaulay's conclusions controversial. His investigation revealed business people often failed to respect the definition of a contract and what a contract is or should be.[8] Simply put, they put the importance of business relationship over the business contract—spurring what has become known as "relational contracts." Why?

First—as for *planning*—many organizations Macaulay studied did indeed make plans in and through their contracts, not least in the form of standard contracts. However, to a surprisingly large extent, many organizations failed to sufficiently plan. For example, expensive machines had been purchased without adequate specifications. Five of seven lawyers interviewed thought that commercial contracting practitioners contracted with limited details in planning. Instead, they were relying on "a man's word."[9] Many contracting practitioners, when bargaining, talked in pleasant generalities but avoided many of the tough details unless forced to face them by lawyers. Furthermore, many organizations entered into agreements based on both parties' standard contracts, which often contradicted each other. The reality? Planning took place, but to a much lesser degree than expected.

Second—on the matter of *inducing performance through legal sanctions*—the picture was even more puzzling. Macaulay found that some contracts were probably not even legally enforceable.[10] For example, he found that a standard contract in the paper manufacturing industry had a pricing clause that a New York court had said was not enforceable. Interestingly enough, everyone in the industry seemed to have known this, but still the same clause was used. Furthermore, Macaulay found that disputes between enterprises rarely ended up in court. Rather disputes were resolved without reference to the contracts (a situation which current research indicates is still prevalent). Many wanted to keep the lawyers out of the picture. Macaulay quoted a contracting practitioner, "You can settle any dispute if you keep the lawyers and accountants out of it. They just do not understand the give-and-take needed in business."[11]

Macaulay's research turned the premise of a contract on its head; businesses wanted contracts, but business people often did not. Often, business people simply ignored their contracts because contracts came with undesirable consequences. Macaulay rightly stated that detailed "negotiated contracts can get in the way of creating good exchange relationships between business units." An insistence on a very detailed contract "indicates a lack of trust and blunts the demands of friendship, turning a cooperative venture into an antagonistic horse trade. ... Business men may welcome a measure of vagueness in the obligations they assume so that they may negotiate matters in light of the actual circumstances."[12]

Against this background, with organizations using neither contracts nor contract law in the ways expected, Macaulay asked two very justified and fundamental questions:

(A) How can a business successfully operate exchange relationships with relatively so little attention to detailed planning or to legal sanction, and
(B) Why does business ever use a contract in light of its success without it?[13]

Macaulay was careful to point out that the answer to these questions needed further studies. However, he gave provisional answers based on what he had learned when conducting the study.

One of Macaulay's answers was that business people used "non-contractual practices" that served the purpose of a contractual planning function. For example, Macaulay found business people felt they did not need detailed planning because everyone knew the customs in their respective industries, filling the gaps in the written contracts. In the same way, core obligations or intent could be addressed through instruments such as a Letter of Intent or Memorandum of Understanding—exchanges with less formality that avoided the need to address potentially contentious issues regarding specific rights, obligations, or consequences. Abundant research into relational contracting shows this is still a common practice today.[14] If the practice is not going away, it is essential for contracting professionals to understand these practices since they provide mechanisms which both make contracts work in practice and outline the consequences.

A second answer Macaulay posited was that personal relationships between individuals of two organizations at all levels often replaced the function of the contract. These personal relationships created informal incentives and social pressure motivating the parties to comply with what had been agreed upon rather than rely on the threat of the court for a formal dispute resolution. This norm of business behavior can still be found in environments and cultures where trade is between parties that know each other well and where the tradition of commercial law is either alien or fails to offer a realistic resolution.[15]

Macaulay pointed to two essential norms:

(1) Commitments are to be honored in almost all situations; one does not welsh on a deal.

(2) One ought to produce a good product and stand behind it.[16]

Simply put, most business people care about reputation, and if you have a reputation for not honoring your word, you won't last long in business. Also, Macaulay wrote, "Not only do the particular business unit in a given exchange want to deal with each other again, they also want to deal with other business units in the future. And the way one behaves in a particular transaction, or a series of transactions will color his general business reputation. ... Thus, often contract is not needed as there are alternatives."[17]

Macaulay's second question—if business people didn't like contracts, why did they still use them—is likely the most significant part of his research.

Macaulay believed a partial answer to this question was that a contract functions as a communication instrument. For example, a "fairly detailed contract can serve as a communication device within a large corporation." The sales manager and in-house counsel may want to communicate with the production manager on what to produce and a sales manager "may want to remove certain issues from future negotiations by his subordinates."[18]

Macaulay also found that formal contract exchanges "are carefully planned when it is thought that planning and a potential legal sanction will have more advantages than disadvantages."[19] This was especially true "where there is a likelihood that significant problems will arise."[20]

Macaulay finally pointed to another crucial reason for using contracts. He pointed to the "relative bargaining power or skill of the two business units."[21] As most business professionals know, bargaining power is not a matter of the size of the parties, but a matter of dependency. As Macaulay rightly said, even "a giant firm can find itself bound to a small supplier once production of an essential item begins for there may not be time to turn to another supplier."[22] Macaulay's point was that the small supplier could abuse the large customer's dependency to its advantage. The risk of dependency has been well researched in the years following Macaulay's iconic article and is now commonly called the *hold-up problem*, a term coined by Victor Goldberg in an article in 1976.[23]

While Macaulay's research provides empirical evidence on why contracts were not used to the extent expected and why contracts were used at all, these answers are not what has made him the most cited academic scholar. Rather, Macaulay's legacy stems from the intriguing questions he posed that have been engaging contract scientists of all disciplines ever since. From a certain perspective, the different branches and dimensions of the science of contracts for the past 50 years can be seen as different attempts to answer these questions and other questions closely related to them.

## A Look Ahead

Chapters 4–6 address the big thinking behind the science of contracting and will highlight a central theme—the different scientific areas of relevance for contracts are not neutral; they come with consequences for how contracts should be entered into, written, and executed to achieve optimal results. These big-thinkers also lay the foundation and play a critical role in the thinking behind this book.

## Notes

1. Jean Braucher, et al., *Revisiting the Contracts Scholarship of Stewart Macaulay: On the Empirical and the Lyrical (International Studies in the Theory of Private Law)* (Oxford: Hart Publishing 2013), p. vii.
2. Fred R. Shapiro, *The Most-Cited Law Review Articles Revisited*, 71 Chicago-Kent Law Review, Vol. 751 (1996). Available at https://scholarship.kentlaw.iit. edu/cklawreview/vol71/iss3/3.
3. Gillian K. Hadfield and Iva Bozovic, "Scaffolding: Using Formal Contracts to Build Informal Relations in Support of Innovation," University of Southern California, Law and Economics Working Paper Series (February 2012). Working Paper 144.
4. Ibid. p. 2, footnote 3.
5. Stewart Macaulay, "Non-Contractual Relations in Business: A Preliminary Study," *American Sociological Review*, Vol. 28, No. 1 (February 1963).
6. Ibid. p. 1.
7. Ibid. p. 3.

8. Note: While Macaulay used the term "business men" and "business man," we have chosen to rephrase to business people.

9. Macaulay, p. 6.

10. Ibid. p. 9.

11. Ibid, p. 11.

12. Ibid. p. 15.

13. Ibid. p. 12.

14. Lisa Bernstein has done significant research into use of informal, non-contractual practices in the grain industry, diamond industry, and OEM parts suppliers. See, for example, "Beyond Relational Contracts: Social Capital and Network Governance in Procurement Contracts," *Journal of Legal Analysis*, Vol. 7, No. 2 (Winter 2015) and "Merchant Law in Merchant Court: Rethinking the Code's Search for Immanent Business Norms," *University of Pennsylvania Law Review*, Vol. 144, No. 5 (1996).

15. For example, in Japan and South Korea where commercial law is a recent development and where "keiritsu" and "chaebol" industry structures have until recently been the norm.

16. Macaulay, p. 13.

17. Ibid. p. 15f.

18. Ibid. p. 16.

19. Ibid. p. 16.

20. Ibid. p. 16.

21. Ibid. p. 18.

22. Ibid. p. 18.

23. Victor P. Goldberg, "Regulation and Administered Contracts," *The Bell Journal of Economics*, Vol. 7, No. 2 (Autumn 1976), pp. 426–448.

# 4

# The Social Science of Contracting

Chapter 3 summarized the seminal conclusion of Macaulay's study that law matters much less than many—especially lawyers—think.[1] This does not imply that businesses operate in a world analogous to the US's Wild West, with no rules nor incentives for correct behavior. Rather, Macaulay astutely observed the fact that in business, there is never only business; all business activities are carried out in society between people. Often these players involved have personal ties affected by shared social norms of what is right or wrong behavior, regardless of what the law says. While the law matters, other mechanisms such as social norms, group pressure, and more informal sanctions often matter much more.

One important branch of contract science Macaulay's research spurred is the social side of contracts, especially the importance of social norms for influencing how the parties act and behave. While Macaulay's research sparked the debate, the original thinking behind the importance of social norms in contracting can be traced back to Emile Durkheim, one of the founding fathers of sociology. In 1896, Durkheim claimed the "contract is indeed the supreme legal expression of cooperation,"[2] fulfilling an essential function in keeping the entire society together.

All contracting professionals should understand the social side of contracts and the role of social norms in all commercial relationships. A vital aspect of the relational contract is, as we will see, to deliberately leverage these social norms to the benefit of both parties, not least by lowering friction. Failing to understand the social context in which almost every commercial contract is

© The Author(s), under exclusive license to Springer Nature Switzerland AG 2021
D. Frydlinger et al., *Contracting in the New Economy*,
https://doi.org/10.1007/978-3-030-65099-5_4

embedded and failing to see the social forces affecting the parties' behaviors will typically lead to at least a partial failure to fulfill the contract.

## Contracts as Instruments for Social Cooperation

If Macaulay sparked some light on relational contracting, Ian Macneil set it ablaze. Macneil was vocal for viewing contracts as an *instrument of social cooperation*. Born in 1929, Macneil joined the law faculty of Cornell University in 1959. In 1980, he became the John Henry Wigmore Professor of Law at the Northwestern University School of Law, a position he kept until becoming professor emeritus in 1999.

Macneil challenged the dominant view in contract law most often called the "will theory," which states that the purpose of a contract, from a legal perspective, is to express the *mutual will* of the parties entering into a contract. Simply stated, will theory assumes that contracts are made between two autonomous and profit-maximizing parties who exchange *promises* at a certain point in time and typically document the promises, expressing this mutual will, in the form of a written contract. The *content of the contract* is, according to this contracting theory, exhausted by the content of those promises.

Macneil challenged this conventional view of a contract.[3] For Macneil, it is artificial, over-simplified, and lacking in realism. For him, a "contract" meant relations among people who have exchanged, are exchanging or expect to be exchanging in the future—in other words, exchange relations.[4] Macneil's core point in his attack on conventional theory was that exchange relations could never be restricted to only a set of promises. While exchanging promises creates a relationship and obligations, the scope of those relationships and obligations always points beyond and exceeds the content of the promises. The social context and social norms almost always come into play even though they are not explicitly expressed in the promises exchanged.

Viewing contracts as a relationship of exchanges and not merely a set of promises allowed Macneil to identify critical functions of the contract, in both the market and society in general, which contracting professionals should never forget.

Economic and other exchanges are typically carried out over time, and this potentially creates an unstable situation. Often, one party performs first with the second party subsequently performing at a future point. For example, a supplier provides a good and the buyer pays a month later. But how can the supplier trust that the buyer will pay him? The buyer may receive and use the goods but refuse to pay. In most cases the buyer would probably pay out of decency, naturally looking out for the other party's interest. But humans tend to be opportunistic and may choose not to pay. Macneil said:

> Man is both an entirely selfish creature and an entirely social creature, in that a man puts the interests of his fellows ahead of his own interests at the same time that he puts his interests first. … Man is, in the most fundamental sense of the word, irrational, and no amount of reasoning, no matter how sophisticated, will produce a complete and consistent account of human behavior, customs or institutions.[5]

The element of time in all exchanges, combined with the uncertainty of the altruistic or egoistic side of the other party, creates uncertainty. This uncertainty creates an inherent risk in all business deals. Social cooperation, without which society would not exist, is always at risk to some extent.

Macneil pointed to the fact that primarily two social norms, or "principles of behavior," are used to mitigate this risk: reciprocity (the obligation to return in kind) and solidarity (the obligation to look out for each other's interests).[6] These norms create conditions for social cooperation—contractual exchanges—to succeed. Consider the example of a supplier that provides a good and the buyer pays a month later. The buyer could decide not to pay the supplier after they have gotten their goods. The norm of reciprocity obliges the buyer to return in kind and the norm of solidarity to look out for the seller's interests. In combination, they induce the buyer to pay, thus solving the tension created by the element of time and man's egoistic-altruistic nature.

For Macneil, norms such as reciprocity and solidarity constituted a part of *all contractual relationships*, although to a varying extent. By entering into a contractual relationship, these and other norms are in essence *activated* and integrated into the relationship. "Activated" is used, as such norms are part of the social fabric in society and exist of any social relationship—be it commercial or personal. In this backdrop, Macneil espoused that *a contract is an instrument for social cooperation.*

To view contracts as only an exchange of promises, where the obligations of the parties never go beyond what they have promised, would ignore that norms go beyond the promises exchanged. It would be akin to an ostrich burying their head in the sand; they *do* exist and must be taken into consideration when writing a contract.

One of Macneil's major contributions is the concept that there are different types of contracts. Macneil observed that exchange "occurs in various patterns along a spectrum, ranging from highly discrete to highly relational."[7] He

**Fig. 4.1** Discrete to relational spectrum

distinguished between two major categories or models of contracts: the *discrete* contract and the *relational* contract. But he rightly concluded these are not distinct entities, but exist on a spectrum or continuum that starts with discrete and evolves increasingly toward relational[8] (see Fig. 4.1).

Macneil believed that discrete contracts are characterized by a short-duration of exchange, for objects with precise measurement and limited personal interaction, which is referred to in this book as a transactional contract.[9] Naturally, a transactional contract will not require much future cooperation. As a result, the "parties view themselves as free of entangling strings."[10]

On the other end of the continuum is the relational contract. Unlike the discrete contract, a relational contract typically covers a longer duration. Examples include employment, franchising, and outsourcing contracts. The objects of exchange may include easily-measured quantities, such as hours worked but also objects not so easily measured or quantifiable, such as customer satisfaction, engagement, innovation, or flexibility. In a relational contract, future cooperation is assumed, which also gives the relationship a different quality: "The entangling strings of friendship, reputation, interdependence, morality, and altruistic desires are integral parts of the relation."[11] At this relational end of the continuum, "the relation has become a mini-society with a vast array of norms beyond the norms centered on exchange and its immediate processes."[12]

One of Macneil's main arguments was that classical contract law was flawed since it treated *all contracts* on this continuum as if they were discrete contracts based on simple exchanges of promises. In fact, in classical contract law, no continuum exists; all contracts are viewed as discrete or transactional in their nature.

It is worth noting that procurement practices supported by more elaborate contracting practices from the late 1990s espoused this transactional view of the world and sought to "commoditize" all purchases. The mantra for many procurement organizations often insisted that complex systems or services should be broken into their component—discrete—parts as commodities so a buyer could compare a supplier's offerings "apples-to-apples" in a competitive bid. This approach was driven by price-based competition and also led to increasing efforts to use contracts as an instrument of risk transfer. Today, there is a growing sentiment that such an approach is not only unsustainable but also undermines the realization of value. In situations where there is higher risk or complexity using a "discrete" approach frequently leads to disputes and disappointment.[13] A critical factor behind this is that the social context in which complex commercial relationships are carried out is ignored.

## How to Have Order Without Law

The existence of social norms in the context of business and law has been widely studied. Ronald Coase—the 1991 recipient of the Noble Prize in economics—wrote a seminal work in 1960 titled "The Problem of Social Cost."[14] The article used several hypothetical examples of how ranchers should solve disputes. Coase's theory was that under the (unrealistic) assumption there was no cost for the ranchers to negotiate solutions; they would always find the solution that would be most beneficial to both parties.

In the 1980s, Robert Ellickson, professor Emeritus of Property and Urban Law, was behind a landmark study to test Coase's theory. Ellickson traveled to Shasta County, California to study how ranchers solve disputes. Ellickson described two key findings in his book *Order Without Law*.[15] First, the Coase prediction was partly verified. Shasta County ranchers had found rules which they applied to solve disputes in ways which over time were the most beneficial for everyone. Simply put, the ranchers had found a system of rules that created a win-win situation depicted by an efficient and fair system. But second, Coase was also proven wrong because the rules applied were not statutory. In the preface, Ellickson wrote: "I did not appreciate how unimportant law can be when I embarked on this project."[16] The rules that created a win-win situation for everyone in Shasta County were not legal rules but instead social norms.

Ellickson found several social norms at work among the Shasta County ranchers replacing the need for legal rules. In this chapter, the focus is placed on only two social norms—loyalty and equity. In later chapters, we focus on other norms.

## The Norm of Loyalty

One of Ellickson's fundamental questions was: what happens if a rancher's cattle wander off and damage a neighbor's crops? Specifically, who should suffer the consequences of the damage, the cattle owner or the neighbor?

It may seem obvious that the cattle rancher should pay. But Ronald Coase had correctly pointed out this is too simplistic. If the cattle rancher is held liable, the result might be for the rancher to restrict the size of their herd and in consequence produce less meat. Why is less meat better than fewer crops? From an economic viewpoint, Coase suggested the problem is to avoid the more serious harm.[17] In the case of Shasta County, meat was much more lucrative and thus cattle ranchers (and perhaps society) in theory would be harmed more than crop farmers.

The environment was ripe for Ellickson's research because the legal situation in Shasta County was itself confusing on the matter. In some areas, the law stated that property owners are strictly liable (i.e., responsible regardless of whether or not negligent) for the damages caused by their cattle. In other areas, the situation was reversed.[18] The fact that the laws were confusing did not seem to matter to the Shasta County ranchers—or perhaps was the reason they ignored them. Ellickson found Shasta County residents had little to no knowledge of the legal rules.

So, what did the Shasta County ranchers do? They did what any neighbor would do; they applied informal social norms of what it meant to be a "good neighbor." Ellickson found that being a good neighbor generally translated into cooperative behavior. When applied to cattle trespasses, it said that livestock owners—regardless of the applicable legal rules—were strictly liable for both intentional and accidental harms inflicted by its cattle.[19] But what would happen when a particularly bad-tempered or sex-starved bull couldn't help itself from wandering off? Well, the neighborly thing might be for the crop farmer to save the cattle rancher the money of repeated damages by castrating the offending bull. Although this would constitute a crime in the eyes of the law and destroys the economic value of the bull, there was a consensus in the community that even violent self-help in response to repeated violations could be justified.

Ellickson's research showed these solutions would in all likelihood minimize the total costs for everyone involved. His reasoning is important. First, it keeps costs low. By applying a simple rule, the ranchers did not need to waste time and money trying to determine whether the harmed neighbor had taken the steps necessary to mitigate its damages. Second, it was cheaper in totality to allocate strict liability to the cattle owners, who knew about barbed-wire fencing and who should act logically to control their herds.[20]

The social norm of developing a solution that minimizes the cumulative costs is a norm of *loyalty*.[21] In its most general form, it is a rule where everyone not only looks out for their interests but also regards the interests of others with equal importance. If a Shasta County cattle owner would argue against being liable for the harm inflicted by its cattle, the counter-argument, based on the loyalty norm, would be that it costs the cattle owner less to control its herd than it costs the neighbors to protect themselves from the cattle.

The loyalty norm is more than what good neighbors live by; it can be seen in action everywhere in society. In his studies of Wisconsin business people, Macaulay found a social norm (not to be found in any law) stating that "one ought to produce a good product and stand behind it."[22] Applying this norm put the risk of product defects on sellers who were typically much better informed about product characteristics and in a better position to control them. As Ellickson pointed out, this informal social norm aligned with Macaulay's findings.[23]

## The Norm of Equity

During his studies in Shasta County, Ellickson also wanted to research how the residents allocated costs for building fences between each other's properties. After all, a fence faces two properties and it is not self-evident who should carry the costs of building them. In economic terms, this is a problem of *public goods* which also includes a free-riding problem: "each adjoining landowner may selfishly delay fence work in the hope of free-riding on efforts of the other."[24] Just as in the case of straying cattle, laws were regulating this issue in Shasta County, but again most ranchers were unaware of these laws.

As in the case of straying cattle, the residents operated with informal social norms to deal with the issue of how to pay for fences. This time, they applied a norm of *equity*, which in practice is a principle of proportionality. Using the norm of equity, they called for "adjoining landowners to share fencing costs in rough proportion to the average number of livestock on the respective side of the boundary line."[25]

As with the other social norms discussed here, the equity or proportion-ality norm is often seen in society. For example, most people think that a person should be rewarded in proportion to his or her efforts. Macaulay's business people in Wisconsin applied a norm saying that commitments are to be honored. But they also applied the equity norm and were relieved from their duty to honor their commitment if, for example, it was impossible, i.e., if the costs of honoring the commitment would be disproportionate to the value of honoring the commitment.[26]

While this chapter focuses on the norm of loyalty and norm of equity, other norms have relevance and impact on successful relational contracting efforts. Another key norm is the norm of reciprocity. Elinor Ostrom, the 2009 co-recipient of the Nobel Prize in Economic Sciences, demonstrated that everyday people, rather than exclusively governments, are capable of creating rules and institutions for the sustainable and equitable management of shared resources, such as oil fields and grazing lands. Reciprocity, along with trust, is essential to a wide range of economic and social transactions: from selecting a spouse to choosing an employer or employee, or one-time transactions such as purchasing a home. Unless one is willing to reciprocate— place trust in the other party and cooperate with them in a non-exploitive manner—the overall benefits from the arrangement will be minimized. We will have more to say about reciprocity in Chapter 5.

## Learnings

The research of Macneil, Ellickson, and others contains essential learnings for anyone drafting relational contracts designed to keep two parties in alignment. The below learnings apply to longer-term, complex contracts:

- Most contractual relationships exist within a social relationship where social norms play an essential role in facilitating communication and influencing the parties toward cooperative behavior
- A contract should be viewed as an instrument of social cooperation, enabling the contracting parties to deal with their diverse incentives of being egoistic and altruistic
- A contract is, therefore, also always more than the written document. To a larger or lesser extent, every contract is embedded in social relations governed by strong social norms
- Loyalty, equity, and reciprocity are three of the essential social norms in most contractual relationships (we discuss the other social norms in later chapters). In a relational contract, they should be explicitly included and transformed into contractual norms
- Contracts exist on a scale from discrete, or transactional, contracts to relational contracts

- The transactional contract is characterized by short-term duration, clear measurement, little personal involvement, and a low need for coordination and cooperation
- The relational contract is characterized by longer-term duration, less precise measurement, more personal involvement, and a high need for coordination and cooperation

## A Look Ahead

In Chapter 5, we look at contracts from the economic perspective, with three different lenses: contract theory, new institutional economics, and repeated game theory. Each theory is addressed in detail—as all three share useful insights into the science of contracting.

## Notes

1. Stewart Macaulay, "Non-Contractual Relations in Business: A Preliminary Study," *American Sociological Review*, Vol. 28, No. 1 (February 1963).
2. Emile Durkheim, *The Division of Labor in Society* (New York: Macmillan, 1984), p. 79.
3. Note that for Ian Macneil, the exchange carried out in this relationship must not necessarily be an economic exchange, even though this is, of course, the most common sort of exchange.
4. Ian Macneil, "Relational Contract Theory: Challenges and Queries", in *The Relational Theory of Contract: Selected Works of Macneil* (London: Sweet & Maxwell, 2001). Hereafter referred to as *Selected Works of Macneil*, p. 366.
5. Macneil, "Values in Contract, Internal and External," in *Selected Works of Macneil*, p. 153.
6. Ibid. p. 154 Macneil uses the term solidarity in the same meaning as the guiding principle of "loyalty" is used in this book.
7. Macneil, "Relational Contract Theory as Sociology: A reply to Professors Lindenberg and de Vos," in *Selected Works of Macneil*, p. 312.
8. David Frydlinger, Kate Vitasek, Tim Cummins, Jim Bergman, "Unpacking Relational Contracts: The Practitioner's Go-To Guide for Understanding Relational Contracts," White Paper by the UT Haslam College of Business, IACCM, CIRIO (2019). Available at https://www.vestedway.com/wp-content/uploads/2019/05/Unpacking-Relational-Contracting_Jan-2019.pdf.
9. *Selected Works of Macneil*, Ibid.
10. Ibid.
11. Ibid. p. 313.

12. Ibid. p. 196.
13. Bonnie Keith, Kate Vitasek, Karl Manrodt, and Jeanne Kling, *Strategic Sourcing in the New Economy: Harnessing the Potential of Sourcing Business Models for Modern Procurement* (New York: Palgrave Macmillan, 2016).
14. Ronald Coase, "The Problem of Social Cost," *The Journal of Law & Economics*, Vol. III (October 1960). Available at https://www.law.uchicago.edu/files/file/coase-problem.pdf.
15. Robert C. Ellickson, *Order Without Law* (Harvard University Press, 1994).
16. Ibid.
17. Coase, Ibid., p. 2.
18. Ellickson, Ibid., p. 42.
19. Ibid., p. 185.
20. Ibid., p. 187.
21. This is the same norm as the norm of solidarity identified by Macneil.
22. Macaulay, *Non-Contractual Relationships in Business: A Preliminary Study*, p. 13.
23. Ellickson, Ibid., p. 190.
24. Ibid., p. 65.
25. Ibid., p. 71.
26. Macaulay, Ibid. p. 13.

# 5

# The Economics of Contracting

Macaulay, Macneil, and Ellickson's findings[1] on the use and non-use of contracts have puzzled many economists. In fact, their work spawned a great deal of research among the economic community.

The classical economic approach to contracting focuses on the economic incentives of the parties. As such, the majority of research into classical economic theory emphasizes the role of material incentives, the assumption being that humans are egoistic and will always act in their self-interest. Under this assumption conflicts of interest will inevitably arise, creating a risk for inefficiencies among trading partners and in the market as a whole. Where and how will these inefficiencies arise and how can they be mitigated or avoided? These are some of the fundamental questions in economic theory, not least theories focused on contracts.

This chapter focuses on three pioneering theories centered on the economic side of contracting: contract theory, new institutional economics, and repeated game theory. Each theory brings critical insights into the science of contracting. While these theories are essential to understanding contracts, we suggest they are incomplete because they do not fully explain how business people behave in real life. For this reason, Chapter 6 builds upon this chapter by exploring the impact of new research in behavioral economics—which studies not how humans *should* act if they were only thinking about their self-interests, but how they *do* act.

© The Author(s), under exclusive license to Springer Nature
Switzerland AG 2021
D. Frydlinger et al., *Contracting in the New Economy*,
https://doi.org/10.1007/978-3-030-65099-5_5

# Contract Theory

Contract theory is a branch of economic theory that refers to a multitude of ideas and theories shared by several economists—the most notable being Oliver Hart and Bengt Holmström, who shared the 2016 Nobel Prize in economics for their separate contributions to contract theory.[2] The common denominator in contract theory focuses on the contract as a way to mitigate conflicts between the contracting parties' interests. Contract theory is an evolving area of study by economists that often uses complex mathematical language to analyze what the optimal contractual solutions would look like (i.e., solutions maximizing the total value of the deal.)

For a contracting professional, the mathematical models developed by economic theorists often provide little value, not least because the models and solutions are based on strict assumptions seldom found in reality. What economists try to solve with mathematical formulas, contracting professionals try to answer in every day real-life drafting and negotiating contracts. You might be thinking, "what is the value of reading about theories?" The answer is simple; economic theorists extensively analyze the problems to be solved. Using an analogy, it is safe to say one can learn a lot by diagnosing the disease properly before recommending a cure.

In this chapter, we focus on the contract theories espoused by Oliver Hart and his collaborators.[3]

At the core of Hart's work is a theory of why contracts are written in the first place—and the consequences of the fact that this purpose of the contract can never be completely fulfilled.

*So, why are contracts written?* This is an important question for all contracting professionals to ask themselves. While Hart, as we will see, has lately adopted a broader view on this matter, his answer in his earlier theory remains fundamental. The starting point in Hart's work is that in most commercial relationships the parties use assets they own or control to provide their part of the exchange. For example, a contract manufacturer may own a factory or machine for producing the goods for its clients. They also control the employees who provide the labor in the factory.

Now let's say the contract manufacturer enters into a long-term commercial relationship with a customer, however *without entering into a contract.* Over time the customer may become very dependent on using the contract manufacturer's resources and it may become costly for the customer to switch to another supplier. This type of dependency is common in many commercial relationships. For example, the contract manufacturer may have built up skills and knowledge about its customer which would be costly for the customer to replicate with another supplier. Or the contract manufacturer may have invested to adapt its manufacturing process to the needs of a specific customer and so on. Contract theory thus considers what economists call *relationship-specific investments* that bind parties and make them dependent on one another, or at least one party very dependent on the other.

These asset-specific investments and the dependency they create give rise to the *hold-up problem*—a phenomenon Macaulay identified in his 1963 article, although under another name. If we assume the parties will act in their self-interest, one party may want to (ab)use the other party's dependency, i.e., hold the other party up. For example, it might be tempting for the contract manufacturer to use the power generated by dependency to force a price increase because they know it will be too hard for the customer to switch in the short term. Likewise, the inverse could happen where the contract manufacturer may feel pressured to agree to their customer's demands because it fears losing such a significant amount of work for their factory could cause layoffs or possibly even closing the factory altogether. This is the hold-up problem.

The hold-up problem—or rather to avoid this problem—is one of the main reasons why contracts are written. From this perspective, a contract seeks to restrict the parties' rights to control assets involved in the commercial relationship that can be used to hold up the other party.

For example, in signing the contract, the contract manufacturer agrees to use its factory, machines, and people to produce the goods for the customer and deliver the goods at a certain point in time at a specific quality.

However—and this is critical to understand for all contracting professionals—all contracting parties will face the problem that their contract will be incomplete. No matter how hard the parties try, they will fail to completely restrict one another's control rights over their assets. Contractual incompleteness is fundamental in Hart's theory, so let's look more closely at this phenomenon.

Let's explore the ways a contract can be incomplete. Here, we highlight two of the most common reasons.

First, the contract may be silent on many points. Simply put, the parties may accidentally leave things out. Second, the contracting parties may have written their intentions about how they should act, but they may have failed to communicate their intent. Research supports this by showing that a high proportion of agreements suffer from a disagreement over scope or goals, frequently resulting in contention over the supplier's obligations and whether particular items are chargeable or should be provided at no extra charge.[4] On even simpler matters of wording, the understanding between the parties or between two people reading the same words may be quite different.

Now let's take a closer look at why contracts are incomplete. The most common reason is there is too little time or it would be too costly to specify everything in detail to avoid unambiguous contract language. Negotiators are often time-constrained and contract drafters simply don't have enough time to completely specify how the parties shall act in different situations that can arise during the contract term. And even if there is enough time, it can require a prohibitive amount of resources to write such complete specifications. In many cases—especially for longer-term contracts—it would be impossible to anticipate every eventuality and craft contractual language for each scenario. The result is a contract having many gaps and omissions, besides being ambiguous.

For the reasons above (and many more), all contracts are therefore more or less incomplete.

Now let's examine what happens when a contract is incomplete. Because of the risk of being held up, one or both of the parties will try to restrict one another's rights over the assets involved in the deal. But they will partly fail since contracts are always incomplete. The control rights over the assets that the contract fails to regulate are what Hart calls "residual control rights," with each party having a remaining area of control over the assets they use under the contract. According to Hart's theory, this is what is incomplete—the restriction of the parties' control rights over their assets. When the parties run into a situation that is not stated or is ambiguous in the actual contract, the parties may find themselves renegotiating the contract as a way to work through any issues. And in renegotiations, because of a party's dependency, the remaining or residual control rights can be a source of power as we saw in the case of the contract manufacturer. This power can be abused to extract value from the other party such as extracting significant value through increased or lowered prices. As such, part of the hold-up problem will always remain.

An essential reason for writing a contract is to avoid the hold-up problem and thereby protect each party's investments made into the commercial relationship. But since all contracts are incomplete, this problem cannot be completely avoided by writing clauses in the contracts. Other mechanisms must be used.

Hart's Nobel Prize-winning work predicted organizations seek to protect themselves from being held-up in different ways by finding ways to reduce dependency. Let's look at three common tactics organizations use to prevent dependency and avoid lock-in. First—and very common—is the practice of using several suppliers instead of only one. This tactic is so prevalent it has been taught since the late 1970s.[5] While using multiple suppliers will protect a buyer from a potential hold-up, the trade-off is that dealing with several suppliers typically is more costly than dealing with only one.

A second tactic is that a buyer may choose to produce some of the goods or services by themselves, e.g., by ensuring it has all the residual control rights through vertical integration. The trade-off here is that the buyer is not necessarily the one who can do the work most efficiently; vertical integration comes with some separate problems.

A third—and also common—way to avoid hold up is to try to write a contract that prevents the other party from using its assets to exercise any form of bargaining power. Many contracting professionals have sought to perfect this approach through an extensive portfolio of contract clauses and details specifying what the other party may or may not do. A recent example of this approach is manifested in a facilities management services contract, which contained over 800 pages and included over 500 detailed metrics—the majority geared toward micro-managing the supplier.[6]

But does seeking to draft the perfect contract work? As we have seen, Hart and other economic luminaries have argued it does not. To write a complete contract is a futile quest. Organizations should face the reality that all contracts will be incomplete, regardless of the number of clauses, pages, and metrics in the contract.

Hart received a Nobel Prize in Economic Sciences for the identification and analysis of the problems of residual control rights, incomplete contracts, and the hold-up problem: a problem that all contracting professionals should know. The formal relational contract we recommend in this book is a way to tackle the problems that Hart identified. Hart's interest in the topic has grown and more recently he has sought ways to shed new light on the problem through the lens of behavioral economics. This new angle is covered in the next chapter.

## New Institutional Economics

Contract theory largely focuses on the costs and inefficiencies of sub-optimal trade-offs which parties make (e.g., use multiple suppliers instead of one) out of fear of being held-up. New institutional economics is a branch of economics that focuses on transaction costs. Simply put, transaction costs are the cost of doing business. For example, there are costs generated when searching for business partners, negotiating contracts, monitoring compliance with the contract, and, in some cases, dealing with disputes.

### Common transaction costs

- Costs associated with developing a Statement of Work/Workload Allocation to define who will do what work in the relationship
- Consulting or legal costs to support one or both of the parties in getting to a formal agreement
- Transition costs to ramp up a new relationship. For example, transition costs for large facilities management outsourcing contracts can easily be over $1 million and include transition costs associated with shifting people to the service provider, ramping up on reporting, and cost associated with transitioning work from the buying organization to the supplier organization (e.g., shifting existing Tier 2 subcontracts such as those for painters, plumbers, elevator maintenance to the new supplier)
- Governance costs to manage the relationship. For example, it is common for an organization to have monthly operations reviews and more strategic quarterly business reviews with suppliers.
- The cost associated with problem-solving when something goes wrong

It is easy to see transaction costs will be affected by the extent to which egoistically acting humans and organizations manage conflicts between their interests, be it before or after the contract is signed. The leading thinkers behind new institutional economics have been asking questions and seeking answers to how and when transaction costs are affected. More specifically, how can organizations conduct business in ways which allow them not to incur or generate unnecessary transaction costs? The questions and the answers are essential for all contracting professionals. In Chapter 9, we advocate that choosing the right contracting model for the right situation is critical to efficiently manage these costs.

There are three main contributors to new institutional economics, all winners of Nobel Prizes in economics: Ronald Coase, Douglass North, and Oliver Williamson. Each is discussed below with the goal to share their key insights which can improve how parties are contracting in the new economy.

## Ronald Coase

Ronald Coase—famous for his eponymous theorem—is credited with initially identifying the concept of the transaction cost. In an article from 1937, Coase asked why firms exist. His research answered the question by pointing to the idea of transaction costs. Essentially, he argued that it is not economically logical for an entrepreneur to offer full-time employment because of the inflexibility this implies. However, the alternative would use the market to hire labor only when required. It is important to recognize the cost of using the market is often far more than the price paid; there will be time and costs of negotiating agreements, managing the suppliers, etc., which may carry economic costs that may outweigh the disadvantages of creating "a firm" or business enterprise. Simply put, sometimes the transaction costs to organize business within a firm (e.g., insource or vertically integrate) are lower than to go to the market (buy).[7,8] But other times, the transaction costs of using the market will be lower. As such, organizations need to exercise greater diligence in the "make versus buy" decision.

Coase's insights led economists to take a keen interest in how different models of organizing business and economic exchanges will affect transaction costs, hence, making coordination cheaper or more expensive. Some of these models for organizing business are called *institutions*. Douglass North was one economist who took this concept further.

## Douglass North

Douglass North's contribution to the research is how those different kinds of rules—formal and informal, political, and economic—shape the incentives of people. People's actions generate transaction costs and can lead to success or failure. According to North, "institutions are the rules of a game in a society or, more formally, are the humanly devised constraints that shape human interaction."[9] The "constraints" that North refers to are, to simplify, constraints to human egoism. The "rules of the game" are what determine if humans and organizations run into conflicting interests. Institutions that don't have clear rules of the game are more likely to have conflicts that generate inefficient transaction costs. Distrust in the rules of the game and high transaction costs may be so high as to dis-incentivize institutions and individuals to not conduct business at all. North's work has been attributed to explaining the economic and political success or failure of entire nations. However, his insights are also crucial for every contracting professional. Why? A contracting professional's job is to set the contractual rules of the game which ultimately affects the success or failure of the business relationship.

Most social relationships—including contractual ones—operate with four types of rules. Let's first look at formal and informal rules. Referring to Macaulay's 1963 study (among others), North explains the difference between informal and formal rules. Formal rules are written laws and written contracts while informal rules are moral norms and habits around which no formal agreement exists.[10] Together both informal and formal rules exist and together shape the parties' incentives and the extent to which they run into costly conflicting interests. For North, the common denominator of the different kinds of rules is to coordinate actions, thus affecting transaction costs.

Now let's look at the distinction between political and economic rules.[11] Political rules broadly define how a state or society is governed. For example, who has decision rights and how can laws be adapted or changed? Economic rules focus more on property rights and exchanges of goods.

North was awarded a Nobel Prize in Economic Science for his work showing how the rules by which institutions play can have a substantial effect on transaction costs. Simply put, having sound rules can help organizations cooperate and avoid conflicting interests.

We address the concept of contracting rules in Chapter 7, where the "rules of the relationship" (i.e., political rules) should be distinguished from the "rules of the business" (i.e., economic rules). As we will see, a strong focus should be put on the rules of the relationship in a formal relational contract.

## Oliver Williamson

Oliver Williamson is also a key contributor to new institutional economics. Like Douglass North, Williamson focused his research on transaction costs and how conflicts of interest generate such costs and how they can and should be efficiently managed. But while North focused on institutions in the format of a system of formal and informal rules, Williamson focused more on how businesses can be organized to best manage transaction costs. Specifically, Williamson dug into when it is better to pursue a "make-decision" and organize and manage the business with employees (vertical integration), versus when is it better to pursue a "buy-decision" and contract with external commercial parties. According to Williamson, the choice is very much a question of how a business optimizes its transaction costs.[12]

Williamson viewed a contract as an instrument to *govern* economic activities. To Williamson, different contracts are different forms of governance of contractual relations. Williamson argued that contracting parties should choose the contract or governance form which minimizes the overall transaction costs by finding the cheapest way to avoid conflicts of interest and coordinate the parties' actions during the term of the contract.

To find the most efficient governance model—and thus the optimal form of contract—it is important to understand which factors affect the transaction costs. Williamson points to three factors of particular importance: (i) relationship-specific assets; (ii) uncertainty; and (iii) frequency. The logic is profound but simple.

i. relationship-specific assets generate a dependency between the parties, which creates opportunities for hold-ups and abuses of power when the contract needs to change
ii. the more uncertain the future, or the more complex the business environment, the greater the risk that unanticipated events will happen which may generate conflicts of interests and thus transaction cost
iii. if the parties frequently deal with each other, they will often be less opportunistic, generating fewer transaction costs compared to a situation where the parties will only meet once or just a few times

Given these factors, Williamson recommended an intuitive yet straightforward approach for minimizing transaction costs: the parties should choose a contracting structure that deals with potential changes during the contract term in the most efficient way.

Williamson proposed a continuum that closely, but not completely, aligns with the thinking of Ian Macneil regarding the difference between a discrete and relational contract. Figure 5.1 illustrates the comparison of Macneil's and Williamson's thinking. We further overlay the graphic with the terminology used in this book.

First, you will notice Williamson used a different terminology than Macneil. Williamson used the term "the market" to describe transactional contracts similar to Macneil's discrete contracts and the word "hybrid" to describe contracts similar to Macneil's relational contracts.

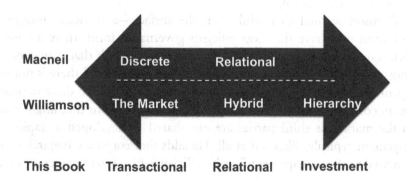

**Fig. 5.1** Difference between Macneil's and Williamson's theories

On the far left of the continuum, Williamson suggested organizations use *the market* as a governance mechanism. To simplify, *competition* is an effective way to optimize for commodity-based discrete or transactional contracts. Williamson argued that if there was a low-level of relationship-specific investments (and therefore low dependency) and uncertainty and frequency were low, coordination will be relatively simple and competition will ensure that opportunism and conflicts of interests are avoided. Think, for example, of a supplier facing the threat of being abandoned; they are more likely to do as the customer wants. Thus, a traditional discrete or *transactional contract* would suffice for simple commodity-like exchanges.

Williamson advocated for what he called "hybrid" relationships for relationships falling between a transactional and a vertical integration governance structure. Williamson suggested relationships with mid-level relationship-specific assets, uncertainty, and frequency should use a hybrid (*relational contract*) approach. Williamson's hybrid relationships are similar to Ian Macneil's relational contracts.

A key difference in Macneil and Williamson is that Williamson added a third dimension to the continuum. Going back to Coase, and the question of why firms exist, Williamson realized that sometimes a situation could be such as to make it much more efficient from a transaction cost perspective to organize a business as a firm through vertical integration (i.e., make). Williamson referred to vertical integration as using a "hierarchy." Vertical integration is depicted in cases with a high-level of relationship-specific investments and high uncertainty and frequency. Williamson argued in these cases, coordination of actions will be complex and costly and will cause a high risk of hold-ups, costly renegotiations, and other problems. In such situations Williamson believed it may be a better choice to use a vertical integration strategy and govern the business through employment contracts. The logic being vertical integration with daily corporate management results in the cheapest governance form.

Williamson warned that while—on the surface—a vertically integrated organization may have the most efficient governance form, there are many hidden transaction costs associated with performing work that is noncore to the organization. One reason is that when work is insourced there is not any competition. Limited competition provides little incentive to drive improvements in cost and/or quality. As a consequence, innovations that might come from the market or third parties are not shared or developed as rapidly as management typically likes—if at all. He adds that corporate hierarchies are "deferential to the management," and inefficiencies lead to bureaucratic costs.

Williamson states "the internal organization is usually thought of as the organization of last resort."[13] In other words, organizations should outsource noncore services whenever possible.

Williamson's work can be summarized with a simple rule of thumb: Use simple transactional contracts for high certainty, low complexity, low dependency situations. However, use vertical integration where there are low certainty, high complexity, high dependency situations. However, recognize there are many situations where a hybrid (relational contract) will be the optimal approach. While Williamson's and Macneil's research came from different perspectives—their conclusions were remarkably similar. The big difference? Williamson put quantitative economic rigor behind Macneil's more qualitative research.

## Repeated Game Theory

Macaulay cited "reputation" as one of the key reasons the business people he studied did not use contracts. If two organizations frequently trade with each other, they both have an inherent incentive to perform if they want to continue to do business in the future: "Both business units involved in the exchange desire to continue successfully in business and will avoid conduct which might interfere with attaining this goal."[14]

This aspect of Macaulay's analysis has been the focus of repeated game theory. Professors George Baker, Robert Gibbons, and Kevin J. Murphy are some of the leading researchers and writers in repeated game theory.[15] In game theory, a distinction is often made between one-shot games and repeated games. One-shot games are played only once, e.g., going to the local market and bargaining for a one-time deal. In contrast, repeated games result in the parties doing repeat business, e.g., an outsourcing contract where the parties must collaborate over an extended period of time. The parties' strategies and incentives are quite different in these two situations.

In repeated game theory, the term "relational contract" is used to refer to "informal agreements and unwritten codes of conduct that powerfully affect the behavior of individuals."[16] It is a form of "collaboration sustained by the shadow of the future."[17] This shadow is the prospect of having to meet again, which creates informal incentives for parties to collaborate today to continue to do business tomorrow.

While there is a wide variety of applications for repeated game theory, the logic at the heart of this theory is rather simple. The starting point—as is usually the case in economics—is that people are selfish and look out for personal benefits. In game theory, the parties can either cooperate or defect. For example, they can provide a product to the agreed quality or abstain from delivering. Or they can pay for a received good or decide not to pay.

Let's focus on the latter case—the choice to pay for a good—in context to game theory. It matters whether the party whose invoice is due is involved in a one-shot or repeated game. In a one-shot game where the buyer will never meet the seller again, it can be rather tempting not to pay the invoice, at least not being for the risk of being taken to court. But if there is a likelihood the buyer will meet the seller again and do more business, the buyer's incentives will look different. She will then have to calculate both the gains from defecting in the next round and the losses associated with the seller defecting in future rounds. If the buyer fails to pay its invoice, it might be beneficial for now. However, it may mean that the seller will never deliver another product which could create losses that may well exceed the gains from failing to pay in the first round. Therefore, in a repeated game, there is often a natural incentive to perform, just as Macaulay also observed.

Important aspects of game theory have proven to be incorrect by behavioral economists. One key learning is that humans cooperate much more in a one-shot game than expected. But the pure economic rationality involved in repeated game theory is also true—people think about future losses when thinking about winning through defection in the short term.

The lessons of game theory have important implications for contracting professionals. Repeated game theory describes a "relational contract" as an informal agreement that cannot be verified by a court but which the parties can still see whether the contract is followed or not. Even though a court cannot verify a breach, the parties can still often observe if a breach is happening. As such, there is an inherent incentive to perform stemming from the fear one's business partner will not want to do business in the future, based not on what they prove—but what they can see.

Academics Robert Gibson (MIT) and Rebecca Henderson (Harvard University) point out the critical importance of at least two factors for a relational contract to succeed: credibility and clarity.[18] The problem of credibility is the challenge to persuade "others that one is likely to keep one's promises."[19] The problem of clarity is in "communicating the terms of the relational contract."[20] While the problem of credibility is about believing in the promises made, the problem of clarity is about *understanding* the promises.

Let's look at Gibson and Henderson's premise in context to informal relational contracts. Informal relational contracts can make up for part of the problem of communicating a verifiable future to the court. However, part of the communication problem remains since it may be difficult to determine if the behavior in which one observes breaches the informal agreement or not.

Most contracting professionals would agree to this analysis and also say the vagueness of the "gentleman's agreement," i.e., the informal relational contract, is precisely why a written contract is so important. A formal written contract brings a relationship from a state of vagueness to a state of clarity. But this is to jump to conclusions too quickly. As Hart, Williamson, and others have pointed out, the formal contract often fails to bring the wished-for clarity because of lack of time to specify in clear enough detail how the parties want to regulate the future.

The key is to find the right balance.

## A Look Ahead

The research and theories of big thinkers such as Oliver Hart, Oliver Williamson, and Douglass North contain essential learnings for anyone drafting contracts in the new economy. But effective contracting practitioners require more. This is why Chapter 6 addresses the psychology of contracting—to understand what motivates the contracting practitioners across the table, as well as internal and external stakeholders, to act in different ways.

## Notes

1. Refer to Chapter 4 for details.
2. See "The Long and the Short of Contracts," *The Royal Swedish Academy of Sciences*, 10 October 2016 press release. Available at https://www.nobelprize.org/prizes/economic-sciences/2016/press-release/.
3. The rest of this section is primarily based on the following articles: S. Grossman, and O Hart, "The Costs and Benefits of Ownership: A Theory of Vertical and Lateral Integration," *Journal of Political Economy*, Vol. 94, No. 4 (1986); O. Hart, and J. Moore, "Incomplete Contracts and Renegotiation," *Econometrica*, Vol. 67, No 4 (July 1988), pp. 755–785; and O. Hart, and J. Moore, "Property Rights and the Nature of the Firm," *Journal of Political Economy*, Vol. 98, No. 6 (1990), pp. 1119–1158.
4. "Most Negotiated Terms Report—2018 (Top Terms)," *IACCM*, published 11 June 2018. Available at https://www.worldcc.com.
5. Porter espoused it was important to understand a company's power over their supplier and customers as a key way to achieve competitive advantage. See Michael E. Porter, "How Competitive Forces Shape Strategy" *Harvard Business*

*Review*, March 1979. Available at https://hbr.org/1979/03/how-competitive-for ces-shape-strategy. See also Porter's "The Competitive Advantage of Nations," *Harvard Business Review*, March–April 1990. Available at https://hbr.org/1990/ 03/the-competitive-advantage-of-nations. Also note Peter Kraljic stressed that dependency was a source of risk and created what he coined as a "bottleneck supplier" which should be avoided. See Peter Kraljic, "Purchasing Must Become Supply Management," *Harvard Business Review*, September 1983 (revised in 2009). Available at https://hbr.org/1983/09/purchasing-must-become-supply-management.

6.  University of Tennessee extensively researched outsource contracts between 2003 and 2009, resulting books, papers and articles, including *Vested Outsourcing: Five Rules That Will Transform Outsourcing* and *The Vested Outsourcing Manual.*

7.  Ronald Coase, "The Nature of the Firm," *Economica*, Vol. 4, No. 16 (November 1937), pp. 386–405.

8.  Modern communication methods have of course proven highly disruptive to the enterprise model. Coase's theories remain entirely valid, but the emergence of new communication techniques, such as the internet, has dramatically altered the cost of communication and facilitated large-scale disaggregation of the enterprise model. Today, this influence has led to "the gig economy," where individual workers are indeed hired and/or rewarded only when work is available.

9.  Douglass North, *Institutions, Institutional Change and Economic Performance* (Cambridge: Cambridge University Press, 1990), p. 13.

10. Ibid.

11. Ibid., p. 47. To be clear, North distinguished between political, economic and contractual rules. North did not realize, it seems, that the difference between "political" and "economic" rules are relevant also *within* a contract.

12. Williamson is famous for his work in Transaction Cost Economics, which can be seen as a sub-branch of new institutional economics.

13. Oliver Williamson, "Outsourcing: Transaction Cost Management and Supply Chain Management," *Journal of Supply Chain Management*, Vol. 44, No. 2 (2008), pp. 5 –16.

14. Stewart Macaulay, "Non-Contractual Relations in Business: A Preliminary Study," *American Sociological Review*, Vol. 28, No 1 (February 1963).

15. See for example: Baker et al., "Relational Contracts and the Theory of the Firm", Quarterly Journal of economics, *The Quarterly Journal of Economics*, Vol. 117, No. 1 (February 2002), pp. 39–84; Baker et al., "Subjective Performance Measures in Optimal Incentive Contracts," *The Quarterly Journal of Economics*, Vol. 109, No. 4 (November 1994), pp. 1125–1156 and Baker et al., "Relational Adaptations", Working Paper, MIT.

16. Baker et al., "Relational Contracts and the Theory of the Firm", p. 1.

17. Robert S. Gibbons, and Rebecca M. Henderson, "Relational Contracts and Organizational Capabilities" (July 18, 2011). *Organization Science*, Forthcoming. Available at SSRN: https://ssrn.com/abstract=2126802, p. 1.
18. Ibid., p. 3.
19. Ibid., p. 3.
20. Ibid., p. 4.

# 6

# The Psychology of Contracting

The social and economic theories we profiled in the previous chapters bring critical insights to contracting professionals. We've explored important reasons why contracts are written, the social context in which all contractual relationships are a part of, and how various risks of conflicts of interests and inefficiencies arise. We now turn to critical insights from psychology and the more psychological branch of economics called behavioral economics.

*Why have a chapter on psychology in a contracting book?* The answer is simple. Psychology and behavioral economics focus on what *motivates* people to act in different ways. Simply put, it is easier to write good contracts when you understand what motivates people and how common biases can slip into decision making.

Let's start with the classical legal and economic assumption that organizations comply with contract obligations because (1) they are materially motivated, and (2) the contract can be legally enforced. In the modern economy it is critical to understand just how flawed this simplified view of human action and motives is. While material interests certainly play an important role, social motives such as fairness and intrinsic motives are equally and often much more important to achieve success in contractual relations. Too strong of a focus on the material interests can even *undermine* and be *counterproductive* to the success of such relations. Therefore, basic knowledge about psychology and behavioral economics is vital for modern contracting professionals.

© The Author(s), under exclusive license to Springer Nature Switzerland AG 2021
D. Frydlinger et al., *Contracting in the New Economy*,
https://doi.org/10.1007/978-3-030-65099-5_6

To set the stage, we start with recognizing Richard Thaler, University of Chicago, Professor of Behavioral Science and Economics), who is widely accredited as the founder of behavioral economics.[1] Thaler—like many of the other big thinkers profiled in this book—received a Nobel Prize. Thaler is credited for putting behavioral economics on the map as a full-fledged branch of economic science.

Behavioral economics disputes the assumption that people are only selfish and opportunistic. For Thaler, the men and women studied by classical economists are just fictions who he calls "Econs." Thaler has spent his life advocating economists should not just study what Econs should be doing because it is what the math models say—but rather what real people (or Humans as he called them) do.

Shifting the focus from Econs to Humans has significant consequences for both understanding the problems and solutions to the problems of contracting. Here, the focus is on just how boundedly rational people are and how unselfish they can often be. Both these aspects have profound implications for how contracts should be written. Let's now explore three essential findings from some of the world's leading psychologists and behavioral economists that shed light on why contracting professionals should care about the psychology of contracting.

## The Cognitive Biases of Humans

One of the prime contributors and inspiring individuals behind behavioral economics is professor Daniel Kahneman. Kahneman is the author of the 2011 bestseller *Thinking, Fast and Slow* and recipient of the Nobel Prize in Economics in 2002. Kahneman and his long-time colleague Amos Tversky used a variety of experiments to explore the nuances and depth of why Humans suffer from bounded rationality. Their research has forever changed the way we can think about rationality and how we, as humans, make decisions.

One of Kahneman and Tversky's main contributions is known as *prospect theory*—a misleading label as the theory has very little relevance to what it is really about.[2] Prospect theory turns—or at least tries to turn—much of classical economic theory upside down. Classical economics is about how people make choices. Since resources are restricted, classical economists create mathematical models that seek to model how people should think about economic choices such as what to produce, how much to consume, and so on. A fundamental assumption in classical economics is that Econs are selfish and rational in their decision making.

With prospect theory, Kahneman and Tversky presented an alternative view of how Humans make choices. The key difference? They had empirical evidence rather than mathematical models about how Humans make decisions.

One crucial finding that Kahneman and Tversky uncovered when conducting psychological experiments was that when Humans make choices they do not assign value to things in absolute terms, but always with a *reference point*. Kahneman and Tversky's premise is easy for most people to recognize. Assume that Peter and Jenny go to the casino for an evening and that both leave the venue with $1,000. Peter entered the casino with $10 and Jenny brought $900. Who will be happier? For a classical economist, it shouldn't matter. A $1,000 payout is a $1,000 payout. Full stop.

But this is wrong, of course; everyone knows that Peter will be happier because his reference point was $10 whereas Jenny's was $900. Peter and Jenny assess their value in terms of the size of the *gains*, not in terms of the value of $1,000. The same applies to losses, however, with a significant difference. Kahneman and Tversky found that Humans suffer from *loss aversion*, meaning they dislike losing more than they like winning.[3]

Kahneman and Tversky found several other ways the human mind seemed to work differently from the assumptions in standard economic theory. Not least, they showed how people suffer from different cognitive biases and fallacies in their everyday lives. In the context of relational contracting, three cognitive biases or fallacies are of particular interest:

1. The planning fallacy
2. Probability neglect
3. The self-serving bias

## The Planning Fallacy

All contracts contain some form of planning. It would, therefore, be good if Humans—especially Humans that are contracting professionals—were good planners. The problem is that Humans are *not* good at planning. In *Thinking, Fast and Slow*, Daniel Kahneman shows how people typically suffer from severe *overconfidence* in their mental capabilities.

First, people tend to think that they understand the past better than they do. Kahneman's student Baruch Fischhoff was one of the first to prove that

Humans have *hindsight-bias*. Think of an event that happened which was impossible to predict in advance—a stock market crisis, a breakdown of a commercial relationship, the success of a product, and failure of another. Suddenly—and only after the fact—it seems very plausible and understandable when looked at in hindsight. The problem is that the human brain does not assess the outcome based on all relevant information but instead on what information is easily accessible afterward, the outcome being part of this information.[4] If the brain comes up with a plausible story of what has happened, it mistakes the story for a degree of truth of the story. For example, stockbrokers placing bets in high-risk companies often suffer, when they have sold the stocks with a high profit, from a hindsight bias when they tell their friends how they "knew" that they were going to be successful.

The tendency for simplicity by the human mind "makes us see the world as more tidy, simple, predictable, and coherent than it really is," writes Kahneman. A core problem is an illusion that understanding the past leads to the illusion of the ability to predict the future: "The core of the illusion is that we believe we understand the past, which implies that the future also should be knowable, but in fact, we understand the past less than we believe we do."[5] This illusion leads us to make overly-optimistic forecasts and predictions about the future, what Kahneman and Tversky called the *planning fallacy*.

There are numerous examples of the planning fallacy, not least from building projects like the Sydney Opera House and Scottish Parliament in Edinburgh, where the actual costs dramatically exceeded the budgeted costs.[6]

It is largely the planning fallacy that leads to the contracting paradox discussed in Chapter 2. When writing a contract, it is necessary to plan. The problem is that we are much worse at planning than we think we are, a fact that our mind unfortunately often makes us neglect.

## Probability Neglect

Writing a contract is not only about planning for the future. It is also about assessing risks and finding ways to deal with such risks. A risk—from an objective viewpoint—is a function of the likelihood of something happening and the negative consequences of it happening. For example, the risk of a nuclear disaster is typically rather low because even if the negative consequence can be severe, the likelihood of one occurring is low.

To be good at assessing risks would be a beneficial competence for a contracting professional. And many contracting professionals *are* good at assessing risks. But the problem is contracting professionals are also Humans, and research shows that even lawyers trained to assess and protect their clients from risk do not assess risks rationally. Instead, Humans often suffer from what Cass Sunstein (Robert Walmsley University Professor at Harvard Law School) calls *probability neglect*. Instead of rationally assessing risks as a function of likelihood and negative impact, Humans get wrapped up in their feelings when assessing risk. If a person can visualize the worst-case scenario for a risk, "little role is played by the stated probability that the outcome will occur."[7]

The "logic" here is all too familiar for contracting professionals, or at least for many who have worked with contracting professionals. How? Contracting professionals often spend significant time and energy focusing on clauses that regulate very unlikely scenarios. Let's assume there is a negotiation about the limitation of liability clause. This clause is all about the worst-case scenario, allocating the risks between the parties if things go bad. Very few have had to apply the limitation of liability clause, simply because the worst-case seldom happens. But for a contracting professional negotiating a limitation of liability clause, the worst-case scenario is somewhat different. If the worst-case does happen, the limitation of liability clause may have a high impact and if the contracting professional has done a poor job negotiating the clause, there is a risk he or she may take the blame. It is not pleasant at all to think about being accused of having done a bad job which made the employer or client lose a lot of money (or not gain money). Probability neglect occurs when a contracting professional, without knowing it, mistakes the strongly negative emotion of visualizing this future with the actual probability of this scenario playing out. Many hours of unfruitful negotiations have been spent due to this kind of unconscious mistake.

The problem can be avoided by a deliberately more sober approach to risks which considers the actual likelihood of a risk occurring and an acceptance that many risks simply cannot be dealt with through explicit clauses in the contract but must be dealt with collaboratively between the contracting parties.

## The Self-serving Bias

The phenomenon of the self-serving bias is known to many as the "above-average effect." It is called this because typically well over fifty percent of respondents in surveys rate themselves as above average in areas such as driving, health, and ethics. For example, one study showed 93% of Americans rate themselves as above average for driving skills.[8] The self-serving bias is explained by the fact the people make judgments that favor themselves and their self-images.[9] Another aspect of the same phenomenon is people's tendency to attribute success to their skills and failure to others or merely bad luck.

The existence of the self-serving bias has been proven in several experiments. Of particular interest are experiments showing self-serving biases when it comes to how Humans view fairness. Not surprisingly, when what is fair is not very obvious to everyone, Humans view the fairest solution as the one best for themselves.[10]

As we will see later in this chapter, the self-serving bias can be a cause of friction in contractual relationships; however, it can also be avoided to a large extent through the use of formal relational contracts. One important way is by ensuring the parties view their situation in light of jointly-adopted social norms like loyalty and equity and have open communication in which they share different perspectives.

## While Humans are Biased, They Do Have a Strong Sense of Fairness

The second critical insight from psychology and behavioral economics is that it is wrong to assume, as is often the case in classical economic theory, that Humans are only selfish. An abundance of studies has proven Humans have a strong sense of fairness.

In a 1986 seminal study, Daniel Kahneman, Richard Thaler, and Jack Knetsch set out to test the assumption made in classical economics that purely selfish economic motives drive people and profit-seeking organizations and that social motives tied to concepts such as fairness plays no role. They did this by asking Humans what they thought about the economics of the supply and demand of snow shovels.[11]

On a typical winter day with normal demand for snow shovels, the price is, say, $15. When a snowstorm comes around the demand for snow shovels increases dramatically. Logically, according to the law of supply and demand, the price of snow shovels will increase. Or will it?

In one questionnaire, respondents were asked[12]:

*A hardware store has been selling snow shovels for $15. The morning after a large snowstorm, the store raises its price to $20. Please rate this action as:*
*Completely fair      Acceptable      Unfair      Very unfair*

Classical economic theory would anticipate that everyone would answer completely fair or acceptable. A feeling for what may be fair should play no role. But the respondents did not seem to have listened to economic theory since 82% rated the action as unfair or very unfair. Other questions gave similar results.

Here is another example:

*A small photocopying shop has one employee who has worked in the shop for six months and earns $9 per hour. Business continues to be satisfactory, but a factory in the area has closed, and unemployment has increased. Other small shops have now hired reliable workers at $7 an hour to perform jobs similar to those done by the photocopy employee. The owner of the photocopying shop reduces the employee's wage to $7.*[13]

The photocopying shop acts rationally under the law of supply and demand. 83% of the respondents, however, viewed the action as unfair. The researchers thought this was puzzling and asked another question. The situation was identical to the one above, with the following difference: The current employee leaves and the owner decided to pay a replacement $7 per hour.

Now, if a large majority of the respondents thought that a $7 wage was unfair in the first example, the same majority would surely think so also in the second example. However, that was not the case. Under this scenario, 73% viewed the wage as acceptable, and only 27% considered it as unfair.

From the standpoint of classical economic theory, this is irrational behavior. What Kahneman, Thaler, and Knetsch found (and this was not the first time) was that the classical *model* of human behavior was wrong, not human behavior.

There are several factors to pay attention to here. What is most important is that many respondents were affected by not only economic—but also *social* motives. The allocation of money between the hardware store and its customers and the photocopying shop and its employee matters to people and should, for many, be *fair*.

As described earlier in this chapter, Kahneman and Tversky showed how people make value assessments in relation to *reference points*. The concept of reference points is equally relevant to fairness. The people made their fairness judgment in relation to a reference point: $15 for a shovel, $7 per hour for work, and so on.

People had *feelings of entitlement* tied to those reference points and reacted negatively when the outcome was worse than the reference point. The one employee in the photocopying shop was entitled to his $9 and it was perceived as unfair to lower his wage. But the replacement employee was not entitled to $9, not having worked there before. Therefore, the market wage of $7 was perceived as fair for the replacement. What made all the difference was the reference point in the two cases.

We will see several examples in this chapter of how feelings of entitlement tied to reference points are highly relevant in contracting.

## Humans Don't Like Abuse of Power

Another way Humans lack economic rationality is shown by examining the use and abuse of power. The hardware store used its position of power (the customers' dependency on the hardware store for snow shovels) to extract more money from customers. Classical economic theory—and many contract writers—view this as uncomplicated. But in the Kahneman, Thaler, and Knetsch study it is not uncomplicated; they note that from the Human perspective "it is unfair for a firm to take advantage of an increase in its monopoly power."[14] Let's look at another example that proves Kahneman's, Thaler's, and Knetsch's point.

> *A grocery chain has stores in many communities. Most of them face competition from other groceries. In one town the chain store does not have any competition. Although the chain store's costs and value of sales are the same there as elsewhere, the chain store sets prices that average 5 percent higher than in other communities.*

Again, the grocery chain is acting economically rational. But in the eyes of the public 76% of the respondents thought that the higher price was unfair, and the chain store was abusing its power. Similarly, using power to discriminate between tenants and to use an auction to respond to a sudden demand for a product were viewed by most to be unfair and an abuse of power.

Behavioral economics studies such as those above do not in themselves refute the law of supply and demand. In the real-world hardware stores may still raise prices of snow shovels in response to increased demand after a snowstorm. Theoretically, they would do this if it would be economically beneficial, which is how long people still accept the higher prices and buy snow shovels.

It's one thing to *feel* you are treated unfairly. But Kahneman, Thaler, and Knetsch also proved that Humans would go so far as to *act* differently because they were treated unfairly. Humans will often *retaliate and punish unfair behavior*. Researchers have devised experiments such as the popular *Ultimatum's Game* where two groups of people are divided into pairs, one being a Proposer and the other being a Responder.[15] The Proposer is given a sum of money, say $1,000, and is asked to propose how the money shall be split between the Proposer and the Responder. If the Responder accepts the proposal, the money is split accordingly. If the Responder rejects, no one gets anything.

Again, classical economic theory has a clear answer and prediction: The Proposer will and should propose a $999/$1 split and the Responder will accept. The Proposer, acting rationally, has no reason to offer more than necessary and the Responder has no reason to reject since he/she will be one dollar richer than before.

Again, however, the predications of classical economic theory fail. A very common result in the Ultimatum's Game is a 50/50 or at least 60/40 split. The results also show that Responders typically reject an offer below a 70/30 split. This result is somewhat stunning since it means that people will punish what they perceive as unfair behavior, *even if it is against their best economic interests*. And a reason Proposers offer fair splits is because they anticipate this reaction.

The Ultimatum's Game has proven time and again that regardless of the culture, country, or the amount of money at stake—Humans punish unfairness despite the fact the decision can make one worse off.[16]

## Reciprocity as a Fundamental Social Norm

In Chapter 3, we showed research supporting loyalty and equity as key social norms. A third crucial social norm is reciprocity. The key concept of reciprocity is to return an action in kind; an eye-for-an-eye, a tooth-for-tooth. It is common sense when you think of it; the way people treat us affects how we treat them should come as no surprise. However, it goes against the teaching of much of the classical economic theory. Professor Ernst Fehr at the University of Zurich and his colleague Professor Simon Gächter share their insight on reciprocity in an article titled "Fairness and Retaliation: The Economics of Reciprocity."

> *Reciprocity means that in response to friendly actions, people are frequently much nicer and much more cooperative than predicted by the self-interest model; conversely, in response to hostile actions, people are frequently much nastier and even brutal.*[17]

In several experiments, Fehr and others have shown how strongly reciprocity and other social motives (in contrast to material motivates) drive people's actions. In one study, some groups of subjects acted as employers while other groups acted as employees. The purpose of the experiment was to find out how offered salaries and work efforts correspond. The employers were asked to offer a salary, and the employees were asked to respond with a voluntary work effort. Three different salary arrangements were tried: a fixed salary, a salary with a salary reduction in case of failed performance, and finally a salary with a bonus for good performance. In all cases, the work efforts were chosen after the salaries had been offered and the employers had no opportunity to respond to the chosen effort levels. The effects of reciprocity were evident; the study revealed a direct correlation between an increase in salary offered and work effort provided in return. Another result was that when the economic incentives were framed as a bonus instead of as a salary reduction, work efforts offered were higher.[18]

Fehr's research is just one of an abundance of research on the Ultimatum's Game, gift exchange games, and similar studies across a variety of countries and cultures.[19] Regardless of culture, it is clear that social norms around fairness, power usage, and reciprocity strongly affect humans all over the world. The assumption that all Humans are pure egoists is simply false. But another conclusion is that not all Humans are the same; some are more egoistic or altruistic than others. Humans exist on a *motivation continuum* from pure self-interest to pure altruism as shown in Fig. 6.1.

Fehr refers to the people lying on the right side of the continuum as *Strong Reciprocators*[20] whereas he calls the people on the left side *Opportunists*. In a group of people, we can predict that both Strong Reciprocators and Opportunists will exist. But who will have the upper hand? Will the Strong Reciprocators or the Opportunists dominate? The answer depends on the context, not least on the rules of the game they play and other circumstances. It may come as a surprise but this is critical for contracting professionals to understand. By writing a relational contract that sets the right rules for the game the contracting professional can create a context in which the Strong Reciprocators will dominate, which will lead to significantly better results for everyone involved. The relational aspects also put a moral compass over the relationship which also lead the Opportunists to start to think of what is best for the group instead of for only themselves.

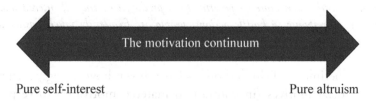

Pure self-interest     The motivation continuum     Pure altruism

**Fig. 6.1** Motivation continuum

# Behavioral Contract Theory

The research results in psychology and behavioral economics presented in this chapter do not have contracts in focus. However, the insights we have made have been used to develop what is sometimes called behavioral contract theory. Here we will focus on Hart's contribution to the theory.

In Chapter 3, we presented contract theory and shared Hart's theories about incomplete contracts, residual control rights, and the hold-up problem. During the 1990s, Hart's theory was vigorously challenged by other economists which led him to expand his theory. Not least, they challenged the claim that the consequences of the persistent hold-up problem could not be dealt with in the contract. As discussed in Chapter 1, Hart revisited his work on contract theory in 2008 with John Moore. Hart and Moore went back to the basics and again asked: "What is a contract? Why do people write long-term contracts?"

Hart's previous answer as to why contracts are written came from the view of an Econ. The answer was that contracts were written to, among other things, encourage investments and protect the parties from each other's opportunistic behavior. Contracts are written to prevent the parties from abusing their power generated by residual control rights over assets to extract value from the other party through tough bargaining during the contract period. But as Hart and others have argued, parties fail to write complete contracts because of a lack of time and resources which will lead to inefficient decision making.

Hart's latest research approached the questions from the perspective of a Human, in particular the research showing Human's strong sense of fairness and tendency to have a self-serving bias. A key finding? While prevention of (ab)use of power to extract value may, as Hart had previously said, be a key reason for why contracts are written, an equally important reason is to avoid the problem of what Hart coined as "shading." *Shading* is a retaliatory behavior in which one party stops cooperating, ceases to be proactive, or makes countermoves because of a feeling of being unfairly treated by the other party.

Earlier in this chapter, we explored the Ultimatum's Game which shows how humans will punish others when they feel unfairly treated. That punishment is a form of shading. Shading happens when a party is not receiving the outcome it expected from the deal and feels the other party is to be blamed or has not acted reasonably to mitigate the losses. The aggrieved party often diminishes their performance in subtle ways—sometimes even unconsciously—to compensate.

Let's expand on the example of shading from Island Health and the Hospitalists introduced in Chapter 1.[21] The Hospitalist physicians care for numerous patients on any given day and one issue was how to manage the variation in the demand for health services. In 2010, the service delivery model changed where community doctors no longer cared for their patients in hospitals. The burden of care suddenly fell on the shoulders of the Hospitalists.

This change was consistent with other hospitals across Canada and the contract did not preclude Island Health's decision to reduce the use of community doctors. The issue was that the Hospitalists felt that the decision was unilateral and unanticipated, resulting in unreasonable expectations of the Hospitalists to meet the new demand levels. The increasing numbers of patients put the Hospitalists under a great deal of pressure as many felt they could not always devote adequate time to patients to provide safe, high-quality care. The Hospitalists responded with a shading action: by not agreeing to take patients from the emergency room they relieved their stress and avoided ethical issues arising from not being able to devote adequate time to patients. A doctor can ethically decline to accept new patients if they cannot reasonably be assured of providing an expected and consistent standard of care both to any new patients and to their existing patient load.

What causes shading? As explained above, shading results from failed expectations from the deal, primarily when the other party is to blame for it. When two parties making a deal fail to communicate their expectations clearly, they run into a risk of failed expectations which can lead to disappointment with one another.

So, let's say, just as we did when we explored Hart's earlier thinking in Chapter 5, that a contract manufacturer enters into a long-term commercial relationship with a customer, but *without entering into a contract (e.g., a 'handshake deal' or a 'gentleman's agreement.')* Both the customer and the contract manufacturer will have expectations of what they will get out of the deal. However, because they have not formally written down their expectations there is a good chance they have not clearly communicated their expectations. Overlay this with the fact that business is dynamic and the parties will likely need to deal with changes over time means there is likely a significant risk of one or both of the parties becoming disappointed. There will be so many situations in which each party will do things that may be perceived as unfair by the other party. While the informality creates flexibility, it can also open the door for shading and therefore for inefficiencies.

How could this problem of disappointment and underperformance be avoided? According to Hart's later theory—by writing a formal written contract. This can help the parties being explicit in what their expectations are and to align those expectations.

While avoiding the problems hold-up problem remains an important reason why contracts are written, Hart thus adds another critical reason—to avoid shading by making explicit and aligning expectations.

However, just as writing contractual clauses can never completely prevent the risk of hold-up from occurring, the problem with failed expectations and shading can, according to Hart, not be completely avoided through the contract. The fact and problem that contracts are incomplete remain. There will not be enough time and resources to write clauses that set the parties' expectations for all future scenarios in the contract. And there will not be enough time to write clauses that address and prevent all possible forms of shading. There are just too many ways in which the parties can abstain from collaborating.

But the parts that *do* get into a formal contract will create expectations about each party's outcome of the deal. The contract, or rather the act of entering into it, will create expectations—or what Hart calls "reference points." Recall the research of Kahneman and Tversky showing that humans do not assess value in absolute terms but relative to a reference point. This concept applies to contracts as well. The contract will become the reference point against which the parties assess if the outcome of the deal is good or bad. This is the reason why Hart refers to his later theory as a theory about contracts-as-reference-points. When something unexpected happens and leads to an outcome perceived as worse than the reference point, the parties will then often be disappointed and start to shade. Therefore, even though contracts are written to prevent shading, part of the shading risk will always remain, just as the risk of hold-ups will.

In several experiments, Hart and fellow researchers Fehr and Zehnder have shown that the most fundamental part of Hart's contract theory is true: contracts do serve as reference points and generate various levels of shading in unexpected situations.

An important aspect of this theory, relevant for the theme of this book, is there is a trade-off to be made in rigid and detailed contracts versus more flexible ones.[22,23] A rigid contract should lower risks of feelings of an unfair treatment since a rigid contract is simple to interpret—one knows what one is entitled to in most situations. The problem is that a rigid contract is just that—rigid. It is not well adapted to change with new circumstances. From this perspective, a flexible contract is preferable. But flexibility also means there are more possible future outcomes of the contract and the self-serving bias will probably make each party feel entitled to an outcome beneficial for themselves. Fehr's, Hart's, and Zehnder's experiments proved this to be true—there is a trade-off between rigidity and flexibility. Something which all contracting professionals must take into account.

Other researchers have also studied the impact of flexible contracts. Brandts, Charness, and Ellman studied the impact of allowing the parties to not communicate, communicate somewhat, or communicate freely during trading in different settings. The researchers found that the contracts where the parties choose a flexible contract and could freely communicate regarding how they would act overperformed relative to the other settings. In particular, clarifications about intended actions, promises, and general friendliness contributed to better results.[24]

Oliver Hart's incorporation of some of the most important insights from behavioral economics into contract theory has fundamental consequences for contracting professionals. Contracts are written not only to avoid the hold-up problem *but also to avoid shading*. To make explicit and to align expectations is as important as the need to avoid being abused by the other party because of dependency. But since the contract will be incomplete, the risk of both hold-up and shading always remains. The traditional contracting mechanisms used to mitigate the risks and consequences of the hold-up problem, e.g., a termination for convenience clause, will not work to avoid or mitigate the shading problem that often may be much more serious than the hold-up problem, not least in long-term commercial relationships. A fresh approach to this problem was needed which ultimately led to Oliver Hart, David Frydlinger, and Kate Vitasek's *Harvard Business Review* article titled "A New Approach to Contracts: How to Build Better Long-Term Strategic Partnerships."[25] The idea is to create formal relational contracts where parties entering into a relational contract can incorporate relational elements such as a shared vision, guiding principles, and robust relationship management processes.

Oliver Hart and David Frydlinger further expanded on Hart's thinking on contracts-as-reference-points, showing the use of guiding principles can help—if not eliminate—then at least to a large extent mitigate the risks tied to the remaining shading problem caused by contractual incompleteness.[26] We argue the guiding principles, together with the other relational mechanisms, will also mitigate the hold-up problem since they will lower the parties' tendency to act opportunistically. From this perspective, the formal relational contract we promote in this book is a way to address and solve the most important problems that anyone writing a contract for a long-term and complex deal will face, identified in economic theory and behavioral economic theory and experienced by many contracting professionals in practice.

## A Look Ahead

Now, the theory needs to be put into practice. In Part 3, we start the journey by sharing how conventional, transactional contracts are different from relational contracts. Also, we share when neither should be used and when perhaps an employment contract or an investment-based agreement such as a joint-venture, should be explored. Later in Part 4, we go into detail about *how* to create a relational contracting using a simple five-step process.

## Notes

1. Richard H. Thaler is an American economist and the Charles R. Walgreen Distinguished Service Professor of Behavioral Science and Economics at the University of Chicago Booth School of Business. In 2017 he received the Nobel Memorial Prize in Economic Sciences for his contributions to behavioral economics.
2. Daniel Kahneman and Amos Tversky, "Prospect Theory: An Analysis of Decision Under Risk," *Econometria*, Vol. 47, No. 2 (March 1979), pp. 263–292.
3. Daniel Kahneman, *Thinking, Fast and Slow* (London: Penguin Books, 2011), p. 283.
4. Ibid., p. 202.
5. Ibid., p. 201.
6. Ibid., p. 250.
7. Cass R. Sunstein, "Probability Neglect: Emotions, Worst Cases, and Law," *Yale Law Journal*, Vol. 112, No. 61 (2002) (See also the John M. Olin Program in Law and Economics Working Paper no. 138, 2001).
8. Ola Svenson. "Are We All Less Risky and More Skillful Than Our Fellow Drivers?" *Acta Psychologica*, Vol. 47, No. 2 (February 1981), pp. 143–148. Available at https://www.sciencedirect.com/science/article/abs/pii/000169 1881900056?via%3Dihub. Also see, "Do Most Drivers Really Think They Are Above Average?" *Smith Law Office*, December 13, 2017. Available at https://www.smithlawco.com/blog/2017/december/do-most-drivers-rea lly-think-they-are-above-aver/. Katia Hetter, "I'm the good driver, you're the bad driver," *CNN*, August 22, 2011. Available at https://www.cnn.com/2011/ 08/22/living/good-bad-drivers/index.html.
9. See, for example, Linda Babcock and George Loewenstein, "Explaining Bargaining Impasse: The Role of Self-Serving Biases," *Journal of Economic Perspectives*, Vol. 11, No. 1 (Winter 1997), p. 111.
10. Ibid.
11. *Thinking, Fast and Slow*, Ibid., p. 311.

12. Daniel Kahneman, Jack L. Knetsch, and Richard Thaler, "Fairness as a Constraint on Profit Seeking: Entitlements in the Market," *The American Economic Review*, Vol. 76, No. 4 (September 1986), p. 729.

13. Ibid., p. 730.

14. Ibid., p. 735.

15. See, for example, Richard H. Thaler, "Anomalies: The Ultimatum Game," *Journal of Economic Perspectives*, Vol. 2, No. 4 (1988), pp. 195–206.

16. See for example Herbert Gintis et al., *Moral Sentiments and Material Interests: The Foundations of Cooperation in Economic Life (Economic Learning and Social Evolution)* (Cambridge, MA: MIT Press 2006).

17. Ernst Fehr and Simon Gächter, "Fairness and Retaliation: The Economics of Reciprocity," *Journal of Economic Perspectives*, Vol. 14, No. 3 (Summer 2000), p. 1.

18. For this reason, this kind of experiment is called a 'gift experiment.'

19. See *Foundations of Human Sociality*, Edited by Joseph Henrich, Robert Boyd, Samuel Bowles, Colin Camerer, Ernst Fehr, and Herbert Gintis (Oxford: Oxford University Press 2004).

20. Ernst Fehr and Simon Gäachter, "Do Incentive Contracts Crowd Out Voluntary Cooperation?" Working Paper No. 34, *Institute for Empirical Research in Economics, University of Zurich* 2000.

21. David Frydlinger and Oliver D. Hart, "Overcoming Contractual Incompleteness: The Role of Guiding Principles," *National Bureau of Economic Research* Working Paper No. 26245, September 2019. Available at https://www.nber.org/papers/w26245.

22. Fehr, Hart, Zehnder, "How Do Informal Agreements and Revision Shape Contractual Reference Points?" *Journal of the European Economic Association*, Vol. 13, No. 1 (February 2015), pp. 1–28.

23. Others have also tested the theory that contracts may set reference points. Of particular interest is a study by Jordi Brandts, Gary Charness and Matthew Ellman, in which they tested how the possibility to communicate during the negotiation process would affect the parties' reference points and choice of actions (J. Brandts, G. Charness, and M. Ellman, "Let's Talk: How Communication affects Contract Design", mimeo.) See also Bjorn Bartling, and Klaus M. Schmidt, "Reference Points, Social Norms, and Fairness in Contract Renegotiations" (March 17, 2014). Forthcoming: *Journal of the European Economic Association*. Available at SSRN https://ssrn.com/abstract=2123387 or http://dx.doi.org/10.2139/ssrn.2123387; R.Iyer, and A. Schoar, "Incomplete Contracts and Renegotiations: Evidence from a Field Audit," 2010, MIT LFE Working Paper LFE-0713-10: R. Iyer, and A. Schoar, "Ex Post (In)Efficient Negotiation and Breakdown of Trade," 2013, Mimeo, MIT.

24. J. Brandts, G. Charness, and M. Ellman, "Let's Talk: How Communication affects Contract Design", mimeo.

25. David Frydlinger, Oliver Hart and Kate Vitasek, "A New Approach to Contracts," *Harvard Business Review*, September–October 2019. Available at https://hbr.org/2019/09/a-new-approach-to-contracts.
26. David Frydlinger and Oliver D. Hart, "Overcoming Contractual Incompleteness: The Role of Guiding Principles," *National Bureau of Economic Research* Working Paper No. 26245, September 2019. Available at https://www.nber.org/papers/w26245.

# Part III

## From Theory to Practice

In Part II, we set out to provide compelling research and science behind why relational contracts should be in every contracting professional's toolkit.

Part III shifts from theory to practice—providing a solid understanding of both transactional and relational contracts and helping you know when to use each model. When contracting parties rely on each other for repeated exchanges they, by default, are engaging in a relationship. As we have seen, a contract serves as both an instrument of social cooperation and as insurance to invest in a relationship. While this book is about relational contracts, we want to stress that not all deals should use a relational contract. Our aim is simple: to help you understand when a relational contract should be used instead of the conventional, transactional contract. Also, we share when neither should be used and when perhaps an employment contract or an investment-based agreement such as a joint-venture, should be explored.

In Chapter 7 we explore the main differences between the transactional and relational contract, comparing both across five dimensions. Chapter 8 addresses a question we often get asked: "*when should I use a relational contract instead of a transactional contract?*" In Chapter 9 we describe a practical process for choosing between the two contract models. Chapter 10 then builds on the learnings to answer a second common question: "*What contract types should be relational contracts?*" This is a great question when you consider there is a myriad of different contract types. For example, on one end of the spectrum, there are simple purchase orders of goods based on standard terms and conditions. On the other end of the spectrum there are complex contracts fraught with uncertainties such as business process outsourcing or construction contracts spanning multiple years. We provide a systemization of contract types to help answer this question.

To help you make the shift from theory to practice, consider the analogy of business being a game. A contracting professional must pay attention to the rules of the game, which interact in complex ways. Using Douglass North's framework discussed in Chapter 7, rules can be divided into informal and informal rules as well as political and economic rules. From a contractual perspective, we find it better to talk about *relational* rules rather than political rules. Social norms—or relationship rules—fill an essential function in facilitating communication and coordination between the parties. We advocate that, when combined, these rules form the foundation of the parties' contract.

The rules contracting professionals create for their relationship affect peoples' motivations and vice versa. As we have seen, reciprocity and intrinsic motivations are a complex phenomenon when it comes to relationships. Humans not only have strong material interests, but they also have a strong sense of fairness and willingness to punish others' unfair behavior.

Together, the motivations and the rules decide if a contractual relationship leads to success or failure.

Conventional contracting practices only address economic motives and legal and contracting norms. Our approach to formal relational contracting expands this thinking to include social and intrinsic motives—as well as formally embedding social norms. When combined, the factors create what we call a *formal* relational contract.

We will show in the coming chapters our relational contracting process enables contracting professionals to have a more holistic view of *all* contracting situations, helping them make wise decisions that can optimize the economic output of their contracts.

Why are we so bold with this statement? Most of today's contracts are written under the assumption that *only* economic motives matter and *only* contractual and legal norms matter. As we have shown in Part II, this is incomplete thinking. When contracting professionals ignore social and intrinsic motives and fail to consider social norms—they make myopic decisions that often create perverse incentives. Likewise, when contracting professionals fail to incorporate the other rules of the relationship (legal and contractual norms), they fail to manage risks and transaction costs wisely. The result? Conventional contracting practices *generate* risks and *increase* transaction costs. A case in point is Island Health and the Hospitalists—which ignored the Human factor for a strong sense of fairness which ultimately led to shading.

In Part III, we will show other cases that illustrate it is simply not possible to efficiently rely solely on economic motives with conventional legal and contractual rules. When complexity and/or relationship-specific investments increase, contracts must be written to include social and intrinsic motives as well as formally address inherent social norms. Only then will the parties be able to coordinate their actions and relationships efficiently to generate a more optimal economic outcome for both parties.

# 7

# A Comparison of Transactional and Relational Contract Models

The main subject of this book is the relational contract. As we have seen with McDonald's, the Royal Australian Navy, and Island Health there is no one-size-fits-all relational contract. Rather relational contracts fall along a continuum from informal to formal (Fig. 7.1).

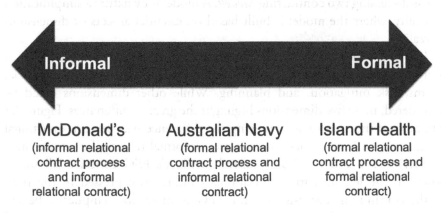

**Fig. 7.1** Relational contracting continuum

© The Author(s), under exclusive license to Springer Nature Switzerland AG 2021
D. Frydlinger et al., *Contracting in the New Economy*,
https://doi.org/10.1007/978-3-030-65099-5_7

| | Transactional Contract | Formal Relational Contract |
|---|---|---|
| **Focus** | The commercial transaction | The relationship |
| **Relationship** | Arm's-length relationship | Partnership |
| **Social norms** | Disconnect from social norms | Explicitly includes social norms as contractual obligations |
| **Risk management** | Use of power and creation of enforceable contractual obligations | Risk avoidance by creation of continuous alignment of interests |
| **Planning** | Aims for complete planning, i.e., contract should cover all future events | Creates a fair and balanced flexible framework |

**Fig. 7.2** Comparison across five dimensions

Individuals seeking to make the shift to relational contracting must first understand how relational contract models are different. It is important to stress that when one uses the terms "relational" and "transactional" contracts one is discussing two contracting *models*. A model is by nature a simplification of reality, where the model is built based on essential aspects or dimensions of reality.

The best way to understand a relational contract is to compare it with a transactional contract across five dimensions: focus, relationship, social norms, risk mitigation, and planning. While other dimensions could be considered, these five dimensions highlight the greatest differences. Figure 7.2 summarizes the comparison showing the difference between a transactional contract and a formal relational contract. Informal relational contracts such as McDonald's and the Royal Australian Navy's FFG contract fall somewhere to the left of a formal relational contract as expressed to the right of the continuum. For example, the FFG contract does emphasize behavioral tenets—but does not explicitly include social norms as contractual obligations.

This chapter provides a deep dive into how transactional and relational contracts differ across each dimension.

## Focus on the Deal or the Relationship

A transactional contract is written to safeguard investments by avoiding hold-up problems and preventing the other party's opportunistic behavior. In contrast, a relational contract is primarily written as an instrument of social cooperation. As such, the focus is different in the relational contract compared to the transactional contract. The purpose of safeguarding investments puts a natural focus on the commercial transaction. The purpose of social cooperation instead puts focus on the relationship. Relational contracts, therefore, focus on the underlying source of value creation for the parties, namely their commercial relationship instead of the commercial transaction.

The choice of focus—deal or relationship—should be reflected in the positions the parties take in the contract negotiation. Even though some organizations are not profit-driven, all commercial contracts are entered into with an aim by both parties to gain positive net benefits. The question then becomes: should these benefits come from a particular transaction or the commercial relationship? If the focus is on the deal, as with transactional contracts, the parties will want to extract empirical value from the deal. A buyer will want to maximize value and minimize price. Likewise, a seller will often want to maximize price or profit. Often transactional deals are treated as a zero-sum game with the misconception that if you win one dollar, I lose that dollar.

In contrast, if the focus is on the relationship, the parties must acknowledge that they are in a repeated ongoing game, a topic covered in Chapter 5. The parties interact under the "shadow of the future" as they seek to shift from exchanging value (I'll give you a dollar if you give me a widget) to creating value. The parties realize that short-term attempts to extract too much value from the other party will most likely generate long-term risks when the other party tries to retaliate. Focusing on the relationship naturally leads to more fairness and consideration of both parties' long-term interests.

World Commerce & Contracting research indicates the vast majority of contracts are transactional.[1] While many organizations set out to have a strategic relationship, they often fall back on conventional approaches, policies, and standard contract templates when it comes time to negotiate and launch the relationship on paper.

So what does this mean in practice to focus on the relationship rather than the deal? In practice, business and contracting professionals spend time, energy, resources, and contract text as they specify the goods or services, quality levels, prices, and deliverables for both transactional and relational contracts. The primary difference is the starting point and mindset they bring to the negotiation. In a transactional contract, the starting (and finishing point) revolves around optimizing "the deal" placed within the four corners of the contractual document. Parties signing a relational contract seek to optimize for the long-term relationship and focus beyond the document—but do not necessarily ignore the document.

An excellent example of this mindset is how organizations negotiate contractual clauses such as limitation of liability, indemnification, and warranties. In a transactional contract, the mindset is typically to protect themselves if something goes wrong. The focus on risk allocation and self-protection has been highlighted by World Commerce & Contracting several years in their annual survey of the most negotiated contract terms (Fig. 7.3).[2]

Focusing on the relationship is a very different exercise. It does not mean that the deal or transaction is unimportant. It also does not mean that the parties are unconcerned with risk, nor that they do not care about limitations of liability, indemnification, or warranties. Instead, parties choose the relational contract model because they realize the deal the parties sign on day one will change as business objectives and circumstances change. In a relational contract, the intent is the relationship will remain throughout the term of the contract even though the specifics of the deal will change.

Prioritizing the relationship over the specific deal points means the parties take a different path to negotiate the standard clauses in the contract. They will negotiate limitations of liability, indemnification, and warranties, but the priorities of what is negotiated changes. For example, the goals, objectives, and guiding principles for the relationship become central topics. Also, the parties will co-create governance structures and procedures which will help the parties maintain continuous alignment.

| 2020 Rank | Term | 2018 | 2015 | 2014/ 2013 | 2012 | 2011 | 2010 |
|---|---|---|---|---|---|---|---|
| 1 | Limitation of Liability | 1 | 1 | 1 | 1 | 1 | 1 |
| 2 | Price / Charge / Price Changes | 3 | 3 | 2 | 3 | 3 | 3 |
| 3 | Indemnification | 2 | 2 | 3 | 2 | 2 | 2 |
| 4 | Delivery / Acceptance | 11 | 10 | 10 | 12 | 8 | 8 |
| 5 | Scope and Goals / Specification | 5 | 11 | 5 | 6 | 5 | 6 |
| 6 | Termination | 4 | 9 | 4 | 8 | 11 | 7 |
| 7 | Payment | 8 | 5 | 9 | 16 | 7 | 18 |
| 8 | Responsibilities of the Parties | 12 | 12 | 12 | 4 | 16 | 12 |
| 9 | Warranty | 6 | 7 | 8 | 7 | 4 | 4 |
| 10 | Liquidated Damages | 10 | 13 | 6 | 20 | 14 | 13 |

Fig. 7.3 Top Ten Most Negotiated Terms 2018

# Arms-Length Relationship or Partnership

Even though the focus is on the deal in the transactional contract, *all* contracts involve some form of a relationship. This is why the second dimension is the *nature of this relationship*. A transactional contract establishes an arms-length relationship between the parties. In contrast, a relational contract establishes a closer, more collaborative relationship, often labeled as a partnership.

What's the difference? Probably the best description of the difference between a partnership and an arms-length relationship was written by professor Ronald Dworkin in his book *Law's Empire.*[3] Dworkin viewed a business relationship as a community between the parties to the contract. Dworkin argued a distinction could be made between what he called "bare" communities and "true" communities.

The community will be a "bare" community if the parties follow the rules of the negotiated agreement but have no sense of obligation toward each other beyond that. The negotiated rules of a bare community represent a compromise between antagonistic interests. Many call this an *arms-length relationship*. A transactional contract is arms-length in nature and can be expressed in the common saying, "Nothing personal, it's business." As the statement implies, the parties have no overall loyalty obligations to look out for each other's interests and no commitment to exceed the strict wording of the contract.

A key goal of the transactional contract, in creating only an arms-length relationship, is typically to limit commitment and to gain as much control over the other party's actions as possible, while relinquishing as little control as possible. Take, for example, a supplier contract. Many contracting professionals eschew the practice of proactively building supplier relationships, stating it is risky to get too "cozy" with a supplier. Conventional logic is that becoming too dependent on a supplier is risky and that buying organizations should avoid "lock-in."

Organizations often use commercial terms to prevent "lock-in," i.e., to keep the relationship at an arm's length distance. For example, termination for convenience clauses combined with comprehensive exit management obligations create powerful tools a customer can use to control suppliers. Another example is an intellectual property rights clause where the customer is given the rights to ideas and innovations created by the supplier or licensor. The goal is to ensure the distance between the parties remains.

Compare the above description of an arms-length relationship with a relationship that can be best described as a *partnership*. To use Dworkin's words, a business relationship will be a "true" community when the parties view the written rules not as an exhaustive list of their obligations, but as being expressions of a set of guiding principles (social norms) that they all agree upon and equally apply. In a business relationship being a true community in this sense, the parties treat each other's interests and needs with equal concern. Dworkin views this kind of business relationship as a fraternal association and says:

> A commercial partnership or joint enterprise, conceived as a fraternal association, is in a way different from even a long-standing contractual relationship. The former has a life of its own: each partner is concerned not just to keep explicit agreements hammered out at arm's length but to approach each issue that arises in their joint commercial life in a manner reflecting special concern for his partner as partner.[4]

In a relational contract the nature of the partnership exceeds the written words in the contractual documents. Contrast this to the nature of a transactional contract where—using Dworkin's words—the explicit agreement is "hammered out at arm's length."

Another way to describe the difference is by using the terminology of professor Richard Thaler, whose concept of Econs and Humans was introduced in Chapter 6. In a transactional contract the parties treat each other as Econs (reflecting the view of conventional economic theory). In contrast, in a relational contract, parties treat each other as Humans (reflecting the view of behavioral economics).[5] When one views the nature of the relationship through the lens of an Econ, it means each party acts as a rational entity, capable of long-term planning, striving to maximize its benefits with little or no sense of fairness beyond what is required by strict business reasons. In a relational contract, instead, the parties act as Humans. While they no doubt are still rational entities, the parties recognize they have limited capacity for long-term planning. It also means they have a strong sense of fairness, as shown in the Ultimatum's Game, which punishes unfair behavior even to one's short-term disadvantage.

In the next chapter, we will share how adopting a view of the other party as an Econ can make sense in some instances but can be highly risky where the relational contract is the best fit.

## Disconnect from or Embeddedness in Social Norms

The third dimension is how much the contracting parties' behaviors are based on social norms such as loyalty, honesty, and reciprocity.

In a transactional contract, there is a *disconnect* from social norms—meaning social norms have little or no role in how the parties approach the contract. Remember, transactional contracts are depicted as arms-length with a focus on the deal. It is common and sometimes even accepted practices that the parties use power and do not look out for each other's interests, that they withhold important information from the other party, and so on. Take, for example, negotiation tactics. Many negotiation books reference that information is power and suggest you should withhold information to get the best deal.[6] Other negotiations experts suggest negotiations are a game you play to win and suggest tactics such as good cop/bad cop and stonewalling.[7]

Contracting parties often create a disconnect from social norms in contractual terms. One example is a termination for convenience clause, which typically entitles the buyer to terminate the relationship even if a contract breach has not occurred, showing there are no loyalty obligations in the relationship. A termination for convenience clause allows the customer to use its power to leave the relationship to extract benefits from the seller. Another example is risk-shifting clauses common in share purchase or outsourcing agreements. Risk-shifting clauses try to push the risk for misses in the due diligence process to the other party. For example, buyers of outsourcing services often want to include a "scope sweep" clause to shift risk to a service provider for failing to accurately price the scope of service in question. Likewise, the service provider will want to reserve the right to change the price based on perceived scope changes discovered after signing the contract. These are just two of countless examples. The key point is that in the transactional contract, social norms play a minor role, or no role because the intent is to build an arms-length relationship—focusing on a particular commercial exchange with as few strings attached as possible.

Compare this to a relational contract that embeds social norms into the foundation of the relationship and agreement. In sociological literature, the term *embeddedness* is used to describe a situation where an economic relationship between two or more parties is only a part of a broader, more social, relationship which includes moral obligations, feelings of friendship, trust, and so on.[8]

Legal scholar Ian Macneil described the relational contract as "a mini-society with a vast array of norms beyond the norms centered on exchange and its immediate processes"[9] and pointed to the norms of reciprocity and solidarity, which is called "loyalty" in this book, as having particular importance. In his groundbreaking study of the Shasta County ranchers, Robert Ellickson found the norms of loyalty and equity helped the ranchers to find solutions to their dealings in the long-term interest of everyone involved.

In a relational contract, the parties deliberately embed their commercial relationship into a social relationship based on social norms, which is converted into contractual norms. Proven norms (also known as guiding principles) include those of reciprocity, autonomy, honesty, loyalty, equity, and integrity—all of which are described in Chapter 14. The resulting contractual Guiding Principles become binding legal obligations and support how the parties interpret the contract with all the other clauses in the contract aligned with the Guiding Principles. We cover *how* to do this in Part 4.

Converting social norms into contractual guiding principles is a means to overcome the challenge that all contracts face—to some extent being incomplete, leading to hold-ups, and the ensuing consequential risk. In the complex, often long-term, commercial relationships where the relational contract is the best fit, the social norms fill in the unavoidably large blanks of the contract to prevent shading. When social norms are included in a relational contract they provide guidance and direction to prevent the parties from abusing their power or embracing a hold-up position to extract benefits from one another to the detriment of the relationship.

Let's revisit a common contractual clause known as a scope sweeper to see how the use of guiding principles are used in practice in an outsourcing relationship. The goal of a scope sweeper clause is to protect the buying organizations from any gaps in the knowledge and understanding of the scope. In essence, if the supplier has not done due diligence, the supplier must bear the risk of the additional scope being "swept" in the contract. In a relational contract, the parties would apply transparency obligations and let the party who would have the lowest cost to either share or find the information carry the risk, applying a principle of loyalty.[10]

Chapter 16 contains many examples of how the contractual Guiding Principles affect traditional contract clauses in the relational contract.

# Risk Mitigation Through Power or Alignment of Interests and Expectations

As addressed in Part 2 of the book, contracting professionals are expected to safeguard the investments made in a contractual relationship from the risks of opportunistic behavior. The *mechanism* to create such safeguards is fundamentally different in the relational contract versus the transactional contract.

In a transactional contract, organizations use *power* to make it costly for the other party to act opportunistically. The two forms of power for mitigating risk are *state power* and *market power*. Both are used extensively in a transactional contract. *State power* simply means the legal ability to enforce contractual obligations. *Market power* is best depicted by the ability to coerce the other party to do as one wants by threatening to leave the relationship. The power to leave is ensured by either a short contract term or a termination for convenience clause, which grants a right to terminate the contract regardless of whether a breach has occurred or not, by simply providing a reasonable number of days advance notice, i.e., 30 days.

Market power is, as with all power, based on a relationship of dependency. In a contractual relationship, a buyer can use market power (via the seller's dependence on the buyer for revenue and margin) to extract benefits from the seller with no corresponding benefits to the seller other than the continued relationship. A typical example is for procurement professionals to request price decreases or other concessions in exchange for a contract extension.

Let's now look at how one mitigates risk in a relational contract. Instead of using power to make it costly to be opportunistic, the parties try to reduce risks by adopting rules intended to keep their interests and expectations continuously aligned. Opportunistic behavior is, by definition, an action in the opportunistic party's interest, but which conflicts with the other party's interests. If the parties do not have conflicting interests, there will be no opportunistic behavior. Hence, opportunistic behavior can be avoided, not by threat of power, but by trying to ensure that no conflicts of interest arise in the first place.

Recall Oliver Hart pointed out that much friction in contracts is generated by failed expectations. The contract creates reference points that generate feelings of entitlements to the expected contractual outcomes. If the parties, through communication mechanisms and other means, continuously attempt to keep their expectations clear and aligned, such friction—shading in Oliver Hart's terminology—can be avoided.

It would be unrealistic to think that contracting parties will never have conflicts of interests or misaligned expectations. So what to do? The parties can mitigate misalignment by adopting interest-aligning relationship mechanisms to enhance communication, ensure clarity of expectations, and promote fairness. Proven examples include co-creating shared goals and objectives, adopting a flexible pricing model that keeps the economics fair and balanced over time, and creating a robust governance structure that seeks to address potential root causes underlying problems. When contracting parties perform below their contractual reference points they can use the relational mechanisms to re-establish alignment.

To be clear, a relational contract should be structured and drafted with the intent of making it legally binding. Why? Most parties enter into contracts with the intent to comply with the contract, so the act of making the contract binding formally elevates their commitment to fulfill the contractual obligations. The fact that litigation is an eventual option to enforce the contract, while usually deemed to be the last resort also becomes compelling to many parties. But even though the relational contract is legally binding, the *primary* risk-mitigation mechanism in the relational contract is through the parties continually aligning their interests.

## Complete Planning or a Flexible Framework

Whether one is building a house or a railroad, seeking to execute a marketing campaign, or trying to ensure access to information technology—one will need to rely on the many activities identified and commitments made by the parties in their contract. Regardless if a contract is viewed as a safeguard for investments or an instrument for social cooperation, the goal is to realize the planned business objectives. As such, the fifth and final dimension we use to compare transactional and relational contracts is in how each approach planning.

The ambition of the transactional contract drafter is to make a complete plan. In contrast, the relational contract drafter uses a flexible framework within which the parties can adjust their plans to continually align with the dynamic nature of business.

Consider the underlying challenge in how organizations plan through their contracting. It is essential to understand there is a tendency for opportunism. A customer organization negotiating a contract may ask: what if we have missed something when planning? What if we realize, after the agreement has been signed, there is additional work we forgot to include in the specification? Will the seller take advantage by trying to increase the price? The answer is most likely "yes," especially in a transactional contract, where there is an arms-length relationship and disconnection from social norms.

Organizations seek to write complete contracts to prevent opportunism. The mechanism organizations use to write a complete contract is known as *presentiation*. The concept of presentiation—coined by Ian Macneil—is the technique of bringing the future into the present by agreeing *now* on how to deal with what may happen *then*.[11] Contracting professionals seek to write complete contracts by trying to foresee everything that can happen during the term of the contract and writing contract clauses to ensure those events become pre-defined. This makes typical transactional contracts *rigid*. There are clear advantages of such contracts, not least since the parties can be very clear on what to expect from each other.

There are however also obvious downsides with contracts that are too rigid. First, if the parties do not allow for changes in the contract if new circumstances arise, the parties can easily find themselves stuck in a deal neither wants. Second, if the commercial agreement is complex and long-term, the attempt to make a complete, rigid contract will most likely lead to a long and complicated contract that the parties will have a hard time interpreting and applying. At some point, the gains from the complete plan may be lost in this complexity, positioning the rigid contract to do more harm than good.

Conversely, flexible contracts can also have their downsides. As covered in Chapter 6, Oliver Hart points out that a key problem with a flexible and "loose" contract is not so much that the parties may abuse a missing piece, but that the parties, being under a self-serving bias, are inclined to interpret flexible clauses to their advantage, increasing the likelihood of creating failed expectations and shading behavior.

So if both have downsides, what should one do? First, it is important to understand that neither approach is right nor wrong. Rather there is tension between the need for rigidity and flexibility in contracts. The answer lies in choosing the best-fit contracting model for one's situation. We cover how to do this in Chapter 8.

The good news is that a well-structured relational contract recognizes the tension between the need for safeguards and clear expectations *and* the need for flexibility and continuous adjustments. How is this achieved?

First, a properly structured relational contract is designed with outer boundaries that create clear and rigid framework rules for the relationship and outline the parties' expectations (e.g., reference points). Second, the more specific aspects of the deal content (e.g., statement of work, pricing) are flexible. For example, rather than a detailed statement of work prescribing how work is done, the parties adopt a more flexible taxonomy of the work and clearly define workload allocation of who does what work supporting the partnership. Last and most important, the parties agree on robust governance mechanisms outlining how the parties will communicate and decide on changes and adjustments to the contract. The governance framework embeds social norms which contractually commit the parties to honor their guiding principles. The result is a well-drafted relational contract which shifts expectations from rigid details in the deal to more general rules and a fair process to deal with changes and adjustments.

# The Definition of a Relational Contract: Revisited

Based on the comparison between the transactional and relational contract made above, it is hopefully easier to understand the definition of what is meant by a relational contract, namely:

> *A legally enforceable written contract*
> *establishing a commercial partnership*
> *within a flexible contractual framework*
> *based on social norms and jointly defined objectives,*
> *prioritizing a relationship with the continuous alignment of interests*
> *before the commercial transactions.*

As shown, the relational contract focuses on the relationship, rather than the deal. A relational contract formally establishes a partnership mentality, embeds the commercial relationship in social norms, mitigates risks with its structure through continually aligning interests via a rigid framework balanced with flexibility in its details. This differs significantly from the transactional contract, where an arms-length relationship simply focuses on the deal. The ambition of a transactional contract drafter is to make a complete plan and mitigate the risks through the market and state power, with social norms playing a minor role.

While we have profiled the two distinct contracting models, the picture is not black or white. Each dimension forms a continuum. For example, the extent of focusing on the relationship or the deal can vary. In some contracts, equal focus may be on both. The degree of embeddedness in social norms may vary. A transactional contract may be rigid but still very fair.

As you sort through your situation to determine if a relational contract or a transactional contract is a better fit, you might be tempted to cherry-pick the aspects of a relational contract you like and simply embed them into your relationship or contract while omitting others. You are not the first to wonder if it is possible to write a traditional, transactional contract with relational elements. While it may be possible, we highly recommend not to do this as we have seen countless attempts where this approach failed. While it may bring short-term successes, our experience is that success is not sustainable.

Why does it not work? Simply put, transactional contracts and relational contracts follow a different logic. A transactional contract views the parties as Econs while a relational contract treats the parties as Humans. The contracting practitioner needs to select one approach and stick with it.

## A Look Ahead

This chapter has explored the most important characteristics of transactional and relational contracts, comparing them across five dimensions. But how does one know which contract model to use in which situation? This is shared in the next chapter.

## Notes

1. Tim Cummins, "Contracting Technology Revolution—Here Today, But Are We Ready?" *Contracting Excellence Magazine*, May/June 2015.
2. See, for example, The International Association for Contract & Commercial Management's *Top Negotiated Terms 2018*.
3. Ronald Dworkin, *Law's Empire* (Cambridge, MA: Harvard University Press, 1986).
4. Ibid.
5. See Chapter 6 for an explanation.
6. See, for example, Roger Dawson, *Secrets of Power Negotiating, 15th Anniversary Edition: Inside Secrets from a Master Negotiator* (Pompton Plains, NJ: Career Press, 2011).
7. A good example of this is from Chester L. Karrass, *The Negotiating Game* (New York: HarperCollins, 1992).
8. See Mark Granovetter, "Economic Action and Social Structure: The Problem of Embeddedness," *American Journal of Sociology*, Vol. 91, No. 3 (November 1985), pp. 481–510.
9. Ian Macneil, "Contracts: Adjustment of Long-Term Economic Relations Under Classical, Neoclassical and Relational Contract Law," in *Selected Works of Macneil*, p. 196.
10. The loyalty Guiding Principle obliges the parties to be loyal to the relationship. Applying the loyalty principle benefits the parties because they can optimize for the total cost of ownership across both parties and ultimately helps prevent a party from making a one-sided short-term decision that might improve one parties' position at expense at the other party. Loyalty to the relationship will come when the parties' interests are treated as equally important.
11. Ian Macneil, "Restatement (Second) of Contracts and Presentation," *The Relational Theory of Contract: Selected Works of Ian Macneil* (London: Sweet & Maxwell, 2001), pp. 182–187.

# 8

# When to Use a Relational Contract

Two questions we often get asked are: *"When should I use a relational contract instead of a transactional contract?"* and, *"When should we rely on employment contracts instead, e.g., use vertical integration as a strategy?"* This chapter sets out to answer these questions. However, before we answer, we want to stress two points.

First, we want to stress that a relational contract is not "better" than a transactional contract or employment. Likewise, a transactional contract is not "better" than a relational contract. Rather, the goal is to ensure the most appropriate contracting model is selected for the situation. In some cases, a relational contract is a better fit while in other situations a transactional contract is a better fit. And sometimes, it is better to organize the business internally, by using employment contracts instead.

Second, it is important to emphasize that while the question of when to use a relational contract might look simple, the answer is not always straightforward. Getting to the right answer is often a matter of first drafting a business case, weighing pros and cons, and making a reasoned judgment based on all facts at hand. The choice of whether one should use a relational or a transactional contract is an economic choice.

© The Author(s), under exclusive license to Springer Nature
Switzerland AG 2021
D. Frydlinger et al., *Contracting in the New Economy*,
https://doi.org/10.1007/978-3-030-65099-5_8

# A Matter of Risk and Dependency

The choice to use a transactional or relational contract or to vertically integrate (e.g., use employment contracts) should be based on the characteristics of the deal and the relationship to be entered into. At a high level, the two most important characteristics to focus on are the *dependency* that will exist between the parties and the *risks* involved in the deal and relationship. The overall logic is simple: the higher the dependency and risks, the more critical it is to apply a relational contract designed to continuously align the interests and expectations of the parties. But when the dependency levels are low and risk moderate, a transactional contract is often a better choice. Sometimes, the dependency and risks will be so high that the best choice is to vertically integrate (e.g., through employment contracts) such as the case where work is considered "core" business. For the rest of this chapter, we assume a company has made a "buy-decision" and the question is whether to use a relational contract or a transactional contract.

# Two Scenarios

Consider dependency and risk through the lens of two global consumer packaged goods (CPG) companies contracting with a supplier for third-party logistics (3PL) support. We look at two scenarios—Scenario High and Scenario Low—which have very different circumstances regarding dependency and risk. While a countless number of scenarios can be analyzed (e.g., both risk and dependency are in the mid-range), these two scenarios share the logic of how to select the most appropriate contracting model for a specific situation.

## Scenario High

In Scenario High, CPG One works with seven third-party logistics suppliers who provide global warehousing support. CPG One has worked with three of the suppliers for over ten years. One of the three suppliers—Global3PL Inc.—has proven its competence in the United States, Europe, and Asia. In total, CPG One spends over $50 million with Global3PL Inc. across all three regions and five business units.

CPG One has been thinking about creating a more strategic relationship with Global3PL Inc. If they entered into a global deal for just the current book of business under the existing scope of Global3PL Inc. the total contract value would be $50 million. However, CPG One is thinking about consolidating the number of suppliers to just three. Here, Global3PL Inc., stands to increase its revenue to over $100 million a year if they are awarded the work of the four other suppliers. A potential deal would have a significant economic value in absolute terms for both CPG One and Global3PL Inc.

The potential agreement is not only significant in terms of spend/revenue for each party but is also of high strategic importance; part of the deal includes Global 3PL Inc. making investments in business-critical IT solutions to improve CPG One's customer service levels and help CPG One optimize their inventory.

CPG One is rightfully concerned about the potential risk of entering into such a large contract with Global 3PL Inc. What if Global 3PL Inc. does not live up to its promises of customizing its IT system with the features CPG One needs? Or what if the parties find themselves in a dispute? In a deal so large and complex and full of uncertainties it could be very costly for CPG One to switch to another supplier. Or worse—what if the switching costs are so high CPG One will be stuck in a bad deal and become the victim of opportunistic "hold-up" behaviors from Global 3PL Inc. abusing the dependency to extract value from the relationship through scope changes and annual price increases?

## Scenario Low

CPG Two is a global consumer packaged goods company that competes with CPG One. CPG Two has been slow to outsource, but the VP of Supply Chain wants to test the thought of outsourcing some of its basic warehousing operations as a proof of concept. The VP has approved a pilot to outsource one of CPG Two's overflow warehouse operations.

CPG Two has completed market research. There are several reputable contract logistics providers in the city where CPG Two's main distribution center is. CPG Two completed a competitive bid to see which service providers could meet their requirements at the best price. The winner was Local3PL Co.

The scope of work is relatively basic. Local3PL Co. will simply store extra pallets for CPG Two and deliver them the next day on a will-call basis when CPG Two places an order before 3 pm. Because it is a pilot, the VP, and general counsel have suggested the contract be limited to a one-year contract with a 30-day termination for convenience. Local3PL Co is keen to get in the door with CPG Two and sees little risk to the short-term contract as they already have the assets available to perform the work. The pilot would provide incremental revenue and help fill up capacity in a warehouse currently only half full.

The level of dependency is low, and there is relatively little risk involved for either party. If Local3PL Co. does not meet expectations, CPG Two can easily switch to another local contract logistics provider at the end of the pilot. The VP of Supply Chain believes even in the worst-case CPG Two can always revert to the way it was working before if the pilot fails since the scope of work is small and it is only for one location.

# Risk

When thinking about risks, a good starting point is to understand the nature of the risks being assessed. Recall a key risk often overlooked is the risk of misaligned interests and expectations which can generate opportunistic behavior and shading.[1]

A case in point is the very public dispute between Volkswagen and two parts suppliers—CarTrim and ES Automobilguss. CarTrim makes seats and ES Automobilguss produces cast iron parts needed to make gearboxes. The dispute centered on a contract that Volkswagen signed with the two suppliers, then later canceled. Both suppliers wanted Volkswagen to pay for plant alterations they made before canceling the contract. The suppliers sought compensation for lost revenue they claimed amounted to tens of millions of euros. Car Trim and ES Automobilguss eventually suspended deliveries after Volkswagen rejected discussions to reimburse the suppliers.[2] This caused Volkswagen to shut down its production lines at significant costs. For perspective, it is estimated that one minute of downtime is incredibly expensive, with estimates ranging from $22,000 per minute to as high as $50,000 per minute.[3] The spat was a classic case of tit-for-tat shading in practice.

Refusing to ship products is a significant decision for a supplier. While the decision halted Volkswagen's assembly lines costing them millions of euros, the suppliers also suffered catastrophically from lost revenue.

So how does one assess the cost of misalignment? A common approach to looking at risk is to view it as a function of negative impact (severity) and negative probability (likelihood). A potential event that costs $1 million dollars is still a low-risk event if it is very unlikely to occur. The same goes for a likely event that only costs a few dollars.

Let's look at the following framework in Fig. 8.1 considering six factors to gauge the likelihood.

| | Factors Impacting the Severity of Misalignment | Factors Impacting the Likelihood of Misalignment |
|---|---|---|
| **The economic value of the contract;** What is the absolute or relative terms (is the contract for $10,000 or $10,000,000)? | X | X |
| **The strategic importance of the contract;** Are the parties dependent on each other for success? For example, need they work together to enter into a new market, gain access to essential competencies, or to improve time to market? | X | X |
| **Costs of failed or weak performance under the contract;** Will failed or weak performance hurt a party's reputation, create dissatisfied customers, and so on? Are there direct and indirect costs if one party does not perform? | X | X |
| **The complexity of the deal;** Is the relationship for a simple commodity? Or is the nature of the work highly sophisticated and/or complicated? | N/A | X |
| **Uncertainty in the deal;** To what extent is the business environment dynamic and will change? Are there unknowns that could affect the economics of the relationship after the contract is signed? | N/A | X |
| **Length of the relationship/contract term;** How long is the relationship needed? What is the likelihood the parties will need to continue their relationship after contract terminates? | N/A | X |

**Fig. 8.1** Factors impacting misalignment

The first three factors can influence both the severity *and* likelihood. This makes sense because the more significant the economic or strategic value on the table, the higher the likelihood for one or both parties to act opportunistically because the stakes are high.

Combined, these six factors can help an organization better understand the risk of misalignment and failed expectations. To make the point, compare a simple purchase of a commodity on a spot market with a large and complex construction contract for a bridge or a shareholder's agreement regarding a growth-stage unicorn. The commodity purchase is straightforward, taking place at a particular moment where after the parties move on from each other, besides possible warranties. The product description is simple and so is pricing, since it is relatively simple for the buyer and seller to assess the value and cost in the deal. And there is no uncertainty. In such a case, there is a low likelihood of misaligned interests harming the parties.

The factors are different when one looks at the complex construction contracts or shareholder's agreements. Due to changing needs and external circumstances, the parties' interests will change over time, increasing the probability of these interests becoming misaligned. Significant relationship friction can arise because of failed expectations, where the contract has created reference points against which the contract outcomes are compared.[4] The more complex the deal and the longer the relationship, the more likely it is that such frictions will arise.

Now recall the CPG organizations under Scenario High and Scenario Low. Both are outsourcing logistics work to a third-party logistics provider. However, Scenario High will have a higher risk of misalignment over the life of the relationship due to the dynamic environment and high stakes for both parties.

## Dependency

The second aspect when discovering whether the transactional or relational contract is the best fit for a particular deal is to look at the dependency between the parties. From one perspective, dependency can be viewed as part of the overall risk analysis. From the other perspective, dependency is so vital that it should be considered separately.

Oliver Williamson made dependency between the contracting parties the most important aspect when assessing which governance model to choose. Williamson used the term "asset-specificity" to describe this dependency.[5] Asset specificity is more commonly referred to as relationship-specific assets or investments. Regardless of what one calls it, the meaning is the same: assets involved in a relationship that are somewhat unique to the relationship.

Sometimes, the relationship-specific assets are obvious. For example, take the case of McDonald's. Ever wonder why a Big Mac is the same everywhere in the world? One reason is that McDonald's has very rigorous standards for its suppliers to have dedicated food processing facilities (e.g., asset specificity) for McDonald's.[6] For example, Lopez Foods meticulously produces beef patties to meet exacting production standards that meet a 100 point inspection every 10 minutes.[7]

But other cases are not so obvious. Take the relationship between an automotive company and a parts supplier. If the supplier builds its factory close to one of their customer's assembly plants to facilitate "just-in-time delivery", the supplier is likely choosing to be further away from other customers. The supplier would have relationship-specific assets that create a dependency between the parties. While the buyer may find a cheaper supplier of the parts, the total costs could become much higher if a switch occurs because of the increase in logistics and inventory costs involved in using a more distant supplier.

In other relationships, knowledge may be the relationship-specific asset. A supplier may have spent years learning to know its customer's business needs and ways of working, and it could cost a great deal for the customer to switch to another supplier that would have to build up this knowledge. In yet other situations, the parties may have integrated their IT-systems or other systems or processes, making it very expensive to unwind the relationship and establish another.

Two of the most important factors to consider when assessing dependency between the parties are *switching costs* and the *availability of alternatives.*

Consider Scenario High and Scenario Low again to see how dependency varies in both situations. As already noted in the description of Scenario High, CPG One has been working with other key suppliers and has found Global3PL Inc. to have the best record for consistently high-quality service. While it is possible to switch suppliers, they would be less than optimal to meet CPG One's needs. Also, the switching costs would be much higher because of the high degree of embeddedness between CPG One and Global3PL Inc. Simply put, trying to untangle the relationship would be much more expensive than the simple 30-day termination of convenience and bringing work back in-house in Scenario Low.

Let's look at more nuanced examples to help make the point. First, consider a situation with high risk and low dependency. A company may need to buy a component to be used for producing the company's consumer goods. If the component does not work, the consumer good will not work, which will make the company lose both money and reputation. However, the component as such is not unique because several suppliers can provide it. While the risk is high, the switching costs would be low if things went awry. Here the buying organization would simply switch suppliers—hopefully before the costs of the risk got too high. But here is the other side of the equation. The seller would know it is easy for the buyer to switch suppliers. This knowledge would likely influence the supplier's behavior in how they acted within the relationship. Why? Often, a seller would prefer to continue the relationship rather than risk the chance of getting their contract terminated.

Now let's look at a situation with high dependency such as a large infrastructure construction project or a long-term outsourcing relationship. In either case, it would cost the buying organization significant time and money to leave the relationship and find another supplier. From a strictly economic viewpoint, the negative impact of the misaligned interests would have to be higher than the total costs of switching before the buyer would leave the relationship. This would mean that the buyer would have to suffer from these adverse impacts—maybe higher prices, lower quality, customer dissatisfaction, and so on—up to a value that equals the switching costs. This is a classic example of the hold-up problem discussed in Part 1 where one party abuses the power created by the dependency to extract value from the other party.[8]

These examples show why the aspect of dependency is so important to assess when looking for the best-fit contract model.

## Assessing Best Fit Across the Five Dimensions

In Chapter 7 we compared transactional and relational contracts across five dimensions. Developing a deep understanding of which contract model is the best fit requires one to compare Scenario High to Scenario Low across all five of the dimensions. In practice, there are many deals where reality is much more complex than Scenario High and Scenario Low. The comparison made here will, however, help highlight the pros and cons of each contact model in the two scenarios.

### Focus on the Deal or Focus on the Relationship

Consider Scenario Low, which has low risk and low dependency. Given this, it makes the most sense to focus on the deal—not the relationship. Why? The economic value is likely moderate and the deal is unlikely to change. As such, there would be a low return on investment to spend a lot of resources building a healthy relationship between the parties. This means contract details such as the description of the services are likely easy to document and negotiating a price should be relatively straightforward. Scenario Low would be a candidate for a transactional contract.

The situation is quite different in Scenario High where there are high risks and high dependency. In this scenario, the parties' needs and other circumstances will most likely change over time, maybe several times over the life of the relationship. The deal will therefore change, while the relationship will remain the same. This means that the economic benefits for the parties are not so much generated by the direct exchanges of goods or services for money or other exchanges, but rather as a factor of the relationship itself. Since the deal will change, it is the parties' assets such as patents, knowledge, culture, strategic relationships with others that will generate benefits over time, not the particular output of usage of these assets in a specific exchange.

In Scenario High, therefore, it makes much more sense to focus on the relationship rather than the short-term deal. Scenario High is a good candidate for a relational contract.

## Arms-Length Relationship or Partnership

In Scenario Low, the parties have a low dependency on each other. In Scenario High, the dependency is high. It should be evident that the former scenario is a candidate for a transactional contract and the latter scenario a candidate for a relational contract. However, getting to the obvious answer is not always straightforward because many organizations' current contracting practices prevent relational contracting. For example, two common contracting approaches are to use a short-term contract duration and a termination for convenience. This makes sense on the surface—especially for buying organizations. Why become locked-in if one can prevent it? One is only contractually stuck with a supplier for the duration one has chosen, and under the worst case, one can fire the supplier anytime (for convenience) if needed. Where the dependency and switching costs are low, this is a perfectly rational way to contract.

While termination for convenience and contract term clauses may be easy to write—they do not reflect reality if one is in Scenario High. Why? Because no contract terms can alter a de facto dependency between the parties created by high relationship-specific assets or low availability of alternative resources. For example, a shareholder of an organization may have no choice but to accept the relationship with the other shareholders unless it wants to sell its shares. A buyer of manufactured parts may have to continue using the parts supplier because of the high switching costs associated with ramping up an alternative supplier with the know-how and specialized tooling to produce the customized part. To aim for contractual mechanisms that foster an arms-length relationship with low dependency is to ignore the reality of high dependency. Simply put, it is like trying to force a square peg in a round hole.

Contracting professionals need to recognize the trade-offs between dependency and independence. While dependency may create a hold-up risk, a hard pursuit for independence also can have a serious economic downside.

For example, one trade-off is that short-term contracts and termination of convenience clauses inherently disincentivizes parties to make asset-specific investments in the relationship. Contractual relationships are increasingly becoming an important factor for organizations to create competitive advantages. A competitive advantage is, by definition, a strength that is unique and is hard for competitors to imitate. If two parties want to generate a competitive advantage through a contractual relationship, the intention must then be to create something unique with the other party. And that means there has to be relationship-specific investments and dependency between the parties.[9]

Second, recall from Chapter 6 that people react negatively to power abuse and unfair treatment. In relationships of high dependency, if one or both parties act as profit-maximizing Econs and ignore the fairness-minded Human perspective, they will most likely create friction in the relationship. For example, in Scenario High, it can be outright damaging for the parties to write a transactional contract that ignores the dependent reality. It is easy to see that the dependency in Scenario High—if abused—could easily create friction. And the friction could not be mitigated by just switching to another supplier or contracting partner since the dependency is high. Therefore, the only rational thing to do is to adopt the relational contract model, where the parties instead view each other as Humans. This acknowledges the parties have to look out for each other's interests and expectations to minimize the frictions that, if they arise, will hurt both parties because of the dependency that prevents them from leaving the relationship.

Sadly, many contracting professionals view dependency as something bad. This mindset deserves an additional review. Firms that embrace a spirit of partnership can generate competitive advantages by consciously embracing and even deepening the dependency between the parties—such as investing asset-specific efficiencies and investments that outperform an arms-length relationship. The better strategy is instead to use a relational contract that establishes a formal partnership mindset and mechanisms between the parties to ensure continual alignment of interests and prevent shading behavior caused by misalignment.

## Disconnect from or Embeddedness in Social Norms

In Scenario Low, social norms don't have to play an important role. Since the deal is simple, the parties will most likely be able to set out most rules of the deal directly in the contract. Where there are gaps, legal rules will probably provide adequate solutions. Also, due to the low dependency in this scenario, the parties will not have to worry too much about frictions generated by breaching social norms.

The situation is quite different in Scenario High. When the dependency between the parties is high due to relationship-specific assets or for other reasons, the parties must avoid the transaction costs generated from shading due to contract reference points not being aligned. They must also be cognizant of unavoidable frictions generated from perceived unfair behavior associated with a breach of social norms. In this scenario, the parties should therefore use a relational contract that embeds the commercial relationship in social norms transformed into contractual norms. This is done by aligning the contract with social norms from the beginning.

Social norms are important in Scenario High for a second reason. Due to the complexity and uncertainty in Scenario High, it is impossible for the parties to write a complete contract. As such, the contract will unavoidably be full of gaps. And in this scenario, legal rules likely cannot fill in the blanks, since such rules are typically written for standardized situations, not addressing all the complexities and nuances that exist and will exist in Scenario High. In such a situation the guiding principles adopted when the parties transform social norms into contractual norms will help the parties keep in a continual alignment of interests. How? Adopting formal guiding principles such as reciprocity, loyalty, and equity can help the parties avoid friction and find ways forward in the hundreds of situations which would be impossible to address with more specific contract clauses.

## Risk Mitigation Through Power or Continuous Alignment of Interests

As raised in Chapter 5, a contract is typically viewed as a safeguard for investments. A dominant number of lawyers and other contracting professionals primarily view the contract as a risk-mitigating instrument to protect the business. This is carried out in practice as evidenced by WCC's "most negotiated terms" report which indicates contracting professionals are stuck in risk-shifting practices.[10] As we saw in the previous chapter, there are two fundamental risk mitigation mechanisms in the transactional contract: market power and state power.[11] Both can be effective in Scenario Low.

The reality is that the feelings of safety, elevated by shifting risk to the other party, are often illusory. Consider market power for Scenario Low. The risk of GPC Two simply leaving the relationship creates strong incentives for Local 3PL Co. to avoid opportunistic behavior. Local3PL Co. is likely to perform, hoping to extend the pilot and/or earn other opportunities within CPG Two.

Now consider state power for Scenario Low. Using contract theory terminology, to demonstrate a breach of contract exists means the breach should not only be observable by the parties, but also verifiable by a court. In Scenario Low, the deal will be reasonably easy to write a clear and complete contract with most facts in the agreement being observable by the parties and also verifiable by a court. Also, the economic value of the contract is low. Combined, the probability of going to court and using state power is weak because it is likely to be much cheaper just to do the right thing.

The situation is different in Scenario High where risk and dependency are high. As shared in the previous chapter, the relational contract primarily mitigates risks by continuously aligning interests and expectations between the parties through joint goals and objectives, guiding principles, and governance processes.

While it might be tempting to think one can use market and state power in Scenario High, it is myopic. As for market power, it is typically a sign of insufficient analysis to conclude that a short contract term or termination for convenience clause will prevent a lock-in effect and generate some market power in a scenario where the actual dependency between the parties is so high. Such mechanisms do not, in reality, create any power since the parties cannot leave the relationship without incurring high costs.

Likewise, state power is likely ineffective in Scenario High. Organizations typically only litigate or arbitrate in very grave circumstances. Why? To do so is the same as signaling that the relationship is over, which can be highly problematic where the dependency between the parties forces them to nevertheless remain in the relationship. Also, going to court is seldom more than gambling for a positive outcome—especially in complex deals. It is often difficult, if not impossible, to write a Scenario High contract that makes a breach both observable by the parties and verifiable by a court. Therefore, the chances of success in the court system will always decrease with higher complexity. With this in mind, it is naïve to primarily rely on risk mitigation through state power for Scenario High contracts.

The bottom line is that the risk mitigation mechanisms of the transactional contract are very weak in high risk and high dependency situations. Also, the arms-length and market-power approaches entering into a transactional contract can generate the risks which the parties are trying to avoid. To ignore an actual dependency and treat each other as Econs, with no obligation to look out for each other's interests, can often generate friction and temptations for opportunistic behaviors in the relationships. The irony is that acting as an Econ and creating a transactional contract can inadvertently create friction and behaviors that the contract is presumably written to avoid.

For these and also other reasons, the relational contract is the best fit for Scenario High.

## Complete Planning or a Flexible Framework

If the contracting parties could specify their respective rights and duties for every possible future state of their relationships their contract would be called a "complete" contract. The contract would not have errors, omissions nor ambiguities.

While some argue it is impossible to write a complete contract, one point is clear; the more complex the contract, the harder it is to draft an almost complete contract. Perhaps this is why Nobel laureate Oliver Williamson astutely wrote, "All complex contracts will be incomplete –there will be gaps, errors, omissions and the like."[12] As we saw in Chapter 5, Oliver Hart pointed to the same fact.

Remember the planning fallacy described in Chapter 6 suggests it is myopic and inefficient to get to a complete contract in a highly complex environment. While the parties may think they can write a complete contract in reality, they cannot. Even if they could, the plan would be so long and complex it would render the contract almost unreadable, thus creating an incomplete contract with significant ambiguity.

Some contracting professionals—especially those who work in buyer-supplier relationships—argue it is ok for the contract to be incomplete at the signing because they can use a trinity of clauses to deal with incompleteness. The triad includes three common clauses: a so-called scope sweeper, change control procedures, and the right to terminate for convenience. Proponents for the transactional contract argue this trinity can prevent abuses of contractual incompleteness.

A scope sweeper clause obliges a service provider—often at no extra cost—to provide the services in not only the service specification, but also any other services that the parties may have forgotten to specify, but which the customer needs. If something was left out of the original scope, the customer can "sweep" that scope into the agreement.

The second mechanism is to use contract change control procedures. Change control procedures allow the parties to set out the process for changing the contract. The service provider must respond to change requests within specified time limits and there can be restrictions on how the service provider can adjust its prices.

The final mechanism in the trinity is a termination for convenience clause. Termination for convenience provides the customer the right to terminate the contract even if the supplier has not breached the contract. The purpose is to give the customer leverage in discussions about scope and changes and disincentivizes the supplier from pursuing opportunistic behaviors.

The strategy behind the trinity of clauses is to ensure the contract is complete by disincentivizing the supplier from abusing the customer's dependency where the contract gaps appear.

While the logic of the trinity of clauses makes sense, experience shows it inadequate. Why? The trinity does not prevent the parties from spending a lot of time arguing whether a change is actually a change to the contract. The friction generated in discussions about contractual changes is an excellent example of the transactional contract generates the risks it aims to avoid or mitigate. The friction results from the misaligned interests and expectations of the parties and are all examples of shading behavior.

A more in-depth review is warranted. Using Oliver Hart's terminology, the signed contract will generate reference points (i.e., expectations) for the parties against which any later outcomes will be measured. For example, a customer will likely have savings or cost targets expressed in an elaborate business case. Likewise, the supplier will have revenue and margin targets shown in their business case. The traditional "battle of the forms" becomes the "battle of the business cases."

When a transactional contract is used both parties will act as Econs and try to negotiate a contract that will ensure their reference points in their respective business cases. The business case reference points often constitute the parties' BATNA's (Best Alternative To No Agreement) or walk-away points. However, prevailing negotiation strategies and practice discourage parties from revealing their BATNA's.

The result? Contracting parties have their contractual reference points fixed when the contract is signed. When something unexpected happens, which may affect either party's business case, the parties will do whatever they can to satisfy their reference points. The customer may refer to the scope sweeper. The supplier may opt to invoke a right for extra charges and create a change order. Because of the phenomenon of loss aversion (discussed in Chapter 6), there will be a lot of resistance during the renegotiations. And if the result is an outcome worse than the reference point, the disappointed party is likely to engage in shading behavior.

Recall the premise of shading. Shading refers to behaviors not expressed in the contract and which cannot be verified by a court, even though both parties can observe that the behavior is anathema to the spirit of the contract. This means that a contract cannot, *by definition*, be written to avoid these kinds of behavior.

For a supplier, such shading behavior could appear in decreased proactivity, diminished productivity, fewer innovative suggestions, lowered quality to a point which does not trigger a contractual breach, or attempts to recoup losses in one negotiation in a later renegotiation. On the customer side, shading may occur when the customer uses another supplier for specific projects or when the customer is very diligent in invoking liquidated damages and penalties. There are countless scenarios where customers and suppliers can become opportunistic and shade—tilting the benefits to their side of the transaction. And when one party shades, it often causes a reciprocal reaction from the other party, fueling their opportunism to get even. Shading and tit-for-tat behavior are, unfortunately, too familiar for many contracting and business professionals.

A key cause of shading stems from using a transactional contract when a relational contract is the best fit. The transactional contract is written to be rigid and will set specific reference points for both parties. In situations of high complexity and uncertainty, it is likely those reference points will never be met since objectives and circumstances will change. It is important to recognize a transactional contract is built to prevent the parties from acting opportunistically, not to avoid opportunism through alignment of interests. As such, a transactional contract simply cannot cope with shading behavior when the relational contract is the best fit. Likewise, high dependency makes market power an illusion.

So which is the best fit contracting model for each scenario from a planning perspective? Scenario Low is a good candidate for a transactional contract. As risks, complexity, and dependency increase (as in Scenario High), organizations should shift to a relational contract. Using a relational contract acknowledges the fact that the contract will be incomplete. The parties should be transparent and state their reference points, allowing them to design a flexible contracting framework and mechanisms (e.g., pricing model vs. a price, relationship management, and governance mechanisms) to maintain the parties in continual alignment.

## A Look Ahead

As one can see from Scenario High and Scenario Low, the decision regarding which contracting model is most appropriate is intricately linked to the characteristics of the anticipated deal and relationship. In the next chapter, the focus will be placed on how the choice of contract model is made.

# Notes

1. See the discussion on the works of Oliver Hart in Chapter 6.
2. Kate Vitasek, "VW's Supplier Dispute Shines More Light on Power-Play Practices," *Forbes Online*, August 27 2016. Available at https://www.forbes.com/sites/katevitasek/2016/08/27/vws-supplier-dispute-shines-more-light-on-power-play-practices/#65f72a753755.
3. SimuTech Multimedia, "Troubleshooting Thursday: True Cost of Factory Downtime, How Downtime Affects Productivity (Tip 67) June 26, 2019." Available at https://www.simutechmultimedia.com/the-true-cost-of-downtime-what-you-dont-know-about-how-downtime-affects-your-productivity/.
4. Oliver Hart, John Moore, "Contracts as Reference Points," *NBER Working Paper No. 12706*, November 2006, revised 2007.
5. Oliver E. Williamson, *The Economic Institutions of Capitalism* (New York: The Free Press, 1985), p. 56. See more about Williamson in Chapter 5.
6. Kate Vitasek and Karl Manrodt, with Jeanne Kling, *Vested: How P&G, McDonald's, and Microsoft are Redefining Winning in Business Relationships* (New York: Palgrave Macmillan, 2012).
7. "Lopez Foods: McDonald's Beef Supplier," *Vimeo*, video. Available at https://vimeo.com/21526300.
8. See Chapter 2.
9. See, for example, Jeffrey H. Dyer and Harbir Singh, "The Relational View: Cooperative Strategy and Sources of Interorganizational Competitive Advantage," *The Academy of Management Review*, Vol. 23, No. 4 (October 1998), pp. 660–679.
10. International Association for Contract & Commercial Management (IACCM), *Most Negotiated Terms Report—2018 (Top Terms)* 11 June 2018. Available at https://www.worldcc.com.
11. See Chapter 7.
12. Oliver E. Williamson, "Outsourcing: Transaction Cost Economics and Supply Chain Management," *Journal of Supply Chain Management*, Vol. 44, No 2 (April 3, 2008). Available at: https://onlinelibrary.wiley.com/doi/full/10.1111/j.1745-493X.2008.00051.x.

# 9

# Choosing a Contract Model in Practice

In Chapter 8, we answered the question, *"When should I use a relational contract instead of a transactional contract?"* The choice to use a relational or a transactional contract should be based on the characteristics of the deal and the relationship, with *dependency* and *risks* being the two primary factors in the decision.

This chapter provides a simple framework for helping make the decision. To do this, we integrate the work of University of Tennessee researchers who have conducted extensive work with procurement (buyer-supplier) contracts.

## Sourcing Continuum

In their book *Strategic Sourcing in the New Economy: Harnessing the Potential of Sourcing Business Models for Modern Procurement*, the authors describe seven Sourcing Business Models that fall along a continuum of seven sourcing business models which customers can use when building supplier relationships (Fig. 9.1).[1]

Sourcing Business Model is a term coined by University of Tennessee researchers and is explained in the groundbreaking book which segments supplier relationships by both relationship and economic models. In the book, the authors provide a Sourcing Business Model Mapping toolkit (which can be downloaded from www.vestedway.com for free) to assess the characteristics of the supplier relationship. The toolkit works by having an

© The Author(s), under exclusive license to Springer Nature
Switzerland AG 2021
D. Frydlinger et al., *Contracting in the New Economy*,
https://doi.org/10.1007/978-3-030-65099-5_9

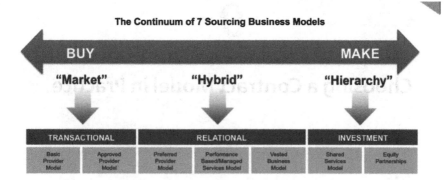

**Fig. 9.1** The Sourcing Continuum

organization "map" 25 business characteristics spanning the following eight dimensions.

- **What level of dependency exists between the buyer and supplier organizations?**
- What is the overall availability of the service/product in the marketplace?
- To what extent is what you are sourcing a "core competency"?
- **To what extent is there a business risk in what you are sourcing?**
- How much potential is there to create a mutual advantage?
- What is the nature of the workscope?
- What is the criticality of the work?
- What are your risk tolerance preferences?

*Risk* and *dependency* (noted in bold above) are the two factors referenced in Chapter 8 for determining the best fit contracting model. These factors are also an integral part of the Sourcing Business Model Mapping Toolkit.[2]

One of the greatest strengths of the University of Tennessee model is that it identifies the relationship contract model as an essential aspect of a sourcing relationship.

Below we provide an example of how a pharmaceutical company "mapped" a potential outsourcing initiative for clinical research services. For context, many pharmaceutical companies are facing a patent cliff with key patents of many vital medicines approaching their expiration date. As the patents expire, competing pharmaceutical companies can legally create generics, eroding the pharmaceutical company's market share and high-profit margins. Many pharmaceutical companies have emphasized speed to market to ensure new drugs are available to replace expiring drugs. However, a bottleneck for getting new drugs to market is the lengthy and complex clinical trials process essential to approve a drug for mass production and distribution. Most pharmaceutical companies have relied on a vertical operational model with in-house professionals dedicated to clinical studies. However, outsourcing has gradually grown among pharmaceutical companies as a way to increase their speed to market.

In the example below, a pharmaceutical company outsourced a small amount of clinical research with success. The company was exploring the viability of approaching CRO (contract research outsourcing) more strategically. A small team from the pharmaceutical company's procurement organization set out to work with various stakeholders to determine which Sourcing Business Model was most appropriate if they entered into a strategic CRO outsourcing deal.

The result of the Sourcing Business Model Mapping effort was a relational contract with an outcome-based economic model. This combination meant the pharmaceutical company should use a Vested sourcing business model for its CRO initiative (see Fig. 9.2).

The pharmaceutical company's complete Sourcing Business Model Map is shared in the following pages with an explanation of why key stakeholders mapped each dimension the way they did. The shading in Figs. 9.3 through 9.10 illustrate their analysis.

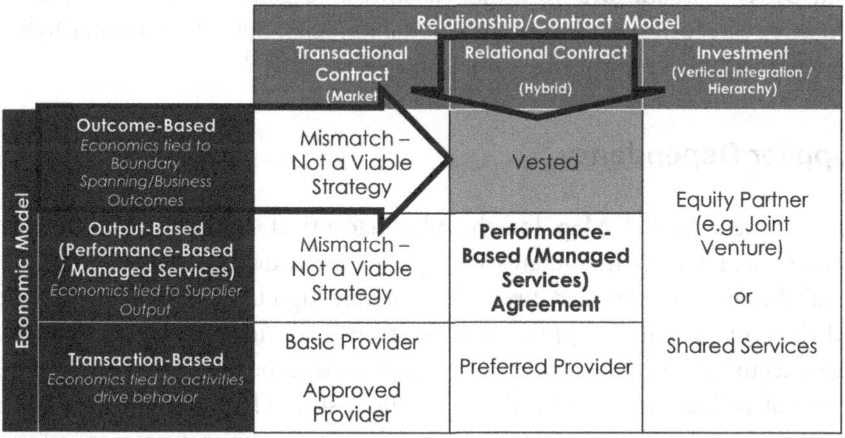

| | | Relationship/Contract Model | |
|---|---|---|---|
| | **Transactional Contract** (Market) | **Relational Contract** (Hybrid) | **Investment** (Vertical Integration / Hierarchy) |
| **Outcome-Based** Economics tied to Boundary Spanning/Business Outcomes | Mismatch – Not a Viable Strategy | Vested | Equity Partner (e.g. Joint Venture) or Shared Services |
| **Output-Based (Performance-Based / Managed Services)** Economics tied to Supplier Output | Mismatch – Not a Viable Strategy | **Performance-Based (Managed Services) Agreement** | Equity Partner (e.g. Joint Venture) or Shared Services |
| **Transaction-Based** Economics tied to activities drive behavior | Basic Provider Approved Provider | Preferred Provider | Equity Partner (e.g. Joint Venture) or Shared Services |

**Fig. 9.2** Business Model Mapping example

| Attributes to Determine Best Relationship Model | Transactional Contract | | Relational Contract | | | Investment Model |
|---|---|---|---|---|---|---|
| | A | B | C | D | E | F |
| **Dependency** | | | | | | |
| The overall cost to switch suppliers | Low | Low | Medium | Medium to High | Medium to High | High |
| Physical asset specificity (location, machinery, processes) | Low | Low | Medium | Medium to High | Medium to High | High |
| Skill level needed for predominant personnel | Unskilled | Semiskilled | Skilled | Professional | Professional | Expert |
| Level of supplier Integration/interface required (systems, support processes) | None | Low | Medium | High | Very High | Critical |

**Fig. 9.3** Supplier dependency (Pharmaceutical company analysis)

# Relationship Model

The UT Sourcing Business Model Mapping Toolkit first helps an organization "map" their business characteristics of a buyer-supplier relationship across three relationship models. The concept of relationship models stems from Oliver Williamson's work that classifies an organization's sourcing needs into three categories: market (transactional models), hybrid (relational/hybrid models), and hierarchical (investment-based models).[3]

## Supplier Dependency

The Business Model Map for the pharmaceutical company indicates the industry scores high in the area of supplier dependency because interviews revealed that CRO suppliers needed a relatively high level of skilled personnel and the cost to switch suppliers can be steep. Also, it was important for the pharmaceutical company's supplier relationships to be integrated with a high degree of collaboration to be the most successful. The business model map points to a relational contracting model as most appropriate to address supplier dependency (Fig. 9.3).

## Availability of Service/Product in the Marketplace

Market research revealed a wide-to-moderate availability of CRO suppliers who could perform the work for the pharmaceutical company. However,

| Attributes to Determine Best Relationship Model | Transactional Contract | | Relational Contract | | | Investment Model |
|---|---|---|---|---|---|---|
| | A | B | C | D | E | F |
| Overall availability of service/ product in the marketplace | Widely Available | Widely Available | Wide to Moderate Availability | A limited number of capable suppliers | A limited number of capable suppliers | Scarcely Available |
| Availability of human resources | High | High | Medium | Low | Low | Low |
| Availability of required technology | Universal | Limited | Restricted | Restricted to Scarce | Scarce | Unique |
| Access to buyer's critical systems and processes | None | Low | Medium | High | Very High | Critical |

**Fig. 9.4** Availability of service/product in the marketplace (Pharmaceutical company analysis)

interviews with key stakeholders indicated the pharmaceutical company would need more sophisticated suppliers under contract than a simple transactional model could provide. As such, the Business Model Map suggested a relational contract for the CRO initiative (Fig. 9.4).

## The Extent that Service Is a "Core Competency"

Key stakeholders were somewhat split regarding whether the clinical trial was a core competency for the pharmaceutical company. All stakeholders agreed innovation was vital to the success, with CRO suppliers playing a critical role in the ability to bring new products to market. The consensus was that while the pharmaceutical company could invest in improving their clinical research work, most agreed the market had matured. Capable CRO suppliers had emerged who could easily perform the work without the need for the pharmaceutical company to make further investments. The result was that stakeholders ultimately felt a relational contract would be the most appropriate (Fig. 9.5).

| Attributes to Determine Best Relationship Model | Transactional Contract | | Relational Contract | | | Investment Model |
|---|---|---|---|---|---|---|
| | A | B | C | D | E | F |
| Strategic Impact/Core Competency for Buyer | No | No | No | Maybe | Maybe | Yes |

**Fig. 9.5** The extent that service is a "core competency" (Pharmaceutical company analysis)

## The Extent of Business Risk

A successful CRO supplier can have a positive (or negative) impact upon the bottom line. The need for regulatory compliance and variability in demand also scored on the higher end of the continuum, indicating a relational contract would be most appropriate (Fig. 9.6).

# Economic Model

The second "map" in the UT Sourcing Business Model Mapping Toolkit helps organizations determine the most appropriate economic model. The concept of economic models has evolved as modern businesses shifted their thinking away from transactional economic models (you pay 218 yuan to print more business cards at your Shanghai hotel) to output-based and

| Attributes to Determine Best Relationship Model | Transactional Contract | | Relational Contract | | | Investment Model |
|---|---|---|---|---|---|---|
| | A | B | C | D | E | F |
| **Degree of Business Risk** | | | | | | |
| Profit Impact (volume purchased, % of total purchased costs, impact on business growth) | None | Low | Medium | High | Very High | Critical |
| Service failure impact on the end customer/brand experience | None | Low | Medium | High | Very High | Critical |
| Service failure impact on internal customer experience | None | Low | Medium | High | Very High | Critical |
| Regulatory compliance policy | Meet Standard | Meet Standard | Meet Standard or Higher | Meet Standard or Higher | Meet Standard or Higher | Meet Standard or Higher |
| Uncertainty of demand | N/A | Manage unanticipated demand spikes with multiple sources | Provider response to unanticipated volume spikes limited | The contractual ability for a supplier to respond to spikes | Contractual flexibility for supplier and client to respond to spikes to optimize the business | Capacity is set based on captive assets plus using market if not asset-specific |

Fig. 9.6 The extent of business risk (Pharmaceutical company analysis)

| Attributes to Determine Best Economic Model | Transaction-Based Economic Model | | | Output-Based Economic Model | Outcome-Based Economic Model | |
|---|---|---|---|---|---|---|
| | A | B | C | D | E | F |
| **Potential to Create Value/Mutual Advantage** | | | | | | |
| Potential efficiency gains | None | Low | Medium | High | Very High | Significant |
| Potential for revenue increase | None | Low | Medium | High | Very High | Constant |
| Potential for innovation | None | Low | Medium | High | Very High | Critical |
| Size of investments needed in to achieve outcomes (buyer or supplier) | Low | Medium | High | High to Invest | Invest | Invest |

**Fig. 9.7** Potential to create value (Pharmaceutical company analysis)

outcome-based approaches (you pay the supplier for achieving a certain output or strategic business outcome). In the book *Strategic Sourcing in the New Economy*, the authors describe three main types of economic models, i.e., models for how the supplier is compensated for its services to the buyer: transaction-based, output/performance-based, and outcome-based economic models. The below examples show how the pharmaceutical company mapped each dimension to determine the most appropriate economic model.

## Potential to Create Value

Stakeholders believed that CRO suppliers had a significant potential to create value for the pharmaceutical company by helping speed to market (increasing revenue) and driving innovation. For this reason, stakeholders believed that an outcome-based economic model was best suited for the CRO outsourcing initiative (Fig. 9.7).

## Nature of the Workscope

Most stakeholders believed that CRO suppliers had control over the outcome to improve speed to market of new drugs—even though there was a considerable shared risk. Most stakeholders also felt the pharmaceutical company should be looking to more strategic KPIs or business outcome metrics versus the transactional metrics they relied upon with existing supplier relationships. Last, stakeholders looked at the ease with which a CRO's task/workscope can be specified. Here stakeholders were split in their opinion because the ease

| Attributes to Determine Best Economic Model | Transaction-Based Economic Model | | | Output-Based Economic Model | Outcome-Based Economic Model | |
|---|---|---|---|---|---|---|
| | A | B | C | D | E | F |
| **Nature of Workscope/Tasks** | | | | | | |
| Degree of supplier control over the outcome | Low | Low | Low | High | Medium-High | N/A |
| Type of success measure desired/required | Transactional Activity Metrics | Transactional Activity Metrics | Transactional Activity Metrics | Output SLA Metrics | Strategic KPI *t* or Business Outcomes | Strategic KPI or Business Outcomes |
| The ease with which task/workscope can be specified | High | High | Medium | Medium | Can Vary | Very Difficult or Impossible |

**Fig. 9.8** Nature of the workscope (Pharmaceutical company analysis)

can vary based on the type of workscope and spans across all areas. When looking at the nature of workscope/tasks on a holistic level, most stakeholders contended that CRO services have a significant potential to create value in virtually all of the categories. For this reason, the pharmaceutical company felt they should strive to create an outcome-based economic model for its CRO initiative (Fig. 9.8).

## The Criticality of the Work

Next, the Sourcing Business Model Map looks at the criticality of the work. Stakeholders scored the risk related to operational safety to be critical because patient safety protocols are the highest priority. They also scored the risk related to operational reliability as high because they felt that performing the workscope to government regulations was essential to the safe and reliable nature of the products being delivered (Fig. 9.9).

## Risk Tolerance Preferences

Last, stakeholders looked at risk tolerance preferences for both themselves and key CRO suppliers who would likely be a CRO supplier partner. Stakeholders found it easy to score their risk tolerance—which fell into a preference for a shared risk approach. However, assessing a supplier's risk tolerance was more difficult because the CRO supplier's risk tolerance spanned all of the categories. In discussions with CRO suppliers, some suppliers were exploring

| Attributes to Determine Best Economic Model | Transaction-Based Economic Model | | | Output-Based Economic Model | Outcome-Based Economic Model | |
|---|---|---|---|---|---|---|
| | A | B | C | D | E | F |
| **Criticality of Work** | | | | | | |
| Risk related to operational safety | Minimal | Low | Medium | High | High | Critical |
| Risk related to operational reliability | Minimal | Low | Medium | High | High | Critical |

**Fig. 9.9**  The criticality of the work (Pharmaceutical company analysis)

| Attributes to Determine Best Economic Model | Transaction-Based Economic Model | | | Output-Based Economic Model | Outcome-Based Economic Model | |
|---|---|---|---|---|---|---|
| | A | B | C | D | E | F |
| **Commercial Preferences** | | | | | | |
| Financial risk Tolerance for buyer | High Risk | High Risk | Medium Risk | Medium-Low Risk | Shared Risk | N/A |
| Financial risk Tolerance for supplier | Low Risk | Low Risk | Low Risk | Medium Risk | Shared Risk | N/A |

**Fig. 9.10**  Risk tolerance preferences (Pharmaceutical company analysis)

outcome-based shared risk/reward economic models. Ultimately, the stake-holders felt that an outcome-based economic model would be suitable—at least with the more progressive and capable suppliers (Fig. 9.10).

# Limitations of Sourcing Business Model Mapping Toolkit

The UT Sourcing Business Model Mapping Toolkit is explicitly developed for buyer-supplier relationships, where a buyer *sources* some input. While it is an excellent resource for identifying the most appropriate contract model for a procurement-focused contract, it has limitations. For example, it is not equipped to map the best-fit contract model for a shareholder agreement or a franchise agreement.

One of the specific drawbacks is that UT researchers made the attribute of "availability of service/products in the marketplace" part of the dependency assessment. This attribute is not necessarily relevant for non-procurement focused relationships. For example, consider a factor referred to as "outside options" in economic terms—a firm's option to choose another business partner instead of the one with which a contract has been entered into. If there are few other business partners in the market with which a firm can contract and obtain the same value, the dependency level is higher than if there are many such firms. In customer-supplier relationships, it is relevant to focus on the availability of other suppliers of the same resources (e.g., skills, knowledge, etc.). But in a shareholder agreement, it is inadequate to think about outside options in terms of available resources. In that case, it is more relevant to think about the availability of other firms willing to invest in the owned organization.

Also, the tool could be further developed. For example, a joint venture would be viewed as an investment-based model, which is an alternative to a relational contract. But a shareholder agreement, establishing the joint venture, can be a great candidate for a relational contract. For this reason we have developed a simplified Contract Decision Matrix (Fig. 9.11).

To ALL contract types—not just purchasing related buyer-supplier contracts.

## Contract Model Decision Matrix

The simplified Contract Model Decision Matrix is presented in Fig. 9.11.

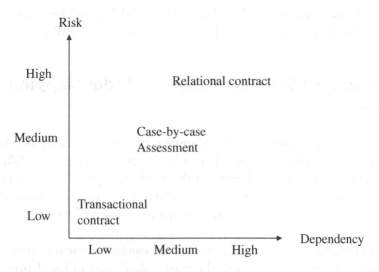

**Fig. 9.11** Contract model decision matrix

As seen in the matrix, the decision is sometimes simple. In cases of low risk and low dependency, a transactional contract should be used. If high risk and high dependency occur, a relational contract should be used. But the graph allows for nine scenarios, for example, low risk/medium dependency and medium risk/low dependency. In these not so clear-cut scenarios, an assessment of the best-fit contract model must be made case-by-case, weighing the pros and cons of each contracting model.

To plot out a deal's position on the graph above, start by separately assessing risk and dependency. A Risk Assessment Matrix and a Dependency Assessment Matrix is shown in Figs. 9.12 and 9.13. The underlying logic of the assessments has been explained in Chapter 7. The Risk Assessment is about the likelihood and severity of the negative impact of opportunistic

| Dimension | Low | Medium | High |
|---|---|---|---|
| The economic value of the contract | | | |
| Strategic importance | | | |
| Cost of failed or weak performance | | | |
| The complexity of the deal | | | |
| Uncertainty in the deal | | | |
| Length of the contract term | | | |
| **Aggregate risk assessment** | | | |

Fig. 9.12 Risk assessment matrix

| Dimension | Low | Medium | High |
|---|---|---|---|
| Cost of finding another contracting party | | | |
| Level of relationship-specific assets (physical, human, intellectual) | | | |
| Other costs of leaving the relationship | | | |
| Level of alternative business partners in the market | | | |
| **Aggregate dependency assessment** | | | |

Fig. 9.13 Dependency assessment matrix

behavior in the relationship. The Dependency Assessment is about the realism of finding—or willingness to spend the money of finding—another contracting party should the relationship fail.

Once one has assessed both risk and dependency, they can then plot the potential deal on the Contract Model Decision Matrix. One's plot will help determine which is the most appropriate contract type—a relational contract or a transactional contract.

## The Importance of Including Stakeholders

Determining which contract model is most appropriate for one's situation is not a mathematical exercise, but will require analysis, judgment, and common sense. For this reason, it is advisable to ensure relevant stakeholders participate in the assessment, especially when there are early indications that a relational contract should be used.

Including stakeholders in the decision is very important. First, a relational contract requires a continuous alignment of interests. Alignment starts *within* each organization. If the business and the legal department think a relational contract is the best fit while the sourcing department wants to use a transactional contract, the disconnect may create friction and derail a relational contract before it ever launches. Therefore, it is important to include all important stakeholders in the assessment of the contracting model.

Second, all contracting parties should have the same view on the best fit contracting model. For example, if one shareholder in a shareholder agreement thinks that a relational contract is the best fit, but the other parties to the agreement do not agree, then there will be problems. The same applies to any customer-supplier relationship. It "takes two to tango" and the parties must agree if a relational contract should be used.

## Organizational Readiness and Maturity

Many organizations acknowledge shifting to a relational contract is the right choice. Some have even used the Contract Model Decision Matrix and have stakeholder buy-in that a relational contract is the most appropriate. However, they struggle with getting traction to get started, citing "organization readiness" or "lack of maturity" as a key reason.

Relational contracting is new to many organizations. As such, organizational readiness or maturity are factors that can limit and even prevent the organization's success. However, an organization's maturity should *not* influence the analysis of which contract model is the best fit. Why? If the relational contract is the best fit, then it simply is the best fit and the organization's readiness to use this contract model will not affect that. If the organization is deemed unready or too immature to make the shift to a relational contract, then it must assess the roadblocks and the costs to overcome the roadblocks.

## A Look Ahead

In this chapter, we shared a framework for determining when it is appropriate to use relational contracts. While a framework is useful, there are hundreds of types of contracts such as supply contracts, outsourcing contracts, franchise contracts, and so on. In the next chapter, we answer the question, *"What contract types should be relational contracts?"*

## Notes

1. Bonnie Keith, Kate Vitasek, Karl Manrodt, Jeanne Kling, *Strategic Sourcing in the New Economy: Harnessing the Potential of Sourcing Business Models for Modern Procurement* (New York: Palgrave Macmillan, 2016).
2. See the UT/Vested post, "Element 1: Business Model Map." Available at https://www.vestedway.com/element-1-business-model-map/.
3. See Oliver E. Williamson, "Outsourcing: Transaction Cost Economics and Supply Chain Management," *Journal of Supply Chain Management*, Vol. 44, No 2 (April 3, 2008).

# 10

# A Systemization of Contracts

Another common question is, *"What contract types should be relational contracts?"* This is a great question when one considers there are myriad different contract types—ranging from a simple purchase order of goods based on standard terms to complex contracts such as business process outsourcing or construction contracts. There are franchise contracts and shareholders agreements. Simply put, there are dozens, if not hundreds, of contract types.

This chapter provides a systemization of contracts to help answer the question of what types of contracts should be relational contracts.

## Systemizing Contract Types

Given the wide range of contract types, it is interesting that little effort has been made in the profession to categorize or systemize contracts. There are likely many ways one might classify contract types. In this chapter, we propose a framework that uses two dimensions—an input/output dimension and a capital resource dimension. These two dimensions were chosen because, in combination, they reflect a view of a business organization as a system where different valuable *resources* (capital forms) are sourced (inputs), put together in production, and after that distributed and sold (as outputs) to customers.

© The Author(s), under exclusive license to Springer Nature
Switzerland AG 2021
D. Frydlinger et al., *Contracting in the New Economy*,
https://doi.org/10.1007/978-3-030-65099-5_10

Later in this chapter, we use this framework to identify which contract types are good candidates to use as a relational contract.

# Dimension 1: The Input/Output Dimension

The input/output dimension is inspired by Michael Porter's view of a business as a *value chain*, which contends that a product moves through a chain of activities and value is added in each step of the chain.[1] Porter identified inbound logistics, operations, outbound logistics, marketing, sales, and services as essential steps in a firm's value chain. While this is a very product-based view of the value chain, other value chains with services and technology are also possible.

The logic of using an input/output dimension is that an organization needs *inputs*—or resources—as a precursor to produce, market, sell, and distribute its value-added *outputs*.

On the input side, an organization integrates its investors and banks, landlords, employees, suppliers, alliance partners, and others. On the output side, an organization integrates with its distribution network—distributors, sales agents, franchisees, and others—and eventually its customers, including businesses or consumers. In all cases, an array of contract types serves as the essential glue which holds the value chain together.

# Dimension 2: Capital Resource Relationships

All supply chain links use capital resources and other various resources to produce their products and/or services—the outputs. Firms must establish relationships, to gain access to the assets they need through their contracts. For this reason we choose capital resources for the second dimension.

While there are hundreds of unique capital resource types, there are four primary categories of value-generating resources: financial capital, physical capital, human capital, and information capital. These four categories encompass the vast majority of contract types or *capital resource relationships*.

## Financial Capital Contract Relationships

Financial capital is the building block to start a business. By financial capital, we mean all financial assets of the organization's cash, stocks, claims, and other financial instruments. For example, the organization may be financed through equity or debt, i.e., by shareholders, other owners, banks, or angel investors. The financial capital is used to acquire all the other necessary capital needed to run the business such as building plants, designing products, marketing services, distributing goods, and so on. Without financial capital, no organization would exist. And without financial capital relationships, a firm's competitiveness is likely impeded by their ability to invest.

## Physical Asset Contract Relationships

The second form of capital a firm needs is physical capital. Physical capital includes all physical things—whether they are owned or not—that an organization uses to produce and sell its products and/or services. For example, business is conducted at some physical location, be it in an organization-owned office building, a leased skyscraper, a production plant, or the owner's garage. Supply inventories are needed, as well as basic items, such as desks and chairs. Machinery and tools—if required—also form part of the physical capital portfolio. Because most organizations cannot generate the physical assets they need to run their business, to add value an organization will need to enter into physical asset relationships through contracts such as supplier agreements.

## Human Capital Contract Relationships

The third necessary resource to start and conduct business is people—human capital. Human capital relationships can typically be divided into two categories—employees and third-party resources.

## Information Capital Contract Relationships

The fourth and final capital form needed to conduct a business is information capital. Information capital is a broad term for an organization's intellectual property rights such as patents, copyrights, trademarks, trade secrets, and, to a growing extent, data. Firms often establish information capital relationships to fill gaps or overcome weaknesses they might have for producing and processing information. For example, an organization may develop relationships and contracts with suppliers to help with some aspect of product design. Or the organization may license software which grants access to an IT infrastructure needed to run the business.

# The Combined View

Based on the logic set out above, it is possible to systematize the various contract types which organizations frequently use when exchanging goods, services, technologies, or other valuables. This framework paints a nuanced picture of the broader contracting landscape and can help identify suitable candidate documents when pursuing a relational contract.

# The Contracting Landscape

## The Input Side of the Landscape

The input side of the contracting landscape is enabled through several common contract types. We provide a high-level overview of the most common types.

### Financial Capital Contracts

There are countless types of contracts used by businesses in the "financial sector," where financial capital is their core business. This analysis focuses on the contracts tied to financial arrangements common to those organizations not operating in the financial sector itself.

Financial contracts appear at two levels—at the operational level and the ownership level. At the operational level, typical financial capital contracts are **loan agreements** that give organizations access to financial capital via a loan. At the ownership level, several contracts cover the purchase and ownership of shares and other financial instruments. Of these contracts, the **share purchase agreement** and **shareholders' agreement** deserve special attention and are discussed below in more detail. The end goal of a shareholders' agreement is to generate value through the jointly owned organization, while a share purchase agreement is used to create that value. While the shareholders' agreement is long-term, the share purchase agreement is simple—shares for the money. **Insurance agreements** are another type of financial capital contract.

A contract type of increasing importance is the **business process outsourcing agreement** used by organizations that wish to outsource some or all of their financial operations processes. Under this agreement, the outsourcing organization has an outside provider manage the organization's business processes, such as accounting, invoicing, and/or other common financial processes. A good example is Microsoft, who outsourced its global financial operations to Accenture in 2007 under a seven-year "OneFinance" contract. Under the agreement, Accenture manages the accounts payable, accounts receivable, and buy desk processes for Microsoft across 95 countries.[2]

Looking at the above contract types from the perspective of risk and dependency, the *shareholder's agreement* and *business process outsourcing agreements* would typically be good candidates for a relational contract. Those agreements often are long-term, cover complex and uncertain circumstances, and the related events, and are often of high value. Also, the parties' dependency is typically high.

The shareholder's agreement deserves special attention. The end goal of a shareholder's agreement is to generate value through the jointly-owned organization. However, shareholder's agreements are often entered into in combination with a share purchase agreement. Share purchase agreements are typically straightforward and dependency is low, at least when there is no need for transitional services from the seller to the target organization. Negotiations related to share purchase agreements are typically very power-based and transactional.

Often, using a power-based approach for a share purchase agreement is acceptable. However, a transactional approach can become problematic if the sale and purchase of shares is the starting point of a long-term relationship regulated by a shareholder's agreement. Why? Since the two contracts are typically negotiated simultaneously, the power-based nature of the share purchase agreement negotiation can destroy the chances of building a relationship based on aligned interests in the shareholder's agreement. Therefore, the shareholder's agreement is typically also written to be a transactional contract, which will then have most of or all the negative consequences of using the wrong contracting model.

While there are no firm statistics, some have estimated that organizations lose millions (sometimes billions!) of dollars in value from choosing a transactional contract for shareholder's agreements. This does not mean that share purchase agreements should be written as relational contracts. Instead, the parties should use another approach to this deal from the beginning. That starting point should not be the share purchase agreement, which is just a means to an end. Rather, the starting point should be the shareholder's agreement, which should be written as a relational contract. The share purchase agreement should then be a component of the creation of the more strategic shareholder's agreement. While the share purchase agreement would still be transactional, it should be written to resemble a relational contract's position on fairness. The purchase of shares can be embedded in the relationship created through the shareholder's agreement.

## Physical Capital Contracts

Many physical capital contracts can be categorized into the **purchase of goods** and **maintenance and support services** tied to the purchased goods. These contracts take many forms. Most regulate very simple purchases on a spot market and can be as simple as a Purchase Order commitment. However, some of these are more strategic and long-term in nature. For example, contracts for custom-built machinery, boats, factories, etc. can be highly complex.

The second type of physical capital contracts is those pertaining to real property. Most organizations do not own their real property but rent the offices and plants they need to run their business. The **rental agreement** is, therefore, a vital contract type. A contract type of growing importance is the **facilities management outsourcing agreement** where an organization chooses a service provider to manage several tasks and processes tied to the organization's offices and other facilities. For example, Procter & Gamble outsources its cleaning, catering, security, maintenance, reception, and event services to Jones Lang Lasalle.[3]

Finally there is the **logistics agreement**—including the third-party logistics (3PL) outsourcing agreements—which is an important physical capital contract. Research shows that over 80% of organizations outsource at least a portion of logistics operations such as warehousing and transportation activities. According to a recent Third-Party Logistics study from Penske Logistics, the vast majority of shippers—93%—report that the relationships they have with their 3PLs generally have succeeded. A higher number—99%—of 3PLs surveyed agree that their customer relationships have typically succeeded.[4] As e-commerce continues to grow, this contract type will likely become an even more critical source of value-add and competitive advantage.

When looking for candidate scenarios for a relational contract, the more obvious ones are the *facilities management outsourcing agreement* and the *logistics agreement*. While not always the case, these deals often involve long-term relationships, high complexity, high value, and high dependency.

## Human Capital Contracts

There are three primary forms of human capital contracts: the **employment agreement**, the **resource consultant agreement**, and the **agreement collective bargaining**.

The employment agreement is often a simple agreement, where the underlying assumption is that the employer will have high discretion in governing the employee's work while compensating the employee with a fixed compensation, sometimes with variable components. The third-party resource consultant or simple staff augmentation agreements typically have the same simplicity.

The collective bargaining agreement can be highly complex, regulating many important areas—salaries, work hours, vacations, benefits, etc.— between the union and the employer organization.

Among these contract types, the collective bargaining agreement is a good fit for a formal relational contract. The relationship between the employer and the union is typically long term, dependency is high, and there are high risks for misaligned interests and expectations causing friction in the relationship. Also, many contracts regarding more complex **managed staffing programs** are often a good fit for the formal relational contract.

## Information Capital Contracts

There is a broad spectrum of information capital contract types. A basic (not always clear-cut) distinction can be made between agreements regulating intellectual property and agreements related to information technology.

One of the most common contract types for managing intellectual property is the **non-disclosure agreement**, which helps organizations regulate trade secrets. There are also various forms of **license agreements** for managing patents, trademarks, or copyrights. The music and media industry relies extensively on license arrangements, where the copyright holder of a piece of music licenses the right to distribute that music.

**Research and development agreements** can also be linked to information capital. For example, the United States Department of Defense (DoD) uses research and development contracts when they work with suppliers to develop new weapon systems such as the F22 Raptor tactical fighter aircraft. Research and development contracts are so essential to the DoD the Federal Acquisition Regulation has an entire section devoted to research and development contracts.[5]

The second broad category of information capital contracts deals with agreements covering information technology (IT). IT contracts range from simple to complex. For example, a **hardware purchase agreement** is typically simple. The **software license agreement** can be either a simple or complex contract, even though the commercial relationship is often non-complex. A good example is Microsoft, which uses enterprise-wide license agreements with large corporate customers for Microsoft Office[TM]. However, Microsoft also sells individual licenses to consumers. For example, you have likely clicked on an "**end-user license agreement**" when downloading software, apps, or music.

**Cloud computing agreements** are becoming popular as more organizations make the shift to the cloud for accessing software and data. Cloud computing is the use of hardware and software to deliver a service over a network (typically the Internet). With cloud computing, users can access files and use applications from any device that can access the Internet. Examples of cloud computing providers are Google (Gmail), Salesforce (CRM), and Microsoft (Dropbox). American Airlines entered into a cloud computing agreement with IBM when American American decided it wanted to have its customers access crucial scheduling and routing data for rebooking flights.[6]

Another set of contracts are **consultancy agreements** and **support and maintenance agreements** tied to applications. As data gains growing importance as a separate source of value, different **data-sharing agreements** have also appeared. In the European Union, with its relatively strict regulation of the processing of personal data, the **data processing agreement** is a vital contract type.

The **IT outsourcing agreement** is also a critical contract type, regulating infrastructure, application development and maintenance, workplaces, and other IT-related services.

A final type of agreement is the **software development agreement**. We want to emphasize this contract type because of the growing use of *agile* software development methodologies.[7] The traditional way of developing software was to use a waterfall method, in which all the features of the software were specified in advance, and then development started. An obvious downside of this approach is that needs typically change over time—often very quickly when it comes to software. The agile approach to software development anticipates changes, thus being much more flexible in developing software that will meet the actual needs.

Among the various common IT contract types, **reasearch and development agreements**, different IT outsourcing agreements, and all software development agreements using some agile methodology are the strongest candidates for the relational contracting model. Sometimes, a license agreement could be a good candidate. These contract types often involve high risks for friction and high dependency between the parties.

## The Output Side of the Landscape

The contract types representing an output dimension can be generally divided into two categories; sales and distribution contracts, and end-customer contracts.

The **agency agreement** is one of the most common contracts used for sales and distribution. Under this agreement, the agent is granted a right to, in exchange for being paid a commission, solicit orders for an organization's products or services, often in a defined geographic area. Cars are often sold under such agreements.

Another important contract form is the **franchise agreement**, where the franchisor grants a franchisee the right to operate under the franchisor's brand. McDonald's is probably one of the world's best-known organizations using franchise licenses where they work with franchise owners and operators who run the majority of their restaurant locations.[8]

The **distributor agreement** is another output-side contract type. An organization can choose between hiring its salespeople to distribute its products, or it can use distributors to provide the same function. The distribution agreement is a contract between an organization having its products distributed and the distributor that specializes in providing that function. Most small businesses use distributors because it is less expensive, facilitates cash flow, and because distributors have more knowledge and experience in the market area.[9] However, many large businesses also use distributor agreements. A good example is Swedish-based giant SKF, which manufactures bearings and lubricants. SKF works with distributors around the world who sell their products to industrial customers.[10]

On the customer side, a fundamental distinction can be made between business-to-business agreements and business-to-consumer agreements. There are myriad different business-to-consumer agreements and it is not relevant for this chapter to address them.

The business-to-business agreements are typically the same contract types already discussed from the input perspective, with the difference that the viewpoint now is from the supplier's side. The difference between the four capital forms is highly relevant when categorizing different contract types on the input side of a business. From a certain perspective, all contracts on the input side have, from a provider or supplier viewpoint, a counterpart on the output side. But there are other types of agreements on the output side which do not easily fit into the distinction between the four capital forms. This is natural: the different inputs are combined by an organization and can be sold as a unique combination. The cloud service agreement is an excellent example of this. From the customer viewpoint, the cloud service agreement belongs in the information capital group. But from a supplier's viewpoint, this agreement regulates the provision of several resources to the customer: data centers, hardware, software, data, employees, etc.

When looking for candidate opportunities for relational contracts, **franchise agreements**, and sometimes the **distributor agreement**, are obvious candidates. In our experience franchise agreements and distributor agreements are obvious candidates—their dependency is often high and there is a potentially high risk for friction due to misaligned expectations and interests.

## A Look Ahead

This chapter concludes Part III. You should now have a clear view of what characterizes a relational contract, when it should be used, how to decide to use it, and why some common contract types should be candidates for relational contracts. Part IV of the book provides a deep dive into *how* to create a relational contract.

## Notes

1. See, for example, Porter, M., *Competitive Strategy: Techniques for Analyzing Industries and Competitors* (Free Press, 1985).
2. "Vested for Success: Microsoft/Accenture One Finance," Kate Vitasek, Karl Manrodt and Srini Krishna, University of Tennessee, (Case Study, 2013). Available at https://www.vestedway.com/wp-content/uploads/2012/09/Micros oft.pdf.
3. Kate Vitasek and Karl Manrodt, with Jeanne Kling, *Vested: How P&G, McDonald's, and Microsoft are Redefining Winning in Business Relationships* (New York: Palgrave Macmillan, 2012).
4. "2020 Logistics Study: State of Logistics Outsourcing." *Penske Logistics, Penn State Smeal College of Business, InfoSys Consulting.* Available at http://www.3pl study.com/3pl2020download.php.
5. "Part 35—Research and Development Contracting," *Acquisition.gov.* Available at http://farsite.hill.af.mil/reghtml/regs/far2afmcfars/fardfars/far/35.htm.
6. See Michael R. Overly, "Drafting and Negotiating Effective Cloud Computing Agreements," LexisNexis, 30 November 2015. Available at https://www.lex

isnexis.com/lexis-practice-advisor/the-journal/b/lpa/posts/drafting-and-negoti
ating-effective-cloud-computing-agreements#:~:text=Cloud%20computing%
20involves%20accessing%20a,customer's%20data%20with%20that.%20prov
ider.&text=As%20such%2Cthe%20most%20critical,applicable%20to%20c
loud%20computing%20agreements,   https://www.ibm.com/cloud/info/adopt-
cloud?S_PKG=&cm_mmc=Search_Google-_-Cloud_Cloud+Platform-_-WW_
US-_-cloud+computing_Exact_&cm_mmca1=000023UL&cm_mmca2=100
08005&cm_mmca7=9060532&cm_mmca8=kwd-6458750403&cm_mmca9=
4de28069-c567-4782-821d-32629f746d36&cm_mmca10=257183580205&
cm_mmca11=e&mkwid=4de28069-c567-4782-821d-32629f746d36%7C4
01%7C1981391&cvosrc=ppc.google.cloud%20computing&cvo_campaign=
000023UL&cvo_crid=257183580205&Matchtype=e.

7.  See, for example, J. Sutherland, *Scrum: The Art of Doing Twice the Work in Half
the Time* (New York: Random House, 2015).

8.  John Maxfield, "What Percentage of McDonald's Restaurants Are Owned by
Franchisees?" *The Motley Fool*, updated 5 Oct. 2018. Available at https://www.
fool.com/investing/general/2016/04/03/what-percentage-of-mcdonalds-restau
rants-are-owned.aspx.

9.  Jill Harness, "What Is a Distribution Agreement?" *bizfluent*, October 31,
2019. Available at https://bizfluent.com/about-6642322-distribution-agreem
ent-definition.html.

10. See the SKF website at http://www.skf.com/us/services/skf-distributor-network/
index.html.

# Part IV

## Five Steps to a Relational Contract

Part II provided an aerial view of the science of contracting to help you connect the dots on the WHY. Part III then shifted the focus from theory to practice by explaining what a relational contract is and when it should be used. That shift now concludes by providing five proven steps the contracting parties can take to create an effective relational contract.

Part IV includes six chapters. In Chapter 11 we introduce why following a formal relational contracting process is essential. Starting with the wrong things, for example, price negotiations often prevents the parties from building a successful partnership. Starting with the right things, such as focus on mutual objectives, and then proceeding through a sequence is a more effective enabler of success. That sequence is:

Step 1: **Lay the foundation for a partnership** based on trust, transparency, and compatibility
Step 2: **Co-create a shared vision and objectives**
Step 3: **Adopt Guiding Principles for the partnership**
Step 4: **Align expectations and interests, architecting the** deal points
Step 5: **Stay aligned** by adopting a robust governance structure and supporting governance processes for relationship management

Chapters 12 through 16 provide a deep dive into each step. We start each chapter by explaining the *what* and *why* of each step. We then go into detail of *how* each step is using real-life examples.

# Part IV

## Five Steps to a Relational Contract

# 11

# The Importance of the Right Process

Parties must embrace an optimal process when developing a relational contract. Let's compare a conventional contracting process with the relational contracting process we outline in this book.

A typical contracting process includes commercially responsible people negotiating the specific deal points such as the scope of work, the solution, and the price. This is followed by one party then sending a draft agreement to the other party based on which the commercial negotiations were conducted. Next, either inhouse or external counsel get involved. The lawyers then send drafts back-and-forth with markups and comments, sometimes followed by the parties sitting down to formally negotiate and clarify their respective positions on critical deal points. Then the bargaining begins with a series of moves and counter moves. Concessions and compromises are made. In most instances, a consensus is eventually reached.

If the parties adopt a relational contract, they must understand and acknowledge the standard way of developing and negotiating simply will not work. There will be temptations to do things the way they are usually done, but giving into such temptations will likely set the parties on the path to either immediate or eventual failure.

In a relational contracting process, the parties use a structured five-step process to collaboratively co-create the contract. The process starts by consciously laying a foundation of trust, followed by developing a shared vision and mutually defined objectives. The parties then establish guiding principles—social norms—for the partnership. Only after the foundation for

© The Author(s), under exclusive license to Springer Nature
Switzerland AG 2021
D. Frydlinger et al., *Contracting in the New Economy*,
https://doi.org/10.1007/978-3-030-65099-5_11

the relationship is established do the parties negotiate the specific deal points such as the scope of work, the solution, and the price/pricing model. In the last step of the process, the parties establish formal governance mechanisms they will use to stay in alignment.

We contend the relational contracting process is as important as the contract content.

First, recall the behavioral economics research referred to in Chapter 6. Nobel laureate Richard Thaler shows people are not "Econs"—i.e., rational and selfish—but Humans. We are only rational to a limited extent and have a strong sense of selflessness. We are all born on a continuum from egoism to altruism, and it will be the surrounding circumstances that will largely decide if it is the egoistic or altruistic side of the people involved that will come forward. A relational contract attempts to build upon and balance our sense of fairness while avoiding the opportunism, high transaction costs, and value leakage associated with transactional contracts. While it is possible to integrate relational contracting components into any point in a relationship, using a deliberate and strategic process to lay a strong foundation at the outset is essential. It is a direct path to success and helps us avoid opportunism from the start.

The importance of this is well illustrated by the research of Kathleen Vohs, professor at the University of Minnesota's Carlson School of Management. Vohs' research shows how money makes us egoistic.[1] For example, in one experiment, individuals were exposed to words and thoughts about money and some were not. The individuals were then tested for their willingness to help others. Those individuals exposed to money before being asked to help others showed a lower willingness to help than individuals not exposed to money. Vohs' work suggests it is critical not to start a relational contracting process by negotiating the deal, where the money is always a key component. Instead, the seeds of a non-opportunistic relationship must first be cultivated, by which our opportunistic tendencies can later be avoided or at least minimized.

A second reason for using a formal process is to ensure organizations and individuals feel there has been a fair process for establishing the contract. The situation is analogous to legislation in a democracy. In legislation, both the content and the process for generating the content matter. A law adopted through democratic voting that denies a group of people fundamental rights will be fair from a process perspective but will be unjust from a substance perspective. Likewise, a law adopted by a dictator giving equal voting rights to men and women will be just from a substance perspective but will be viewed as unfair from a process perspective. If the process is perceived as unfair, the adopted laws will lack legitimacy and the people's willingness to follow them will be diminished. The process of negotiating and jointly creating the relational contract is not just a means to get to the written document, but an important part of creating what is actually in focus: the collaborative relationship.

A third reason for using a formal process, with a certain sequence of defined steps, goes to the heart of what a relational contract intends to achieve—risk avoidance and mitigation through continuous alignment of interests and expectations.[2] Recall the research by professor Oliver Hart referenced in Chapter 6. Hart identified a primary reason for entering into a contract is to align the parties' expectations, thereby avoiding disappointment, disputes, and preventing shading. By serving as a reference point, the contract brings the parties onto the same page. This is true for *any* contract, including transactional contracts. However, the emphas is in a relational contract is to develop a contract with mechanisms aimed at keeping the parties' interests and expectations in continual alignment when business happens.

If the parties start by discussing the specifics of the deal, i.e., scope, services, quality, price, etc., they will most likely focus on specific matters which will be highly relevant in the early stages of the relationship. However, the deal points will change over time and require adjustment. As highlighted in Part III, a relational contract should be used in complex deals with medium to high dependency and risk, which span long periods. This is why a formal relational contract espouses the specific deal points should be flexible while the general framework should be somewhat rigid. The shared vision, objectives, and guiding principles provide this general framework for the relationship. By focusing on these broader matters first, the parties lay the foundation for a long-term alignment of expectations, guiding them as they develop the specifics of the deal.

One might ask whether it is *necessary* to use the formal process outlined in this book when architecting a relational contract. They might argue that creating a solid relationship should come naturally and should not feel "forced" with the process. There needs to be clarity on this point. Many organizations have created very successful relational contracts and did not use a formal process. Instead, they discovered the journey for themselves, often by intuitively implementing the components suggested in this book. While developing and drafting an effective relational contract can occur without using a formal process, those who follow the simple five-step process significantly increase the likelihood of their success. Adages such as "even a blind squirrel occasionally finds an acorn" and "a broken clock is correct twice each day" come to mind when addressing the argument offered by those who suggest, "we do not need to be constrained to a process." The relational contracting process we share has repeatedly and reliably led to superior outcomes.

## A Look Ahead

Chapters 12–16 each address one of five steps in the process and lay out how to complete each step with the greatest effect.

## Notes

1. Kathleen Vohs, Nicole Mead, Miranda Goode, "The Psychological Consequences of Money," *Science*, Vol. 314, No. 5802 (December 2006), pp. 1154–1156.
2. See Chapter 4.

# 12

# Step 1: Lay the Foundation for a Partnership

The first step of creating a relational contract is to lay the foundation for the partnership. In Chapter 7, we highlighted the first characteristic of the relational contract is to focus on the commercial relationship instead of simply the commercial transaction—or "deal" (Fig. 12.1).

This chapter explains this characteristic in more detail and shows *how* to turn the theory into practice using real examples. We end the chapter with tips/tools for putting the step into practice.

## What Does This Mean?

So, what does it mean to *focus* on the commercial relationship instead of the commercial transaction? Jim Collins provides an excellent analogy of what it means to have a long-term view versus a short-term perspective in his best-selling book *Built To Last*, co-written with Jerry Porras.[1] Some organizations succeed because they have amazing products and services, but their success fades when those products and services fade in popularity. Those organizations are "time tellers." Other organizations have successful products and services because they are created by amazing organizations—what he calls "clock builders"—who generate profits year after year by always producing new products and services the market wants. Collins eloquently argues that in the race of the market, it is always the clock builders that win in the long run.

© The Author(s), under exclusive license to Springer Nature Switzerland AG 2021
D. Frydlinger et al., *Contracting in the New Economy*,
https://doi.org/10.1007/978-3-030-65099-5_12

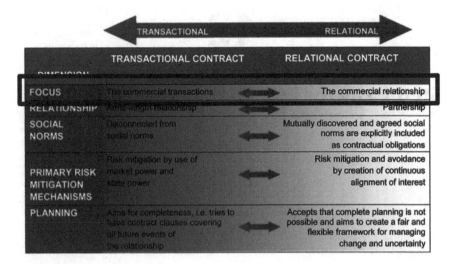

**Fig. 12.1** Focus on the relationship

The comparison between time tellers and clock builders can also be used to illustrate the difference between transactional and relational contracts. In transactional contracting, the focus is on the deal which is analogous to telling the time. When the exchanges planned for in the deal have been carried out, the relationship terminates and no more value is created. A relational contract is analogous to building a clock because the relationship can continue to generate value when all the transactions and deals from the initial relationship phase are complete.

Organizations that focus on the relationship do so because they believe they will generate more value from the commercial relationship over time than they will benefit from just focusing solely on today's deal. When one views a potential partner through the lens of the relationship instead of the lens of a deal, the entire foundation of the contract is flipped on its head. For example, it becomes crucial to start by examining if the parties have what it takes to eventually form a partnership (the second characteristic of a relational contract). This is why the first step of the relational contracting process is to lay the foundation for the relationship where the parties seek to understand and agree if they have what it takes to get to the second characteristic—a partnership.

Laying a solid foundation for a potential relationship varies depending on the situation. For example, do the parties have an existing relationship, or are they new to each other? Many organizations that pursue relational contracts do so with existing customers/suppliers, citing they feel comfortable elevating their relationship to the next level. While it is almost always easier to "flip" an existing transactional contract to a relational contract, it is also possible to develop a relational contract between parties who have never worked together before. Based on one's starting point, laying the foundation for a partnership will mean slightly different things in these two situations. Both situations are discussed later under "how."

Regardless of whether a new relationship is built or an existing one is transformed, laying the foundation for the relationship always starts by creating internal and external alignment on *trust*, *transparency*, and *compatibility*. Many relational contracting practitioners have found that attaining internal alignment is often more challenging than building external alignment.

*Trust* is a complicated phenomenon without a clear definition. A core component of trust is a feeling that the other party is aligned in its words and actions; individuals and organizations do what they say they will do. Conversely, organizations do not do what they say they will not do. It is a feeling that the other party will not be opportunistic nor take advantage of commercial partners for unilateral benefits. Instead, the parties focus on mutual interests. Without some degree of trust, no relationship—commercial or social—can be built. And in a partnership formed by a relational contract, trust is absolutely core.

*Transparency* is closely connected to trust. In a relationship with high transparency, the parties share information about their intentions, interests, their financials, and other vital factors. With high transparency there is an atmosphere of open communication where issues can be brought up without generating too much tension, and where concerns can be addressed and joint planning can be carried out. Remember that the key purpose of a contract, as discussed in Part II, is to align interests and expectations. A relational contract is effective in complex deals where the future is hard to predict and where continuous communication will be needed to maintain alignment. Without high transparency, this will simply not be possible to achieve.

*Compatibility* manifests itself when the parties are a good "cultural fit." It is essential to point out that compatibility does not equate to "you are like me, so I will be like you." Using this logic ignores the value of team diversity, which is a proven driver of success.[2] Instead, compatibility is an alignment of preferences for decision making (hierarchical vs. flat), innovation (values change vs. values steady-state), or teaming (collaborative vs. a silo mindset). These and other factors constitute the organization's DNA, with which there needs to be a threshold of cultural alignment with a commercial partner's DNA for the parties to have a healthy working relationship with minimal friction.

Trust, transparency, and compatibility are the fundamental building blocks of a relationship and are essential for creating a sound clock versus merely telling time.

A key part of Step 1 is for the parties to have an open and candid dialogue over not only their existing levels of trust, transparency, and compatibility between each other but also on their preferred viewpoints for trust, transparency, and compatibility for the relationship as they move forward. The goal is to align on potential opportunities, barriers, issues, and potential for improvement. Based on such analysis and discussion, the parties will become ready and move forward to Step 2.

Keep in mind it is unlikely relationships will have complete trust, transparency, and compatibility. Moreover, if the parties are too different from each other, there is a high potential for misunderstandings, distrust, ignored risk, and lost value. The aim of Step 1 of the relational contracting process is not to achieve such completeness. Instead, the objective is to ensure alignment where there is *sufficient* trust, transparency, and compatibility to build a successful partnership.

## Why Should You Do It?

Many ask why they need to lay the foundation first, citing they already know they have high levels of trust, transparency, and compatibility. It is a good argument. To understand why this first step should be taken it is necessary to look back at learnings from Part II, where the Science of Contracting from a social, economic, and psychological perspective was discussed.

As shared in Chapter 4, Professor Ian Macneil pointed out that contracts are *an instrument for social cooperation*,[3] emphasizing that a contract is first and foremost formed and based on a social relationship, not an economic relationship. In his criticism of conventional (legal) contract theory, Macneil pointed to the fact this social side of the contract is too often ignored.

This ignorance is not only true in theory but also practice. There exists a significant degree of unawareness or ignorance of a key fact—that entering a contract of some complexity is never limited to building a simple economic relationship where a service or good is exchanged for money. Some kind of social relationship is always created, whether between two individuals or sometimes hundreds or even thousands of individuals who work under the partnership. Each individual has their perspectives, experiences, education, culture, language, ambitions, and aspirations. It is within the social relationship between those individuals the economic transactions will be carried out and economic value is built. This is true for all contracts, but especially for relational contracts, which often involve a multitude of people from the partnering organizations. The first step in the relational contracting process explicitly recognizes that the parties are building a social relationship, based upon social norms—not just drafting a contract document.

Consider also the lessons from Oliver Williamson and Oliver Hart shared in Part II. Both have done seminal research on the concept of incomplete contracts. Incomplete contracts are particularly vexing where long-term relationships with high complexity are essential because it is impossible to predict all of the possible situations and market changes that will occur over the life of the relationship. As such, many aspects and events will simply not be addressed in the contract; and, where there is wording in the contract to deal with a particular situation, this wording will usually be open to different interpretations.

Incomplete contracts would not be a problem if Humans were always altruistic, looking out for each other's interests, always trying to be fair, and helping each other in difficult situations. But this is not the case with most people. Based on behavioral economics research as highlighted in Chapter 6, we know that people can be simultaneously altruistic and egoistic. So which behavior will dominate when the contracting parties have conflicting interests and learn the contract is incomplete? The altruistic or egoistic side? In highly dependent relationships it is likely that the egoistic side of the people involved will start to dominate over time, leading to the hold-up problem where the parties abuse each other's dependency for their benefit. Or perhaps shading behavior creeps in where the parties abstain from cooperative behavior or retaliate for perceived unfair actions.

The risk of hold-up and shading behavior can only be avoided to a limited extent by how the deal itself is crafted. To some extent, those risks must be mitigated within and through the commercial relationship. At the end of the day entering into a relational contract is about finding and maintaining continuous alignment of interests and expectations between the parties, despite business and market factors evolving. In the words of sociologists, the parties must *embed* their deal into their social relationship to create continuous alignment and mitigate the inevitable conflicts between interests and failed expectations (which can lead to shading) that the parties will endure. To a large extent, this demands the parties align on the more Human side of contracting, including the soft and subtle components of the relationship. The relational contracting process means aligning on components like how the parties will consciously build trust, embrace transparency, and seek to create ways to maintain a certain level of compatibility. This focus will inevitably lead to internal tension as the commercial and relationship teams engage their legal resources to draft contractual elements. In contrast, legal colleagues will often be unfamiliar with—and perhaps even reluctant to—translating these aspects into effective contract language.

## From Theory to Practice

It's one thing to "get" the need to do Step 1. But how exactly do you do it? The answer is, "it depends."

One of the most significant factors depends on whether you are starting with a new or existing relationship. And if you are starting with an existing relationship, is it a healthy relationship with a high degree of existing trust, transparency, and compatibility or one fraught with distrust? This section contains real examples of how actual organizations put Step 1 into practice.

## Existing Healthy Relationship (Discovery Health)

The healthcare market in South Africa—like most countries—is dynamic and evolving. Adrian Gore—an actuary by trade and entrepreneur in spirit—saw this as an opportunity for disruptive innovation. Gore founded Discovery Health in 1992 with a focus on making people healthier and enhancing lifestyles. Discovery Health launched what would become one of the most progressive insurance platforms for individuals and employers to fund medical treatment (called a Medical Scheme in South Africa).

In 1998 South Africa passed the Medical Schemes Act to regulate the industry. The Act required medical schemes to become non-profit entities governed by an independent board of trustees. To comply with the Act, the Discovery Health split into two entities: The Discovery Health Medical Scheme (the Scheme) and Discovery Health (Pty) Limited (DH), a medical scheme administrator. The Scheme ultimately contracted with DH to provide administration and managed care services as an outsourced service provider.

When Milton Streak joined the Scheme in 2009 as the Principal Officer, he immediately realized the strong collaboration between the Scheme and DH was as a source of the Scheme's competitive advantage. There was no doubt the Scheme had an excellent working relationship with Discovery Health. As the Principal Officer, Milton Streak knew the Scheme would need to dig deeper into best practices for outsourced contracts. His research led him to the University of Tennessee's research on Vested outsourcing for creating highly collaborative win-win relationships.

In 2015, the Scheme's Board of Directors commissioned a formal review of the relationship and contract, engaging Dr. Andrew Downard as a neutral third party. The report was very positive. The Scheme and DH had set up an excellent outsourcing contract producing solid results—with one caveat: the parties failed to incorporate the very successful relational aspects into their contract.

Dr. Downard facilitated a workshop between the parties where the parties candidly discussed trust, transparency, and compatibility. For example, some members worried  whether the relationship could sustain its high levels of trust, transparency, and compatability if Streak and Dr. Jonny Broomberg, DH's CEO, left the helm. Likewise, the parties had never considered the benefit of being more transparent regarding developing a win-win pricing model.

The review triggered the Scheme and DH to restructure their existing contract to a formal relational contract, capturing the intent and informal collaborative governance mechanisms which proved to be so successful. The initiative required documenting the overall intent of the relationship, incorporating the softer aspects of the relationship that were a genuine source of success, and creating formal governance mechanisms to keep the parties aligned over time.

The results were exceptional. Under the leadership of Streak and Broomberg, the Scheme grew to South Africa's largest open medical scheme, documenting dozens of innovations—leading to lower costs for members and improved services and product offerings.[4]

## Existing Unhealthy Relationship (Island Health)

Canada's Vancouver Island Health Authority (Island Health) and South Island Hospitalists, Inc. (Hospitalists) offer an excellent example of applying Step 1 of the relational contracting process in an existing unhealthy relationship.

Island Health was a pioneer in developing Hospitalist services in British Columbia in 2000, establishing a small group of Hospitalists to work at two hospitals. However, enthusiasm for the practice waned each time the Island Health Administrators and the Hospitalists met to renew their contract.

Between 2000 and 2014 Island Health and the Hospitalists met four times in what can be best described as increasingly long, acrimonious, and difficult negotiations. It is safe to say when their fourth contract expired on June 30, 2014, neither side was optimistic about how negotiations would proceed. The parties continued to work under the expired contract, but distrust only increased as the parties fell into a tit-for-tat cycle that intensified with payment delays and the controversial and highly emotional suspensions of some physicians in March 2015.

Both parties recognized the critical need to build a new relationship and changed personnel in the fall of 2015 to get the relationship back on track. But the relationship was so broken that contract negotiations went into a standstill; neither side knew how to proceed. Simply put, both sides were stuck. They decided to explore relational contracting in 2016, two years after their conventional contract had expired and countless hours of contentious negotiations failed. The parties used the University of Tennessee's Vested methodology to embark on the five-step relational contracting process.

To start the process the parties agreed to a three-day "Alignment Workshop" held at an offsite location at the University of Victoria. The workshop was facilitated by a neutral third party hired by both parties. In their case, the neutral was a boutique consulting firm professionally trained and certified in the Vested methodology—The Forefront Group.

Day One of the workshop started with a 360-degree relationship review. A key part of the review was a hard look at the gaps in foundational components of their relationship using the Compatibility and Trust (CaT) Assessment developed by Dr. Karl Manrodt and Dr. Jerry Ledlow. Fifteen Administrators and forty-one of the Hospitalists took the CaT online self-assessment before the workshop. Of those, twelve Island Health Administrators and nine Hospitalists attended the Alignment workshop in person. Bonnie Keith was one of the facilitators. "You could feel the tension in the room. The air was so thick you could cut it with a knife," Keith recalls.

As part of the CaT, the participants were asked to list three adjectives they would use to characterize their relationship. The words from each participant were compiled into a Wordle™ (see Fig. 12.2) that aptly illustrated where they stood at the beginning of the three-day workshop. The larger the font of a word, the more times the word was used to describe the current state of the relationship. Predictably, 84% of the adjectives were negative, with the majority of responses describing the relationship as "distrustful," "strained," and "broken."

Courtney Peereboom (Director, Special Projects and In-Facility Care at Island Health) was disheartened by what she saw, leading her to confess,

**Fig. 12.2** Wordle™ of adjectives describing the relationship going into the workshop

"Seeing the words on the Wordle from that survey was very disturbing. When you look back at it, we were in a terrible place."

Before providing the results of the CaT survey, The Forefront Group facilitators had the workshop attendees write three adjectives describing an ideal relationship between Island Health and the Hospitalists. During a break, a second Wordle™ was created—but this time the words represented hope for a "Future State" for the relationship (Fig. 12.3).

The "Today" and "Future State" Wordles™ were posted at the front of the room with The Forefront Group challenging the parties to think about how they might change their behaviors to begin to "live into" the Future State.

**Fig. 12.3** Wordle™ of adjectives describing the desired future state of the relationship

Dr. Milvi Tiislar, MD, CCFP was a Hospitalist who had just returned from maternity leave during the "troubles" in 2015 and was part of the first Alignment Workshop. Dr. Tiislar described her reaction to seeing the words. "It was very powerful to see a graphical depiction of all the negative emotions. And then there was the huge contrast describing what we all wanted the relationship to be. It was both eye-opening and nice to see that we had all described the same fundamental things that we wanted."

A key part of the Compatibility and Trust Assessment was to understand perception gaps. "I remember the CaT started with a question for us to grade ourselves and to grade your partner," Kim Kerrone (Island Heath's Vice-President, Chief Financial Officer, Legal Services & Risk) says. "We gave ourselves a B and the Hospitalists a D, and they did the exact opposite. For some, the perception was, 'We are the good guys and they are the bad guys.' It was interesting because the Hospitalists thought the exact same thing from their perspective! That was very illuminating."

The detailed CaT assessment provided a "spider web map" showing how the parties viewed themselves across five behavioral dimensions—and how they perceived the other party (see Figs. 12.4, 12.5, and 12.6).

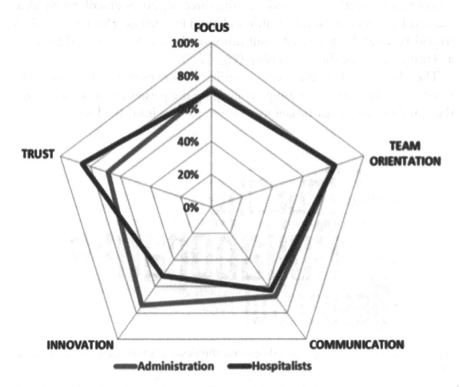

**Fig. 12.4** Administration and Hospitalists combined self-view

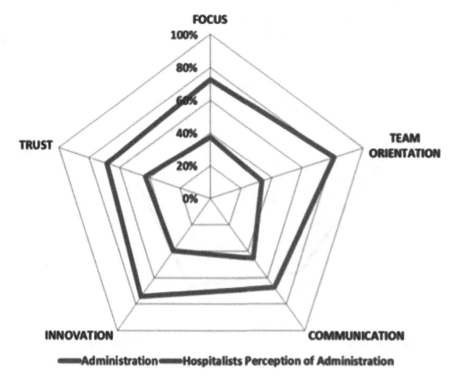

**Fig. 12.5**   Administration and Hospitalists' perception of Administration

Figure 12.4 shows the self-assessments of each group across each behavioral dimension, revealing there was relatively good alignment between how the Administrators and the Hospitalists viewed themselves. There was tight alignment across three of the five dimensions. Peereboom explains, "The results of the CaT were interesting. We all went into the workshop thinking we were so far apart from each other, but what the CaT revealed was that at our core we were somewhat aligned in our values, which was surprising."

Figures 12.5 and 12.6 show how the two parties viewed each other—showing perception gaps. The key point is that while the parties had a similar view of how they approached key aspects of the relationship, they viewed the "the other guy" as being far from aligned.

Dr. Ken Smith, MD, CCFP, summed up the cause of the perception gaps. "Simply put, neither side knew what the other was doing: the Hospitalists had no idea what the Island Health budget was for them, and Island Health Administrators did not know how the Hospitalists scheduled patient care. It was easy to see how there were such huge perception gaps." A lack of transparency and the lack of visibility were an underlying cause of significant distrust.

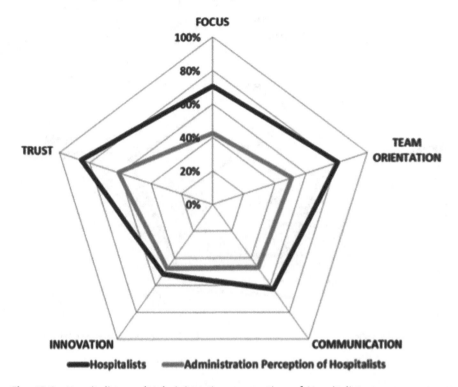

**Fig. 12.6** Hospitalists and Administration perception of Hospitalists

As lunch drew near, the facilitators introduced the concept of the "buddy system" where Administrators and Hospitalists would pair off in groups of two or three and have lunch with the sole purpose of getting to know "the other guy" on a more personal level. Dr. Maskey remembers thinking, "Like really? We're all going to have lunch together. That was amazing, especially after only one morning together!"

Dr. Maskey had lunch with Dr. Brendan Carr, who was the President and CEO of Island Health at the time. Dr. Maskey said she invited Dr. Carr to lunch "because he was someone I did not know very well and had a somewhat fraught relationship with when we had encountered each other in the past."

Dr. Maskey explains the power of getting to know the person behind the business side of negotiations. "During lunch we began to established a different relationship. We both seemed to be able to appreciate that our prior tensions were related to the Hospitalists' passion for their work, and a desire for a respectful relationship, and a lack of understanding and knowledge between our two groups."

That first morning created a safe environment with a candid discussion about the relationship, giving the parties just what they needed. Both the

Administrators and Hospitalists realized they could have a trusting, transparent, and compatible relationship. It was a turning point for Dr. Maskey and the others. "We were no longer interested in just developing a contract, but in building excellent relationships at multiple levels that would allow all of us to be leaders in Canadian healthcare, whether as Administrators or Hospitalists."

## New Relationship (Telia)

Step 1 is vital when entering into an entirely new relationship intending to create a relational contract.

The journey of Telia Company AB (a Swedish listed telecommunications company and mobile network operator) is a perfect example of how to lay a strong foundation for a potential strategic outsourcing relationship. Telia began its journey like most organizations: wanting to understand if shifting away from a conventional transactional contract would unlock the potential of a more strategic outsourcing relationship.

Andreas Sahlen, Telia's Head of Estate Mgmt. & Real Estate Law, was keen to conduct a pre-study before Telia made any significant decisions. The pre-study revealed several key concerns. First, Telia had "stiff contracts" that were inflexible in allowing suppliers to optimize maintenance operations. Telia uncovered how the existing budgeting process led to Telia putting its money in the wrong places and the way it was handling the maintenance part of the business was not optimal. Sahlen recounts, "We were saying we wanted a strategic partner, but we were operating in a very traditional transactional manner with our suppliers. With twenty plus suppliers, our contracting approach was at best typified by an Approved Provider model."

The problem for Telia? Which of the twenty suppliers would be the best fit for a more strategic relational contract? Telia turned to Cirio Law Firm and the EY advisory group to facilitate them through a Request for Partner process, with EY providing expertise in facilities and project management and Cirio Law Firm providing expert legal advice on how to write a relational contract. The Request for Partner (RFPartner) process is a highly collaborative competitive bidding process used when a buyer is actively seeking not just a strategic solution from a supplier but also the ability to assess multiple providers' cultures, mindsets, and willingness to engage in a collaborative relational contract.[5]

Telia began the Request for Partner process by down-selecting the suppliers based on capabilities. Once three suppliers were short-listed, the focus shifted to picking the supplier based on the best fit. Key to this was ensuring Telia was selecting a partner with solid compatibility, a willingness to be transparent, and consciously committed to building a trusting relationship.

An essential part of the RFPartner process was to spend time in stakeholder workshops designed to have a high degree of supplier interaction where Telia and potential partners developed operational knowledge of each other's team and how well the parties work together (i.e., cultural compatibility). For example, one of the collaboration workshops was for Telia and the potential partners to develop a high-level roadmap for transformation. Robin Warchalowski—an EY consultant certified in the Vested methodology—explains: "Most competitive bidding processes are designed for the buying organization to write a spec and have the supplier bid on the spec. The winning supplier is typically the one with the best capabilities at the lowest price—or the best value. The RFPartner process is different because it is designed for the buyer to share their problem and to have the supplier develop a solution for how they will help the buying organization transform to the desired future state. The approach and face-to-face nature of the workshops enable the parties to really gel (or not). It often becomes evident very quickly which supplier has the best fit in terms of trust, transparency, and overall compatibility."

Two suppliers emerged out of the RFPartner process as potential partners: Veolia and another leading facilities management supplier. With two potential partners and solid experience from the workshops, Telia and each supplier completed a Compatibility and Trust (CaT) Assessment. The results of a Compatibility and Trust Assessment showed that Veolia was a highly suitable partner for Telia, especially in the areas of trust, focus, and team orientation, as seen in Fig. 12.7.

Ingrid Wallgren, the Telia Senior Sourcing Manager on the initiative, comments, "In the beginning it was a huge discussion. But the RFPartner workshops revealed the obstacles and risks were not as big as we feared and we discovered ways of working through the risks in a productive manner. We also knew from the Compatibility and Trust Assessment that we were picking a partner that was a great cultural fit with Telia."

## What to Do if You and Your Potential Partner Are Misfits?

As the parties jointly discover if they have enough trust, transparency, and compatibility, the parties may uncover that they have insurmountable gaps

**Compatibility and Trust Dimensions**

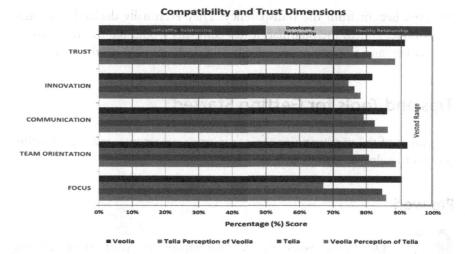

Fig. 12.7 Telia and Veolia compatibility and trust dimensions

in trust, transparency, and compatibility—or one, or both, is unwilling to invest in closing the gaps.

One example of organizations not willing to lay the needed foundation is a pharmaceutical company that outsourced its facilities management to a leading service provider. Both organizations were very frustrated with their existing relationship and quickly recognized that many destructive behaviors had crept into their daily ways of working—causing what UT researchers have coined as Outsourcing Ailments.[6] Both parties were keen to explore how a relational contract could improve their relationship similar to how Island Health and the South Island Hospitalists did.

The parties entered Step 1 with eyes wide open. They quickly learned the reason for their discontent—gaps in the foundational elements of compatibility. The pharmaceutical company's corporate culture was very creative and innovative. It placed a lot of weight on creativity, and thus valued flexibility with a high tolerance for constant change—almost to the point of manifesting the corporate equivalent of Attention Deficit Disorder. On the other hand, the service provider's organization was founded by engineers. Its corporate culture was steeped in process rigor. It disliked change. Change agents were seen as threatening. The service provider effectively shut down the organization's frequent requests for change in the name of efficiencies and process standardization. There was a genuine culture clash.

Ultimately the parties determined there was simply too much of a foundational cultural misalignment between the parties. The ultimate decision was that it would be best for the parties not to move forward. The parties did, however, benefit from the transparency. They eventually decided that once the contract ended, the pharmaceutical company would bid out the work to the market, and the service provider would decline to bid on the RFP.

## Tips and Tools for Getting Started

Regardless of the starting point of one's journey, we recommend the following process to help you complete Step 1.[7]

### Pre-work

- Determine who should participate in your trust-building workshops
- Determine if you will use a professional facilitator. We highly recommend a neutral third-party facilitator, especially for organizations wanting to restructure an existing relationship such as Island Health and the Hospitalists.
- Have team members complete the CaT assessment (or other trust assessment instrument) before your workshop.

*It is often helpful to do a comparison of each organization's mission statement, ethics statements, values, etc. Bring this to the workshop as a handout and discuss it as part of the compatibility discussion.*

### Step 1: Kickoff

**Purpose:** To make sure that everyone is clear with the objectives and deliverables they will create during the workshop.

- The kickoff typically takes 10–15 minutes and is led by a facilitator
- Start your meeting stating the objective for the day: to identify and close gaps in trust, transparency, and compatibility.
- Do introductions if people present do not know each other. What is everyone's role? How do they envision themselves contributing to the success of the relationship?
- If you have a large group, consider splitting into smaller sub-groups. Determine who will be in each sub-group. It is helpful to have cross-organizational groups.

## Step 2: Discussion

Use the provided discussion questions as prompts to help you ask (and answer) questions about trust, transparency, and compatibility. If this is a new relationship, discuss and agree on the philosophies for how you will approach each area.

 *Ask yourself...would you treat your partner differently if you worked for the same organization?*

## Discussion Questions: Trust

*How Trustworthy Are You?*

- How do you define trustworthiness?
- In what ways do you act in a trustworthy manner?
- What challenges to trustworthiness do you face?
- What excuses do you make about not being trustworthy?
- Do you clearly communicate your intentions and then follow up by fulfilling your promises?
- Do you act with integrity? (Can individuals and organizations depend upon you to act consistently with how you acted in the past?)

*How Trustworthy Is Our Organization?*

- Who (list names) in our organization do you need to build a trusting relationship?
- Who (list names) in our organization can damage trust by acting in an untrustworthy manner? Why?

*How Trustworthy Is Our Partner?*

- How does each of our organizations define trustworthiness? Are our definitions similar? If not similar, how could this inconsistency in definition cause confusion?
- Has either one of our organizations said one thing and done another in the past? What was the impact?

- How does each organization contribute to any untrustworthy behaviors? What are these specific behaviors that need to be addressed?
- Do different individuals show different degrees of trustworthiness? Who? How should we address that issue?
- Does either organization have any reason not to trust each other? What are those reasons?
- Has either organization had opportunities to act in their short-term self-interest without doing it? What was the impact?

## Discussion Questions: Transparency

*Are you wiling to share the following? If not, what is holding you back from sharing?*

- Complete financial data for helping to truly get to total costs (not just price)
- Your internal objectives and their corresponding importance to the organization
- Accurate forecasts and projections
- Your intent and details regarding strategic initiatives
- Potential problems, issues, or concerns that could harm your partner if the risk were realized
- Your intentions or insights regarding potential changes in policies, regulation, or personnel
- Your organizational goals and targets, including your metrics, used to determine bonuses (e.g., sales representatives earn a % on revenue, procurement earns a bonus for achieving annual price reductions, a project manager earns a bonus for getting the project delivered on time, etc.)
- Your Best Alternative To a Negotiated Agreement (BATNA)

*Questions to ask—share your perspectives*

- Can your partner be trusted not to abuse your trust by using the information to gain an advantage at your expense?
- What can I share that will bring value to the relationship and build trust?
- Will the information foster transparency and encourage better decision making?
- Are there any potential negative consequences (privacy or regulatory issues)?
- Who should be consulted before sharing information?

- Who should approve the decision and the nature of the information?
- Does your partner have appropriate confidentiality policies and practices in place to prevent the dissemination of information beyond the intended recipients?
- If we cannot, or will not, share some information (specific financial data, for example), is there alternative data we can share that will still promote trust, honesty, and better decision making?

## Discussion Questions: Compatibility

Concerning compatibility or cultural "fit," the parties engaging in a relational contracting partnership should have enough commonality to foster an atmosphere of trust and open communication needed to solve problems as they arise.

*Questions to ask—share your perspective*

- What characteristics do we need from our partners to improve our compatibility/cultural fit?
- What is your process to ensure personnel working in this relationship have at least a minimum level of compatibility?
- What are you willing to do if your partner complains about a compatibility issue between personnel?

## Step 3: Capture Overall Learnings

If one has smaller breakout groups, it is beneficial to come together and share learnings. Document any observations, notes, and action items that emerge, especially related to how one will close gaps in trust, transparency, and compatibility.

 *It is helpful to refer to these notes as you for creating your statements of Intended Behaviors (Step 2, next chapter)*

 *If you are in an existing relationship, and it is adversarial, consider working with a professional facilitator trained in relational contracting.*

## A Look Ahead

Once the parties believe that the partnership has the requisite level of trust, transparency, and compatibility—or if they are willing to work on a new or existing relationship to develop the necessary trust, transparency, and compatibility—they can feel confident in moving on to Step 2, where they will develop a shared vision and a common set of guiding principles.

## Notes

1. Jim Collins and Jerry Porras, *Built to Last: Successful Habits of Visionary Companies* (New York, Harper Business, 2004).
2. See, for example, Juliet Bourke, Bernadette Dillon, "The Diversity and Inclusion Revolution: Eight Powerful Truths," *Deloitte Review*, No. 22 (January 22, 2018). Available at https://www2.deloitte.com/us/en/insights/deloitte-review/issue-22/diversity-and-inclusion-at-work-eight-powerful-truths.html.
3. Ian R. Macneil, *Contracts: Instruments For Social Cooperation* (South Hackensack, NJ, F B Rothman, 1968).
4. The complete Discovery Health case study is available at the University of Tennessee's dedicated research library at www.vestedway.com.
5. See the University of Tennessee/Vested White Paper "Unpacking Collaborative Bidding: Harnessing the Potential of Supplier Collaboration While Still Using a Competitive Bid Process." A free download available at https://www.vestedway.com/wp-content/uploads/2017/08/Unpacking-Collaborative-Bidding_2017.pdf.
6. Kate Vitasek, Mike Ledyard, and Karl Manrodt, *Vested Outsourcing: Five Rules That Will Transform Outsourcing*, Second Edition (New York, Palgrave Macmillan, 2013). The ailments are discussed in Chapter 3.
7. In addition, the University of Tennessee offers an online Getting to We course and toolkits, which are very relevant to relational contracting practitioners.

# 13

## Step 2: Co-create a Shared Vision and Objectives

The second step of creating a relational contract is to co-create a shared vision and strategic objectives for the relationship. As addressed in Chapter 7 one of the characteristics of the relational contract is to promote a "partnership" versus an arms-length relationship (Fig. 13.1).

In this chapter, we go into more detail about this characteristic. We show why it is essential as well as provide real examples of how one can achieve this. This chapter will end with tips/tools for putting the step into practice.

## What Does It Mean?

Co-creating a shared vision and common strategic objectives for the partnership is straightforward; the parties sit down and discuss what they want to achieve together, both long term and short term, and at both a high level and a low level. A long-term, high-level shared vision is formulated for the partnership as the strategic "north star" for the relationship. Lower level, more concrete goals are formulated into strategic objectives for the partnership. The Shared Vision and Strategic Objectives can be as big—or small—as the parties desire. For example, the overarching goal might be to simply achieve tactical continuous improvement efforts from more collaboration. Or the parties may be seeking significant boundary-spanning desired outcomes that require a highly strategic partnership where both parties are investing in a

© The Author(s), under exclusive license to Springer Nature
Switzerland AG 2021
D. Frydlinger et al., *Contracting in the New Economy*,
https://doi.org/10.1007/978-3-030-65099-5_13

| | TRANSACTIONAL ← → RELATIONAL | |
|---|---|---|
| **DIMENSION** | **TRANSACTIONAL CONTRACT** | **RELATIONAL CONTRACT** |
| FOCUS | The commercial transactions | The commercial relationship |
| **RELATIONSHIP** | Arms-length relationship | Partnership |
| SOCIAL NORMS | Social norms | Mutually discovered and agreed social norms are explicitly included as contractual obligations |
| **PRIMARY RISK MITIGATION MECHANISMS** | Risk mitigation by use of market power and state power | Risk mitigation and avoidance by creation of continuous alignment of interest |
| **PLANNING** | Aims for completeness, i.e. tries to have contract clauses covering all future events of the relationship | Accepts that complete planning is not possible and aims to create a fair and flexible framework for managing change and uncertainty |

**Fig. 13.1** From a relationship to a partnership

business endeavor, such as a transformative outsourcing initiative, or creating a statewide health system through a formal alliance partnership.

Whatever the aspirations for the relationship, formulating the Shared Vision and Strategic Objectives is first and foremost an *alignment exercise*. As outlined in Chapter 6, alignment is a key characteristic of a successful relational contract in which risks are avoided through continuous alignment of interests and expectations, and less through threats or exercising market power.

As the parties go through Step 2, they align their interests and expectations at the highest level. At the start of the relational contracting process the parties typically have a vague idea of what they want to achieve. Also, the parties will likely also have divergent perspectives that need to be clarified and aligned. When potential partners start at the highest level and align to a single shared vision, then work their way to more concrete strategic objectives, the parties become aligned with their views and perspectives on what they will achieve together. And if they cannot align at this high level? Then it is a leading indicator they should forego the effort and not enter into a contract! The work completed in Step 2 will guide the rest of the process since the entire relationship and deal will be oriented toward the shared vision and objectives.

To be clear, adopting a shared vision and strategic objectives is merely the first step in the alignment process. The parties must continue to align as they work on Steps 3 through 5. But the path to eventual success starts with the Shared Vision and Strategic Objectives.

# Why Should You Do It?

To understand why a shared vision and strategic objectives should be adopted, it is first necessary to look back at Chapter 7 which shows the characteristics of a relational contract and highlights one of the characteristics as *risk mitigation*. The main mechanisms to mitigate risks in the transactional contract are state and market power. These mechanisms are often weak in situations with high dependency because high dependency creates significant switching costs. This typically means that the parties will likely not go to court or leave one another unless there is an extreme situation justifying the switch. At the same time, high complexity creates a high risk of misalignment of interests and expectations with the verbiage of the transactional contract, which focuses on tangible aspects in an arms-length relationship. A relational contract mitigates these risks by creating a *continuous alignment of interests and expectations*. Such alignment starts with a common view of what is to be achieved by the parties.

Let's do a quick review from Part II—the Science of Contracting—to see how academic research and theory supports developing a shared vision. First, recall the work of Robert Gibbons (MIT) and Rebecca Henderson (Harvard University). Their work provides an interesting perspective on why aligning on a formal shared vision and strategic objectives are important. The strength of the informal ties created when the parties repeatedly interact becomes much stronger if the parties have *clarity* on what to achieve and expect.[1] However, to understand the importance of a shared vision and strategic objectives, one needs to take a step further into the analysis. Reflect on the lessons from Nobel laureate Richard Thaler discussed in Chapter 6.[2] Humans are both opportunistic and altruistic. They are opportunistic and want the best possible deal for themselves; however, they are also endowed with a strong sense of fairness.

Lastly, recall the work of Oliver Williamson. Williamson based much of his analysis on an assumption that humans are opportunistic and will take advantage of one another if given the opportunity. For opportunism to flourish, there must be conflicting interests. A buyer may want a lower price, while the supplier does not want a lower margin. An investor wants more control, whereas an entrepreneur may want more freedom to act. Power cannot overcome opportunism. Aligned interests place the contracting parties in the same boat and disincentivize their opportunism, enabling a partnership to flourish. In some successful relational contracts, opportunism does occasionally exist—but only when a mutual benefit is at stake. As one business executive astutely observed after going through the relational contracting process, "If we are opportunistic, it is like we are a cannibal eating our own arm off. It just doesn't make sense to hurt the other party when you too will be hurt from your actions."

While aligned interests during the contracting process are essential, we should also recall the later theory of Oliver Hart who has shown that the contract also serves, and should serve, as a reference point for expectations. One of the best ways to create clarity of expectation is to co-create a formal shared vision and mutually define strategic objectives.

Many argue that creating a formal shared vision and strategic objectives seem vague or abstract. They ask, "Why not spend the time detailing out specifications and metrics as a way to gain clarity?" Granted, a highly specified contract can address this issue. However, it only partly solves this problem and does not get the parties entirely on the same page. In complex situations with numerous unforeseen events, the only realistic way to get the parties on the same page is to try to reduce the complexity of the world with a common view of the future. When unforeseen events happen the shared vision and strategic objectives become a beacon to keep the parties on track, reminding them of the intent driving their partnership.

Let's be clear: solely establishing a shared vision and strategic objectives are insufficient. The complete intent of the relationship cannot simply be captured in a short shared vision and strategic objectives. The shared vision and strategic objectives serve as the starting point. They constitute the parties' shared view of success once the value is created. The shared vision and strategic objectives are established as the direction ahead of the relationship, and the parties need to continually align with the remaining three steps, including architecting the specific deal points in Step 4. The deal itself consists of the products or services to be delivered, compensation to be paid, capital investments to be made, allocation of shareholder rights, and terms of exit, etc. The deal should be drafted as the parties' best hypothesis on how they will achieve the vision and the objectives. It is mostly in the specific deal points where the parties' interests and expectations are aligned or misaligned. And when business happens, which causes one or both parties' expectations to not be met, the vision and the objectives are the beacons guiding the parties in adapting their contract, ensuring continued alignment. This fact will be further explored in Step 4 (alignment of interests and expectations) and Step 5 (living in the agreement).

# From Theory to Practice

In a formal relational contract, the shared vision is coupled with the parties' strategic objectives which they intend to achieve through the relationship. A well-written shared vision focuses on the future and creates a sense of direction and opportunity—and in many cases—provides a source of inspiration. The shared vision and the strategic objectives serve as a compass point—or true north per se—for the relationship.

Much has been researched on the power of having a shared vision.[3] Take for example the power of John F. Kennedy's shared vision with NASA of putting a man on the moon within less than a decade. People working together with a clear common goal are much more likely to achieve success than those who have no shared direction.

Coupled together, the shared vision and strategic objectives align the contracting parties toward a common goal and transcend the self-interest of each organization, serving three purposes:

1. It sets forth a larger purpose for the business relationship
2. It exposes all stakeholders (managers, employees, and even customers) to the desired future state
3. It keeps the parties focused on how to drive the business forward as "business happens," providing clear direction for decision making

In a formal relational contract, the Shared Vision and Strategic Objectives are one of the first passages people read in the contract. Figure 13.2 shows how

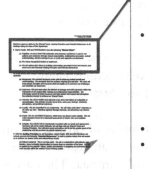

**The Island Health – Hospitalist Shared Vision**

- Together, we are a team that celebrates and advances excellence in care or our patients and ourselves through shared responsibility, collaborative innovation, mutual understanding, and the courage to act, in a safe and supportive environment
- We will be recognized leaders in healthcare
- We will achieve this vision by building relationships grounded in trust and respect, and anchored in the Guiding Principles and Intended Behaviors

**Fig. 13.2** Shared Vision in context to the contract Island Health/SIHI

| SIHI - Hospitalists | | | |
|---|---|---|---|
| (labor services agreement) | | | |
| **Shared Vision** | | | |
| • Together, we are a team that celebrates and advances excellence in care or our patients and ourselves through shared responsibility, collaborative innovation, mutual understanding, and the courage to act, in a safe and supportive environment<br>• We will be recognized leaders in healthcare | | | |
| **Achievement is reflected in the Strategic Objectives** | | | |
| 1. A Sustainable and Resilient Hospitalist Service | 2. Excellence in Patient Care | 3. Relationship Health Excellence | 3. A Best Value Hospitalist Service |

**Fig. 13.3** Island Health/SIHI Strategic Objectives

Island Health and SIHI incorporated their Shared Vision right upfront into their written contract.

Co-creating the Shared Vision builds on the work Island Health and SIHI completed in Step 1. Kim Kerrone reflects on the Shared Vision exercise: "One major game-changer was the creation of a Shared Vision that patient care is our North Star. When the Hospitalists realized that was what the Administrators also wanted, it was a breakthrough."

The Island Health–Hospitalist Shared Vision is coupled with four Strategic Objectives as shown in Fig. 13.3.

Dr. Kenneth Smith, was one of the leaders representing the Hospitalists. He comments "I could really feel a turning point after the Island Health administrators and the Hospitalists had completed the Statement of Intent. In the beginning, it was very difficult when you are in Step 1 and you are talking and trust (and lack of trust). But at some point, during Step 2 there was a profound change as we started working together on what our goals were. We sat side by side and the physical nature of co-creation helped us start to develop interpersonal relationships where we were seeking common ground and started to function like we're all in the same boat together. It became more of a 'we need to solve this together.'"

Over the years the University of Tennessee has worked with over 50 organizations that have adopted formal relational contracting. Figure 13.4 provides three additional examples of Shared Vision and Strategic Objectives in practice.

These examples in Fig. 13.4 provide real-life examples of Shared Vision and Strategic Objectives, and share samples of how one can create a Shared Vision and Strategic Objectives set for their relational contract. The parties start with creating their Shared Vision, followed by developing their Strategic Objectives.

| Intel - DHL | | | | |
|---|---|---|---|---|
| (forward logistics example for Costa Rica logistics contract) | | | | |
| **Shared Vision** | | | | |
| *To create a logistics operation that continuously improves on cost while improving or maintaining other key operational indicators* | | | | |
| **Achievement is reflected in the Strategic Objectives** | | | | |
| 1. Increase Cost Savings | 2. Improve Delivery Performance | 3. Reduce Shipment Damage | 4. Maintain Safety Scores | 5. Maintain Intel Customer Satisfaction Scores |

| Microsoft – Accenture | | | |
|---|---|---|---|
| (business process outsourcing contract to transform Microsoft's financial operations) | | | |
| **Shared Vision** | | | |
| *Best-in-class finance functions, enabled by process standardization, solid internal controls, and effective performance management. Achieved by hiring & developing the best people and using integrated applications that showcase Microsoft technology.* | | | |
| **Achievement is reflected in the Strategic Objectives** | | | |
| 1. Best-in-Class finance operations | 2. Process Standardization | 3. Solid internal controls | 4. Effective performance management |

| Facilities Management Example | | | |
|---|---|---|---|
| **Shared Vision** | | | |
| *We are aligned to deliver innovative and sustainable real estate solutions that create **unparalleled value** for our stakeholders. Our success is mutually dependent. We attract and retain top talent, promoting a culture of loyalty and **brand excellence**, resulting in **legendary** Customer and Employee **experiences** on our journey to be the Better Bank.* | | | |
| **Achievement is reflected in the Strategic Objectives** | | | |
| 1. Drive economic value to the organizations through fair and transparent financials | 2. Be an environmental leader | 3. Provide holistic, world-class real estate services | 4. Be an innovative organization |

**Fig. 13.4** Three examples of real-world Shared Visions and Strategic Objectives

# Tips and Tools for Getting Started

While a shared vision may be drafted on the back of an envelope or over a cup of coffee with as few as two people, it is recommended that the parties bring the key stakeholders together from each organization and co-create the shared vision the reason is simple: the shared vision is only as good as the support from those who will make it happen.

We find using a facilitated workshop is an excellent approach. We provide a step-by-step process for developing a Shared Vision and Strategic Objectives. The example provided comes from a Telecommunications company that used the five-step relational contracting process outlined in this book to create a strategic joint venture for customer installation, support, and maintenance operations.

## Create Your Shared Vision

### Step 1: Brainstorm "Inspiration" Words

**Individual Exercise:** Have each person spend 3–5 minutes writing down three words or short phrases they feel represent what the "future state" of their relationship should look like. For example, "world-class," "operational excellence," "patient and resident-focused," "ONE-TEAM," "safe."

**As a group:** Have each person share their words/phrases with the group, having a facilitator noting each unique word on a flip chart or virtual whiteboard. If more than one person has the same word simply make a tick mark to note the frequency with which the word was used.

You will use the list of words for Step 2 (Fig. 13.5).

> **Tip!** *Some teams find it helpful to have team members do Step 1 as pre-work, especially if there is a large group. The facilitator can then create a Wordle® (e.g., using WordleIE or another free web-based application) to generate the word cloud.*

**Fig. 13.5** Wordle™

**Step 2: Develop a First Draft of Your Shared Vision (Fig. 13.6).**

 Develop the first draft of your Shared Vision. This should be short, preferably one sentence but not more than two sentences.

 *For groups larger than six, divide into smaller groups of 3-6 people.*

 *For inspiration, use the examples above. Below are other examples you can leverage.*

**Sample Shared Vision 1 (Telecommunications joint venture for customer installation, support, and maintenance operations)**

We excel at servicing our customer's connected world with passionate people and smart solutions.

**Sample Shared Vision 2 (Vancouver Coastal Health and Compass)**

Patient and resident-focused environmental services that are consistently high in quality and reliability. Our commitment to innovation, collaboration, and shared governance will drive mutual value and create an exceptional healthcare environment.[4]

**Sample Shared Vision 3 (Jaguar and Unipart)**

**Fig. 13.6** Example of first draft Shared Vision

To support Jaguar dealers in delivering a uniquely personal ownership experience to Jaguar drivers worldwide, ensuring industry-leading owner loyalty—through partnership and world-class logistics.[5]

Once the parties are happy with their draft, they should write it on a flip chart to share with the larger group.

## Step 3: Vote for Your Favorite Draft

 If you split the teams up into smaller groups, bring the entire team back together; Have team post the flip charts with each team's draft Shared Vision at the front of the room or use a virtual white board. Everyone now gets to vote for their favorite three statements.

- Have each team share their draft and explain what they like about what they have done. Then have other team members say what they like about each draft or what may be missing.
- Once the teams have shared their drafts, everyone will get to vote on their favorite. A digital poll works well in workshops.
- Use a voting indicator such as self-adhesive dots (e.g., as shown at right). If you don't have dots, you can simply use a marker and place tick marks to denote votes.
- Each individual can vote for three separate draft statements (a person should not vote for a statement more than once).

The draft Shared Vision with the most votes will become the "baseline," to be used in Step 4.

## Step 4: Fill Gaps in Your Baseline Shared Vision

- Re-write the "baseline" draft Shared Vision neatly on a flipchart or virtual whiteboard
- Have the group pick out the "must-have" words or phrases that other teams used that might be missing in the baseline version. Add these words/phrases to the bottom of the baseline
- You will use the baseline draft with notes on missing words/phrases to create a new draft in the next step

### Step 5: Refine Your *Shared Vision*

- Create a refined second draft.
- Go through "rounds" of feedback until you develop consensus. To gain consensus, do a Fist-To-Five on the combined statement, asking "are you 80% comfortable and 100% committed?"
- For anyone at a four or less, ask them to state WHY they don't feel they can be 100% committed.
- Modify the Vision Statement to address the concerns.
- Repeat until all parties are at a Five (80% comfortable and 100% committed) for supporting the Shared Vision.

 *We find it typically takes three "rounds" of editing to gain consensus; however, we have seen it take up to six rounds.*

## Developing Your Strategic Objectives

### Step 1: Review Your Shared Vision

Your Strategic Objectives should support your Shared Vision. Start by reviewing the Shared Vision you already created. To show how this step works, we will use the following Shared Vision created by a Telecommunications company used for creating a joint venture with its network operations partner.

> *We excel at servicing our customer's connected world with passionate people and smart solutions.*

 *Teams often find it helpful to post a very large printout or a flipchart of the Shared Vision at the front of the room as an easy memory jogger. In virtual meetings, one can use a "sticky pad" app.*

### Step 2: Brainstorm One-Word "Outcomes"

An excellent way to start this exercise is to review the one-word adjectives you used when you created your shared vision (Fig. 13.7).

As a group, the parties decide on the words/phrases they believe should be encapsulated into their Strategic Objectives.

**Fig. 13.7** Wordle™ of Adjectives

## Step 3: Create Short Phrases

Create five or fewer short phrases to describe the future state of a successful partnership. For example, in the case of the Telecommunications team a large team (divided into four smaller groups was each asked to list their Top 5). Collectively the group came up with a list of twenty. Once duplicates were eliminated, the following remained (Fig. 13.8):

| | |
|---|---|
| • Market leader | • Higher profitable |
| • Provide amazing customer experience (ACE) | • Better ROI |
| • Operational Excellence/Efficiency | • Value Sharing |
| • High Quality measured by KPIs | • Innovation – Products |
| • Value | • Innovation – Services |
| • Lower TCO | • Passionate people |

**Fig. 13.8** Short phrases used in a Shared Vision

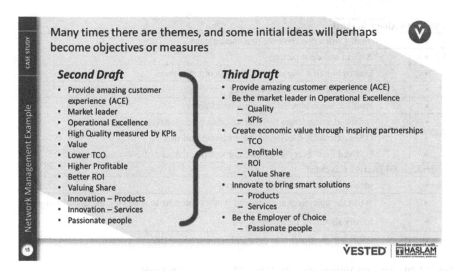

**Fig. 13.9** Refined objectives

## Step 4: Document Your High-Level Strategic Objectives

 Look for ways to streamline your Strategic Objectives to have five or less. Often, items can be combined because they are similar or removed (because they are duplicates) with the sub-bullets being objectives and/or metrics you will use in the physical contract. The example in Fig. 13.9 shows how the Telecommunications company and its service provider refined its Strategic Objectives.

 *For inspiration, use the examples above*

**Tip!** *If you are stuck, use "sticky dot" voting to learn what the group feels are the Top 5. Try hard to limit your Strategic Objectives to five or less. Remember, some items can become objectives or metrics!*

## Contract Work

Once the team has agreed on the Shared Vision and Strategic Objectives, they will combine these with their Guiding Principles (to be completed in Step 3 in the next chapter) to form an overarching Statement of Intent (SOI). See Appendix 1 for two examples in practice.

Once the parties have completed their Shared Vision and Strategic Objectives, they can use the following checklist in Fig. 13.10 to ensure their Shared Vision and Strategic Objectives have optimal impact.

| Shared Vision Checklist | |
|---|---|
| • | Short – often one sentence or a short phrase |
| • | A vivid and clear picture |
| • | Description of a bright future for both organizations |
| • | Memorable and engaging wording |
| • | Realistic aspirations (if there is a timeframe) |
| • | Balanced, considering both organizations perspectives |
| • | Often externally focused on the customer/end-user |
| • | Is "lived into" every day – often repeated at the start of every meeting |
| **Strategic Objectives Checklist** | |
| • | Ideally five or less to provide focus |
| • | When the objectives are achieved it will contribute to achieving the shared vision |
| • | Ideally should be measurable |
| • | Balanced, considering both organizations perspectives |

**Fig. 13.10**   Shared Vision and Strategic Objectives checklists

# A Look Ahead

Once the parties have created their Shared Vision and Strategic Objectives they can feel confident moving on to Step 3, where they will discover and document the Guiding Principles for their partnership.

# Notes

1. Robert S. Gibbons and Rebecca M. Henderson, "Relational Contracts and Organizational Capabilities" (July 18, 2011). *Organization Science* (forthcoming). Available at SSRN: https://ssrn.com/abstract=2126802.
2. Richard H. Thaler, "Anomalies: The Ultimatum Game," *Journal of Economic Perspectives*, Vol. 2, No. 4 (1988), pp. 195–206.
3. See, for example, Michael Henry Cohen, *The Power of Shared Vision: How to Cultivate Staff Commitment & Accountability* (Minneapolis, Creative Health Care Management, 2015); James M. Kouzes and Barry Posner, "To Lead, Create a Shared Vision," *Harvard Business Review* (January 2009).
4. "Vested For Success: How Vancouver Coastal Health Harnessed the Potential of Supplier Collaboration," *University of Tennessee* (Case Study, 2016) by Kate Vitasek, Jeanne Kling and Bonnie Keith (2016). Available at https://www.vested way.com/downloads/VCH_Case_Study_collaborative_bidding_Mar6.pdf.
5. Unipart / Jaguar Relationship "Perhaps the Best Example of Performance-Based Logistics," *Unipart Group Press Release*, February 16, 2009. Available at https://www.unipart.com/wpcontent/uploads/2017/09/Jaguarbestpractice.pdf. See also Amy Roach Partridge, "A New Day Dawns for 3PL Partnerships," *Inbound*

*Logistics*, February 15, 2011. Available at https://www.inboundlogistics.com/cms/article/a-new-day-dawns-for-3pl-partnerships/ and Adrian Gonzalez, "3PLs and Software Vendors: Keep Innovating Your Business Models," *Logistics Viewpoints*, November 28, 2012. Available at https://logisticsviewpoints.com/tag/uni part-logistics/?ak_action=reject_mobile.

# 14

# Step 3: Adopt Guiding Principles for the Partnership

The third step of creating a relational contract is to adopt guiding principles for the partnership. Chapter 7 explained one of the key characteristics of a relational contract is to mutually discover and agree on social norms, which will be explicitly included in the contract (Fig. 14.1).

This chapter explains how to put social norms into practice by explaining what it means and why it is essential. At the end of the chapter, we provide real-life examples of how to turn the theory into practice along with tips and tools for putting the step into practice.

## What Does It Mean?

While there are several social norms, we focus on six: reciprocity, autonomy, honesty, loyalty, equity, and integrity. Combined, these six social norms form the guiding principles for the relationship and become the foundational anchor of a formal relational contract.

We are often asked, *"So just what is a social norm? And what does each social norm mean?"* Read on for the answers to these esential questions.

© The Author(s), under exclusive license to Springer Nature
Switzerland AG 2021
D. Frydlinger et al., *Contracting in the New Economy*,
https://doi.org/10.1007/978-3-030-65099-5_14

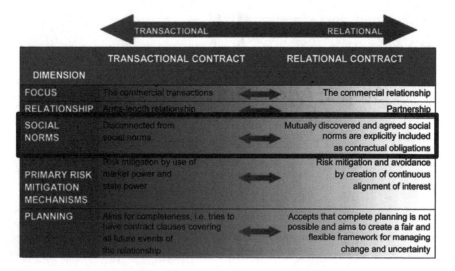

**Fig. 14.1** Guiding Principles

## What Is a Social Norm?

*So just what is a social norm?* Social norms are unwritten rules about how to behave in a particular social group, culture, or circumstance. From a sociological perspective, social norms are informal understandings that govern the behavior of members of society. In the field of social psychology, the roles of norms are emphasized—as they guide behavior in a specific situation or environment as "mental representations of appropriate behavior."[1] Each social situation has its own set of expectations about the "proper" way to behave, which varies from group to group. For example, Concordance Health—a $1 billion-plus healthcare distributor based in Ohio—has a strong social norm: never be late to meetings. Likewise, most of the large oil and gas organizations have created an industry-wide norm to exercise safety precautions well beyond where other industries operate. Social norms can drive good—or bad—behaviors and set behavioral expectations for the group.

A relational contract formally embeds the proven social norms mentioned above into the parties' relationship as guiding principles, converting the social norms into contractual norms. Contracting parties should start by "discovering" each norm through collaborative dialogue where they jointly agree on the appropriate behavior for their relationship. The parties then transform these social norms into contractual norms by formally drafting and documenting them into the foundation of their agreement—preferably at the beginning of the contract. In doing so, the parties set the expectations for how they intend to behave throughout the life of their agreement. These behaviors guide individuals in both how they approach projects that fall under the scope of the relationship and how the organizations approach the overall relationship.

The Guiding Principles fulfill several functions in a formal relational contract, including:

- Being the foundation of the contract architecture
- Being reflected in the contract clauses
- Forming the basis for interpreting and fulfilling the contract after it is signed
- Regulating any changes to the contract
- Being "lived in" as part of governance

The Guiding Principles will—together with the Shared Vision and the strategic objectives—form the foundation for architecting the deal. Architecting the deal means to come to an agreement by defining the commercial aspects of a contract. For example, the parties need to specify the scope of the work, determine the allocation of responsibilities and risks, and agree on compensation. It also means ensuring general terms and conditions such as termination rights, liabilities, and warranties align with and reinforce (rather than contradicting) the deal. This concept is discussed in detail in Step 4 in the next chapter.

This leads to a common question: "What are the six guiding principles and what do they mean?"

## What Are the Six Guiding Principles and What Do They Mean?

We advocate a formal relational contract should incorporate six proven social norms into the fabric of the relationship—and the contract. These six are reciprocity, autonomy, honesty, loyalty, equity, and integrity. Combined, they create what we call the Guiding Principles of the partnership.

While there exist many other social norms, we argue these six social norms—when combined and when followed—have the inherent power to replace opportunistic *What's in it for Me* behaviors with healthier *What's in it for We* behaviors. Following these six social norms enables the parties to align interests and expectations in a fair and balanced manner not only during contract development but also well after the contract is signed.

Let's explore the fundamentals of each social norm.

## Reciprocity

Reciprocity obligates parties to make fair and balanced exchanges. Many people learn about reciprocity in early childhood. Children are taught it is important to share toys. Reciprocity applies equally to business relationships because fair and balanced exchanges build trust, and trust is the foundation of all successful relationships.

Many consider reciprocity (making fair trades) the most fundamental social principle. Elinor Ostrom (2009 Nobel Prize winner in Economic Sciences) shares extensive research on why reciprocity is a foundational social norm for success in the book *Trust and Reciprocity: Interdisciplinary Lessons for Experimental Research.*[2] Robert Axelrod's book *The Evolution of Cooperation* highlights his renowned research in the "Prisoner's Dilemma," which showed the best strategy is "tit-for-tat" with the parties cooperating for mutual success.[3] Tit-for-tat is best described when one party mirrors the response of the other party (reciprocates). For example, when one party cooperates, the other party is likely to cooperate.

In a personal relationship, reciprocity obliges individuals to return favors granted and gifts given. When negotiating a contract, reciprocity obliges the parties to allow for a fair opportunity for each party to earn a return on investment when an investment is made. Likewise, when risks are taken, the party taking the risk should receive an appropriate risk premium unless the other party takes on commensurate levels of risk. Positive reciprocity enables parties to create more value through cooperation than non-cooperation. Conversely, negative reciprocity can create a destructive cycle of value-reducing behaviors (e.g., if you are not fair to me, I will retaliate and do something not fair to you).

## Autonomy

In a collaborative relationship, the parties must commit to the principle of autonomy or abstaining from imposing power upon one another. However, for many organizations, autonomy in commercial relationships is not commonly seen. Why? The infamous specter of bargaining power has been promoted heavily since the 1970s with management concepts—such as Michael Porter's Five Forces. Porter outlines the power between suppliers and customers as two of the primary forces which create a competitive advantage. A party with a strong position instinctively uses its power to gain short-term benefits. That power comes in many forms, ranging from demands for unilateral concessions such as hiding known risks or shifting known risks to the weaker party, or micro-managing the other party.

Experience and economic theory show, however, that the prevailing strategy deployed by the more powerful party is flawed. Instead of trying to force their will upon each other, relational contracting parties should promote the principle of autonomy: enabling independent decision making by each party. In Chapter 6, we referred to the research by Ryan and Deci which showed how important autonomy is for people's intrinsic motivations. We also referred to the research of Nobel laureate Daniel Kahneman and others, showing that people react negatively to abuses of power. But there is more.

Mihály Csíkszentmihályi[4] (in *Flow: The Psychology of Optimal Experience*), Malcolm Gladwell[5] (in *Outliers: The Story of Success*), and Daniel Pink[6] (in *Drive: The Surprising Truth About What Motivates Us*) have brought the importance of autonomy to the forefront with compelling analysis in their popular books. At the individual level, autonomy refers to the ability to act based on reasons and motives which reflect the individual's values and convictions. The same applies to business relationships. People want to make their own decisions, free from the power of another. They want to work as equals and want to be part of a process that allows them to make decisions for the broader group.

A relationship characterized by autonomy has several benefits. Autonomy leads to greater innovation, which ultimately can lead to a competitive advantage. Autonomy acts as a "facilitator" by allowing the parties to live the other core principles, such as reciprocity, honesty, and loyalty—why should anyone be honest and loyal to someone who tries to force their will upon them? In turn, those principles lead to more creative problem-solving and innovation. And autonomy, like the other principles, strengthens trust. When a stronger party chooses not to use its strength, it shows the trust that the other party will still act in both parties' interests.

## Honesty

Parents tell their children that "honesty is the best policy." How often, though, are "little white lies" justified by adults? Or how often does someone (an individual or an organization) bury their head in the sand instead of confronting brutal facts?

While the virtues of honesty have been espoused since the beginning of mankind, Dan Ariely has put the importance of honesty in business relationships front and center in both his research and popular books.[7] Ariely—a professor of psychology and behavioral economics at Duke University—has authored multiple books on the topic, including *The (Honest) Truth About Dishonesty: How We Lie to Everyone—Especially Ourselves*,[8] which is thought-provoking.

Ariely encourages individuals and organizations to call out dishonesty immediately. It's not just the impact of the transgression—but the impact which can arise when dishonesty becomes a social norm in day-to-day business practices. Ariely points out that cheating can become contagious, and that group dynamics and behavior laden with cheating can have a powerful effect on each individual. He calls this "wishful blindness" and explores the concept as it relates to the Enron collapse in 2001.

Honesty can have a significant impact on an organization's willingness to be transparent. Many business people ask, "If I am open and honest with them, is the other person being open and honest with me? How will I know?" Experiences with opportunism can produce fears that a dishonest party will take advantage of honest discourse by using information against the honest one. This in turn drives further opportunism. The argument is: "I don't think that they are being honest with me, so I'll withhold a little information. It isn't all that important so it's no big deal." Unfortunately, the other party is maintaining the same argument. Both have justified their dishonesty.

Simply put, honesty builds trust. Without that trust, organizations cannot break through WIIFM (What's In It For Me) thinking.

## Loyalty

Loyalty is a key relational contracting principle because it obliges the parties to be loyal *to the relationship*. Loyalty to the relationship—or maintaining "relationship first" thinking—will come when the parties' interests are treated with equal importance. Loyalty is *not* being loyal under all circumstances to one party. It is not about sticking together no matter what, nor does it take priority over one's fiduciary duty to one's organization. Loyalty is about loyalty *to the relationship as a single entity*.

The principle of loyalty is used to allocate risk and rewards, as well as burdens and benefits between the parties. It promotes continuous focus on what is best for the relationship as a separate entity. If effectively applied by the parties, the principle of loyalty will keep the costs low for all and the quality of the service provider's services high, to the benefit of each party.

There are three main aspects of loyalty to the relationship: appropriate allocation of risk and workload; a relationship that has its interests; and elimination of information asymmetries.

First, risk allocation. Traditionally, each party tends to allocate as much risk as possible to the other party, regardless of who can best mitigate those risks. Take for example a typical business process outsourcing contract where an organization outsources its back-office finance operations including accounts payable and accounts receivable. It is common for the buying organization to try to shift risk to the supplier by negotiating extended payment terms, currency conversion risk, and inflation risk. We argue that while it might be possible to shift risk, it is often not smart because in many cases simply shifting the risk does not mitigate the risk. In fact, shifting risks can even increase. For example, a supplier unable to mitigate risks will compensate for the potential risk by adding a "risk premium" to the overall costs of the project. Yet, if the risk (e.g., inflation or natural disaster) does not occur, the project costs are not reduced. The principle of loyalty obliges the parties to allocate risks to the party able to eliminate the risk or, if that is not possible, to the party best able to manage and mitigate the risk in the most cost-effective manner.

Also, most business relationships are plagued with information asymmetries where information is distributed unequally between the parties. According to the Nobel laureate Douglass North, referred to in Chapter 5, this lack of information symmetry leads to higher transaction costs, since information is needed to understand how to value goods and services.[9] An effective way to eliminate any information asymmetries is to simply share information. Loyalty obliges the parties to show a great deal of transparency as it significantly decreases the overall transaction costs for the relationship. The benefit of increased transparency and openness also increases trust and yields a better decision-making process.

## Equity

Some businesspeople view a relationship as a balance sheet. Both sides should be equal. This is especially true in Western democracies where equality is a fundamental social norm. The principle of equity, however, is different. It obligates parties to look more critically at distributing resources. It might be easy to split things 50–50 to ensure they are equally shared, but it might not be viewed by all as fair.

Equity, as a legal principle, arose centuries ago out of the limitations perceived in English common law. Two aspects of equity are relevant to business: proportionality and remedies.

First, the principle of equity obliges that parties share rewards in proportion to their contributions, resources invested, and risks taken. Equity prevents tensions in the relationship because equity addresses the inequalities which arise over time.

The second aspect of equity stems from the Courts of Chancery, which remedied the limitations and inflexibility of common law by supplementing common law with decisions meant to make the parties equitably whole again. This concept shares the same name, but not the same intention as a remedy in the sense of a corrective action or sanction. Equity in the form of a remedy that addresses contractual limitations serves an essential purpose in relationships: It allows people to do the right thing even if the contract does not call for that action. Organizations can try to conceive of all possible contingencies, but business happens. If the contract does not provide a solution, the parties may find an equitable solution instead.

By defining equity, each party is taking responsibility for keeping the relationship in balance. Sometimes organizations may get an unequal proportion of cost savings or will agree to take on different levels of risk. The key is to have a common definition to help people navigate those situations with an eye toward overall balance within the relationship.

## Integrity

Integrity adds the final ingredient to a robust strategic relationship. Integrity means *consistency in decision making, words, and actions.* For example, the principle of integrity is applied when one makes similar decisions in similar situations. Integrity applies to individuals—but also collectively to organizations.

There are two obvious ways to know when integrity is missing. First, an organization will face the same set of circumstances but make different decisions. Inconsistent decisions breed distrust. Second, one's actions do not match their words.

Intuitively, people understand integrity; they want to be able to rely on each other to make the same decision, convey the same message, and take the same action under the same set of circumstances. People want to know that they will get consistent results. Integrity promotes trust between the parties by creating predictability—since what has happened in history forecasts what is expected to occur in the future. Integrity thus reduces both risk and complexity.

Integrity is rarely discussed as a principle to govern business relationships. However, references to concepts such as the spirit of the contract implicitly refer to the principle of integrity. If you have ever looked at a contract and thought, "You might be right if you look at the letter of the contract, but that does not mean the decision is the right thing to do," then you understand the principle of integrity. Applying the spirit of the contract and maintaining integrity in decisions are needed to win the hearts and minds of those you need to rely on in the long term to get things done.

Of course, every organization encourages its employees to act with integrity. Unfortunately, conflicting priorities can easily emerge and send mixed signals. Take for example an oil and gas company that has a strict policy for suppliers to not do work without a Purchase Order. The supplier received a mixed message when their vendor manager asked them to replace the HVAC system in a local subsidiary in August and hold off invoicing them until January when the new budget kicked in.

Naturally, people will look for ways to justify why they are not making the same decision when presented with the same set of facts, citing the need to be agile and responsive to explicit objectives and wishes. The purpose of discussing and defining integrity is to keep everyone committed to fulfilling their roles while performing according to the best interest of the relationship.

## Why Should You Do It?

In Part II, we shared strong scientific—therefore commercially compelling—reasons for adopting guiding principles in a formal relational contract.

We pointed to legal and economic theorists such as Macaulay, Macneil, Ellickson, and North who identified ways organizations use social norms to avoid conflicts of interest. For example:

- Macneil pointed to the norms of reciprocity and solidarity (which we here call loyalty) as crucial to mitigate the risks of the breakdown of the social cooperation involved in all contractual relationships[10]
- Ellickson showed how the Shasta County inhabitants applied the norms of loyalty and equity to deal with and avoid disputes[11]
- North showed how people and organizations use both formal and informal rules to avoid transaction costs caused by conflicts of interest[12]

We addressed the psychological research of Thaler, Fehr, Ryan, and Deci, which points to the psychological dimension of social norms. A fundamental insight into behavioral economics—to use Thaler's terminology—is that people are Humans and not Econs. This means that Humans have a strong sense of fairness among other things. A sampling of the psychological research supporting social norms includes:

- The Ultimatum Game—as well as other experiments—has shown that people often turn to retaliatory behavior when treated unfairly, even if it is against their best economic interests[13]
- Ernst Fehr has shown how reciprocity often provides a much stronger incentive for cooperative behavior than negative, or even positive, economic incentives[14]
- Ryan and Deci's self-determination theory shows the importance of autonomy in generating intrinsic motivations to perform well, where intrinsic motivations are far stronger than extrinsic motivations[15]

Last—but not least—we addressed the economic research of Nobel laureate Oliver Hart. *Conflicts of interests and failed expectations* are the key sources of problems in contractual relationships. Contracts are written to prevent conflicts of interests and ensure fulfilled expectations.

It's one thing to align interests. However, it is also important to align on expectations. Oliver Hart's work has shown it is essential to gain alignment of expectations versus only aligning interests. The written contract sets reference points for what the parties believe they will achieve out of the relationship. But since all contracts are incomplete, there will always be a risk of failed expectations when business factors change after the contract is signed. Failed expectations easily lead to what Hart calls "shading" behavior in which cooperation is withdrawn and the parties start to follow the letter instead of the spirit of the contract.[16] Hart has shown, together with David Frydlinger, that the adoption of guiding principles can fulfill an important function of overcoming this problem with contractual incompleteness, by ensuring that the parties behave fairly when it becomes necessary to deal with unexpected events.[17]

Conventional transactional contracts mainly use state and market power to protect organizations against opportunism. But as explored in Chapter 7, state and market power becomes less effective as dependency and risk increase. Incorporating the guiding principles into a relational contract aims to use cooperative efforts to create continuous alignment of interests and expectations throughout the term of the relationship rather than relying on market and state power.

All this research proves the parties can avoid conflicts of interest more effectively by applying social norms in their relationship than by using power. Furthermore, research shows that (ab)use of power can generate conflicts of interest and lowered motivations to perform.

It is hard to argue against the case for applying social norms to mitigate conflicts of interests and align expectations in a contractual relationship where the relational contract is a good fit. We find that once contracting professionals take the time to understand the research and logic there is little debate that having contractual relationships grounded in the guiding principles is a good thing. The debate then becomes should contracting parties go one step further and transform the social norms into *written contractual norms and make them contractually binding?*

We argue the answer is YES! Contracting parties should formally incorporate the social norms into the written contract with a commitment to make them legally binding. We explore the reasons why below.

## Not Making the Guiding Principles Legally Binding Creates Confusion

Over the years, we have seen many contracting professionals push back on putting the guiding principles into the contract to make them legally binding. These skeptics offer two alternative approaches for dealing with the guiding principles. The first is to simply agree to use guiding principles informally—but not formally put them in the contract. The second approach includes putting the guiding principles in the formal contract, but then explicitly writing a clause stating the guiding principles are not contractually binding.

Either approach is folly. Why? In both cases, the parties place themselves in a confusing situation, at least from a legal viewpoint. To understand why these two scenarios create confusion, one needs to wear legal glasses. A duty of good faith exists across most jurisdictions—either a general duty of good faith such as in the United States or, in the case of the United Kingdom, more specifically in relational contracts. The six guiding principles outlined in this chapter in essence guide what exactly good faith means to the contracting parties. As such, it seems meaningless to agree not to follow them.[18] Add to this the fact there is risk of a court still interpreting their good faith duties in light of the implicitly agreed-upon principles. A party that has violated the guiding principles may not want to assume the risk that a judge or jury will interpret the contract and the party's behavior.

By adopting the guiding principles outlined in this chapter, the contracting parties eliminate confusion about what "good faith" means. Rather, contracting parties gain clarity by establishing the meaning of their contractual duty to act in good faith. The act of transforming social norms into the contract itself makes them contractually binding—and therefore enforceable.

## A Strong Signal of Trust

A second argument for making the guiding principles legally binding is that it sends a strong signal for building trust—and conversely for preventing distrust. Simply put, the parties send very mixed messages by *not* making them legally binding. It would be as if the parties said "yes, we will follow these guiding principles, but we don't *have to* if we don't *want to*." Consider it in context: "Yes, I promise to be honest, but don't hold me accountable when I am not." In any relationship, sending this kind of message would most certainly and unnecessarily lower trust levels.

## Risk Mitigation

The third argument for making the guiding principles legally binding relates to risk mitigation. As Macaulay showed in his seminal article described in Chapter 3, there often exists a discrepancy between the formal contract (the "paper deal") and the actual relationship (the "real deal").[19] It is not uncommon for an organization to have a transactional contract which can be very one-sided but they *act* differently in the "real deal" by applying basic social norms such as reciprocity and loyalty. When this happens, the parties are *informally* leveraging the guiding principles to solve conflicts and ensuring aligned interests. This typically works well as long as both parties abide by social norms. However, if one or more individuals forming the relationship leave and a "new sheriff" comes into town, they may not know about nor feel bound by the parties' history, the spirit of their relationship, nor any prior course of doing business.

The "new sheriff in town" has the power (purposefully or unknowingly) to destroy a perfectly healthy relationship. Recall, for example, the case of Chrysler where the new Daimler executives shifted back to power-based approaches eroding trust and value.[20]

In other cases, the shift in philosophies can happen not because of a new sheriff, but simply because an existing sheriff has obtained new orders—often from senior executives or corporate headquarters. The following statement is from an Account Executive for a large IT contract[21]:

*I was often pushed (by the CEO) over the last 12 months to maximize the results for us (the supplier) at the cost of the buyer instead of living into our win–win gentleman's agreement. It really put me between a rock and a hard place. How do I do what is right for the client when the CEO is breathing down my back to find ways to improve our short-term profits? We might have had a gentleman's agreement when we signed the deal – but now I was being forced to not live into the intentions of the deal. It really didn't sit well and I eventually left the company.*

In this case, trust was destroyed, friction increased, and risks arose—all without breaching the contract. Either way, either the existing or new sheriff is entitled to destroy the relationship by going back to the letter of the contract, or by simply using power to renegotiate it. By making the guiding principles legally binding, a breach of the guiding principles constitutes a breach of the contract. In this way, the parties mitigate this risk of short-term opportunism. The contract thus serves as a mechanism to disallow opportunistic behavior by people in their organization. In essence, by formally adopting the guiding principles, *the parties are protected from themselves*. This concept is taken one step further below.

## A Security Measure Against Breach of Contract

The fourth and final argument is that making the guiding principles contractually binding serves as an insurance policy against a breach of contract. To understand this argument, let's return to the relational contracting framework laid out in the introduction to Part III of this book. The framework shows contractual relationships are decided by the combination of the parties' motivations and the rules of the game by which they play. The rules consist of social, legal, and contractual norms. By making the guiding principles contractually binding, the parties create a strong alignment between the three categories of norms.

Consider the analogy of a rope used to tie a boat or ship to a dock. The boat and the dock represent the contracting parties. A high-quality rope is made by intertwining smaller separate strands of rope—the social, legal, and contractual norms. Each strand can bear so much weight; however, when braided, the weight capacity significantly increases. When one removes one of the strands or does not braid them, the rope is weaker.

Many organizations find themselves in situations where they are— consciously or unconsciously—weakening a partnership by removing or unbraiding the rope of norms. Consider the following. It is not legally possible to agree on contractual norms being in breach of mandatory legal norms. However, organizations can agree on contractual norms that are not aligned with social norms. This happens all the time. Transactional contracts are written where the stronger party is allowed to exercise power in contradiction to the autonomy norm; risks are allocated in breach of both the loyalty and equity norms. Also, where a contract is incomplete, ambiguous, or silent, the parties may act opportunistically—again, in breach of social norms. To be clear, this misalignment between contractual and social norms is not necessarily bad in all cases. But in those relationships where a relational contract is more appropriate (those with medium to high dependency and risk), such misalignment can be a significant source of friction, value leakage, and shading. By contractually agreeing to the guiding principles such misalignment is avoided. We will see in Chapter 17 what it means to make the guiding principles contractually binding.

Earlier we made the point that the risk mitigation mechanism of state power—basically contractual enforceability—is very weak in deals where the relational contract is a good fit. But now the point is being advocated to make the guiding principles contractually binding. On the surface, this may seem a contradiction, but it is not. It is a nuance that serves to keep ethical organizations ethical. Why? The key motivating force for following the guiding principles will be to avoid a breach of contract. As such, making the guiding principles legally enforceable makes good commercial sense since very few want to be caught breaching a contract.

Simply put, making the guiding principles legally binding is a security measure for ethical organizations. Few people will want to be caught breaching a contract, even though the other party may not sue the breaching party. And the simple fact that one could be successfully sued helps one live according to positive and productive social norms that drive commercial success.

For contracts requiring a strong relationship component, it becomes increasingly essential to integrate social norms with the legal and contractual norms. Doing so ensures a fair and mutually beneficial deal for all parties at the signing of the contract. But more importantly, the parties will have the power to weather tough storms as the social norms serve to help contracting parties continuously align their interests and expectations over the term of the relationship.

## From Theory to Practice

A *formal* relational contract is different from an *informal* relational contract. What both have in common is the parties follow positive social norms that create a healthy environment—something that is essential when the parties operate in a dynamic environment where changes in the business environment can cause misaligned expectations and shading. What is different about a formal relational contract is that the social norms are formally agreed and physically embedded into the actual contract. These mutual commitments to documented social norms are known as "Guiding Principles."

In a formal relational contract, the Guiding Principles are coupled with the Shared Vision and Strategic Objectives into a concept referred to as a "Statement of Intent (SOI)." In many cases, the contracting parties augment their by outlining and committing to other key expected behaviors. Figures 14.2 and 14.3 provide a snapshot of the Island Health and SIHI contract, providing an excellent example of how they put the theory into practice.

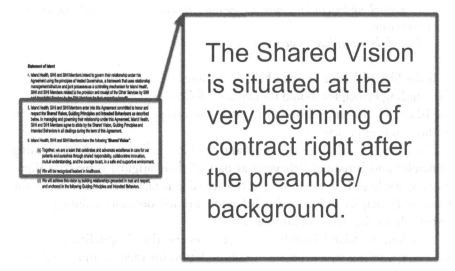

**Fig. 14.2**  Incorporating the Island Health/SIHI Shared Vision

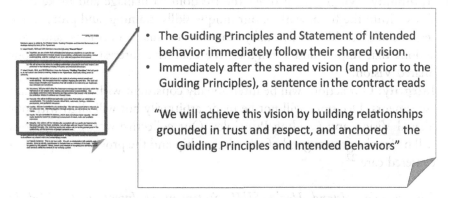

**Fig. 14.3**  Incorporating the Island Health/SIHI Guiding Principles

One of the very first things in the contract is the parties' Shared Vision. Figure 14.2 shows how Island Health and the Hospitalists incorporated the Shared Vision in their contract.

The Shared Vision states:

*Island Health, SIHI and SIHI Members have the following "**Shared Vision**":*

*Together, we are a team that celebrates and advances excellence in care for our patients and ourselves through shared responsibility, collaborative innovation, mutual understanding, and the courage to act in a safe and supportive environment.*

*We will be recognized leaders in healthcare.*

If the Shared Vision is one of the first things a reader sees in the contract, the Guiding Principles should immediately follow. Figure 14.3 illustrates how the Island Health and Hospitalists made the bridge from the Shared Vision to the Guiding Principles.

The Island Health Administrators and the Hospitalists drafted the Guiding Principles and Intended Behaviors as part of their original three-day Alignment Workshop. It is worth noting the actual contract stresses the use of the Guiding Principles and Intended Behaviors in their decision-making process, "especially during times of adversity."

Together, the Island Health Administrators and the Hospitalists agreed on the exact wording which became the foundation for their contract. Take for example the parties' guidance on autonomy and integrity:

- **Autonomy**: We give each other the freedom to manage and make decisions within the framework of our unique skills, training, and professional responsibilities. We individually commit to make decisions and take actions that respect and strengthen the collective interest to achieve our Shared Vision.
- **Integrity**: Our actions will be intentionally consistent with our words and agreements. Decisions will not be made arbitrarily but will align with our Shared Vision and Guiding Principles. Our collective words and actions will be for the greater good of the relationship and the provision of patient-centered care.[22]

*The complete Island Health-SIHI Statement of Intent is provided in Appendix 1.*

Dr. Jean Maskey, former site chief of the Hospitalists group, shared why the Statement of Intent is such a crucial part of a formal relational contract.

"The Statement of Intent and the environment in which we developed it was crucial in developing trust. It gave all of us permission to speak up, as well as permission to relax and have real conversations and exchanges of ideas as equal partners. The fact that that it works both ways is critical."

Dr. Manjeet Mann, a cardiologist and Island Health Executive Medical Director, felt the change happening as the parties drafted their Guiding Principles and Intended Behaviors. "Something remarkable began to happen. Those attending began to see that the Vested relational contracting process just might break the impasse and bring us to alignment on a collaborative labor services agreement that would fit the needs of their unique situation."

All participants agreed that the three-day Alignment Workshop was a pivotal turning point for the Island Health Administrators and the Hospitalists. By the end of the third day, the Administrators and Hospitalists rallied behind the theme of "A New Day, A New Way" which was grounded in their newly-minted Statement of Intent. Glenn Gallins—the attorney who represented SIHI—commented: "I thought the focus on relationship building in the Vested methodology was absolutely brilliant. Towards the end of day three, most of the doctors were at the point when they said, 'Well, when are we actually going to discuss the contract?' I took that to be a good sign."

Reflecting on the three days, Dr. Ken Smith said, "The Vested relational contracting process allowed us to see each other's needs and goals and how to blend the two into a positive working framework that could work going forward. The concept of working together as 'we' was a unique experience. The three-day workshop and the Vested methodology had created a safe environment for everyone to move forward." He added, "When you looked at the Wordles$^{TM}$ with the words of how we felt at the beginning of the three days and how profoundly negative it was and then you look at the words at the end of the three days, there was all this hope." Dr. Mann described the workshop as "therapeutic," commenting on how the Vested process helped Island Health Administrators and Hospitalists begin to have a strong feeling of empathy.

Kerrone attributed the transformation over the three days to a combination of things but summed it up nicely: "The bottom line was we were sitting in the same room talking to people as people. This was just what the group needed. It was enough to get us going."

As the third day ended, the Island Health Administrators and the Hospitalists were aligned not only with a Statement of Intent (Shared Vision, Guiding Principles, Statement of Intended Behaviors) but also with a renewed sense of hope and a willingness to move forward using the Vested relational contracting methodology to restructure all aspects of their contract. At the end of the meeting, all of the Administrators and Hospitalists passed around the pages of their existing contract and symbolically tore the pages into confetti symbolizing the celebration for "A New Day, A New Way." Dr. Maskey commented, "Those three days definitely validated that we could move forward. We could begin to see there was enough alignment to help us get past our past troubles."

Together, the Island Health Administrators and Hospitalists had laid the foundation for a different kind of contract—a formal relational contract. They were ready to move on to Step 4 where they would begin to address the core of their agreement more effectively.

## Tips and Tools for Getting Started

Creating the Guiding Principles for the relationship may seem odd, but it is relatively easy when one follows the proven approach outlined below. However, if one is in an adversarial relationship (such as Island Health and the Hospitalists) or forging a new high stakes relationship, it is exponentially easier to complete this step if one uses a neutral third-party facilitator.

The physical aspect of creating Guiding Principles is similar to creating a Shared Vision—both are only as good as the buy-in from the stakeholders in both organizations, especially those who will need to operate within the social norms. For this reason, the best path to alignment on the Guiding Principles is not simply going through the motions of each step, but taking time to discover what each principle means and how it will (or will not) change behaviors in both organizations as the parties move forward.

The following is a proven approach for creating the Guiding Principles for one's relationship.

### Pre-work

Use the Statement of Intent toolkit you downloaded as a free resource from the University of Tennessee's dedicated website to Vested (www.vestedway.com).

For those wanting additional support, consider enrolling in the University of Tennessee's *Getting to We* online course and/or engaging a Center of Excellence for professional neutral third-party facilitation.

*It is helpful to have either a hard copy print-out of the toolkit or access to a soft copy so team members can physically see the definitions in front of them.*

 *Some teams have found it valuable to include extended Stakeholders and Leadership team members in this portion of the workshop to get their inputs based on customer perspectives, alignment to organization strategies, and buy-in.*

## Step 1: Review the Definitions

As a group, review the definitions of each of the Guiding Principles. Each of the six Guiding Principles is based on known "social norms" that help societies and organizations thrive.

**Reciprocity**: Reciprocity obligates the parties to make fair and balanced exchanges. If one party accepts a business risk, the other must be prepared to do the same. If one party commits to invest time and money in an important project, the other party must be prepared to reciprocate.

**Autonomy**: Autonomy means abstaining from using power to promote one party's self-interest at the expense of the other.

**Honesty**: Honesty obliges the parties to tell the truth, both about facts in the world and about their intentions and experiences.

**Loyalty**: Loyalty obliges the parties to be loyal *to the relationship*. Loyalty to the relationship will come when the parties' interests are treated as equally important.

**Equity**: Equity obliges parties to look more critically at the distribution of resources. It might be easy to split things fifty-fifty, but it might not be fair.

**Integrity**: Integrity means *consistency in decision making and actions.*

## Step 2: Review the Guiding Principle Against Your Experiences

For each Guiding Principle above, "discover" each one by discussing the following questions. Completing this exercise will help each person internalize the importance of each of the Guiding Principles.

- Do you recognize this norm from your personal life?
- What does this norm look like if someone is living that principle?

- Do you recognize this norm from your professional life (at work, between your relationship with your business partner, etc.)?
- What happens if this norm is *not* followed in professional life?
- What happens if this norm *is* followed in professional life?
- Why/how should that this norm be applied in the now relevant commercial relationship?

## Step 3: Create Your Guiding Principles

 Use the sample language in Appendix 1 for each Guiding Principle (or the toolkit if you are using it). As a group, discuss and document the wording you will use to express each of the six Guiding Principles in your agreement (Fig. 14.4).

| Guiding Principles Checklist | |
| --- | --- |
| | Did you include all six of the Guiding Principles? |
| | Does everyone fully understand why the Guiding Principles are essential? |

**Fig. 14.4**  Guiding Principles Checklist

 *It is acceptable to translate the wording to something that works for you, but the foundational concept of each principle should not change as they are based on societal social norms known to establish trust.*

*Use a process to refine your Guiding Principles similar to how you refine your Shared Vision and objectives. This generally requires three rounds to gain consensus.*

## Contract Work

Once you have agreed to the wording you will adopt for each of the Guiding Principles and Intended Behaviors, you will then combine them with your Shared Vision statement and your Intended Behaviors to form an overarching Statement of Intent. The Statement of Intent should be physically included in your agreement, preferably in the beginning of the Master Services Agreement.

## A Look Ahead

Once the parties have completed their Statement of Intent, they can feel confident to move forward with Step 4 where the parties will begin aligning interests and expectations as they architect the specific deal points for their contract.

## Notes

1. Henk Aarts, Ap Dijksterhuis, "The Silence of the Library: Environment, Situational Norm, and Social Behavior," *Journal of Personality and Social Psychology*, Vol. 84, No. 1 (2003), pp. 18–28.
2. Elinor Ostrom and James Walker, editors, *Trust and Reciprocity: Interdisciplinary Lessons for Experimental Research (The Russell Sage Foundation Series on Trust, Vol. 6)* (New York: The Russell Sage Foundation, 2003).
3. The winner of the tournament was a game called "tit-for-tat," using the strategy to start with cooperation and thereafter do what the other player did on the previous move. As long as the other party cooperated, the party using tit-for-tat also cooperated. If the other party defected, tit-for-tat defected, and so on. Tit-for-tat won since it was the strategy that had obtained the greatest rewards when the game was finished. Tit-for-tat was the strategy that created most value during the game.
4. Mihály Csíkszentmihályi, *The Psychology of Optimal Experience* (New York: Harper & Row, 1990).
5. Malcolm Gladwell, *Outliers: The Story of Success* (New York: Little, Brown and Company, 2008).
6. Daniel H. Pink, *Drive: The Surprising Truth About What Motivates Us* (New York: Riverhead Books, 2009).
7. Dan Ariely is the author of several provocative and entertaining books, including *Predictably Irrational* and *The Upside of Irrationality*. His Website is at http://danariely.com/.
8. Dan Ariely, *The (Honest) Truth About Dishonesty: How We Lie to Everyone— Especially Ourselves* (New York: HarperCollins, 2012).
9. Douglass C. North, Nobel Prize lecture, "Economic Performance Through Time," December 9, 1993. Available at http://www.nobelprize.org/nobel_pri zes/economics/laureates/1993/north-lecture.html.
10. See Chapter 1; see also Ian R. Macneil, *Contracts: Instruments for Social Cooperation* (Hackensack, NJ: F. B. Rothman, 1968). Also see The Relational Theory of Contract: Selected Works of Ian Macneil (Modern Legal Studies), 2001.
11. See Chapter 4; see also Robert C. Ellickson, *Order Without Law* (Harvard University Press, 1994).

12. See Chapter 5; see also Douglass North, *Institutions, Institutional Change and Economic Performance* (Cambridge: Cambridge University Press, 1990), p. 13.

13. Richard H. Thaler, "Anomalies: The Ultimatum Game," *Journal of Economic Perspectives*, Vol. 2, No. 4 (1988), pp. 195–206.

14. See Chapter 6.

15. See Chapter 6.

16. See Chapter 3.

17. David Frydlinger and Oliver Hart, "Overcoming Contractual Incompleteness: The Role of Guiding Principles," *Vox CEPR Policy Portal*, November 7, 2019. Available at https://voxeu.org/article/overcoming-contractual-incompleteness-role-guiding-principles.

18. In Chapter 17, we put forward arguments for why the parties should adopt the guiding principles even though they are to a large extent already included in the good faith doctrine.

19. Stewart Macaulay, "The Real and the Paper Deal: Empirical Pictures of Relationships, Complexity and the Urge for Transparent Simple Rules," *The Modern Law Review* Vol. 66, No. 1 (January 2003), pp. 44–79.

20. Refer to Chapter 1 for more on how Chrysler fell victim to the "New Sheriff in Town."

21. Interview on March 6, 2020. Individual wished to remain anonymous.

22. From the Vancouver Island Health Authority—South Island Hospitalists Inc. Service Contract signed by all the parties on July 1, 2018; the effective date was made retroactive to April 1, 2018.

# 15

# Step 4: Align Expectations and Interests (Architect the Deal Points)

As shared in Steps 1 through 3 (Chapters 12–14), alignment of interests and expectations starts with the parties laying the foundation for the relationship with a Statement of Intent. Organizations such as Island Health think of it as the true north for their relationship; others suggest it analogous to the constitution of the relationship. Whatever you call it, simply doing Steps 1–3 is not enough. The parties also need to align on the specific deal points that represent the business and commercial aspects of the contract.

Let's return to Chapter 7 where we highlighted that a fundamental difference between a transactional contract and a relational contract is around how each deals with risk mitigation. A relational contract looks at risk through a lens of risk mitigation and avoidance by creating mechanisms that enable continuous alignment of interest and expectations (Fig. 15.1).

This chapter goes into detail about how to put this characteristic into practice. It explains what this means and why it is essential. We then provide real examples of how to turn the theory into practice. The chapter ends with tips and tools for putting Step 4 into practice.

## What Does It Mean?

If alignment starts with a Shared Vision and Strategic Objectives, it must also continue as the parties negotiate specific deal points. For example, the

© The Author(s), under exclusive license to Springer Nature Switzerland AG 2021
D. Frydlinger et al., *Contracting in the New Economy*,
https://doi.org/10.1007/978-3-030-65099-5_15

| DIMENSION | TRANSACTIONAL CONTRACT | RELATIONAL CONTRACT |
|---|---|---|
| FOCUS | The commercial transactions | The commercial relationship |
| RELATIONSHIP | Arms-length relationship | Partnership |
| SOCIAL NORMS | Disconnected from social norms | Mutually discovered and agreed social norms are explicitly included as contractual obligations |
| PRIMARY RISK MITIGATION MECHANISMS | Risk mitigation by use of market power and state power | Risk mitigation and avoidance by creation of continuous alignment of interest |
| PLANNING | Aims for completeness, i.e. tries to have contract clauses covering all future events of the relationship | Accepts that complete planning is not possible and aims to create a fair and flexible framework for managing change and uncertainty |

**Fig. 15.1** Aligning Expectations

parties need to agree on the products or services delivered (scope and responsibilities), the economics (a price or pricing model), and how the parties will measure success (metrics). The parties also need to determine the appropriate legal terms such as levels of liability, term, termination obligations, and a litany of other legal clauses. As the parties discuss the specific deal points, it is common each party may assume risks based on the decisions made. For example, the buyer may have a 90-day payment term policy. If the supplier agrees, they will bear the cost of capital risk associated with performing the work before getting paid.

In Step 4, the parties will *architect* the agreement, agreeing on mutually beneficial deal points that best support the agreement rather than undermining it.

While the concept of architecting a commercial relationship may be new to some, negotiating the underlying deal is not. The difference is in how one approaches Step 4. Architecting a deal means the contracting parties enter Step 4 with the *What's In It For We (WIIFWe)* mindset they have integrated into Steps 1 to 3. Architecting a deal requires the contracting parties to resist the urge for traditional *What's In It For Me (WIIFMe)* behaviors. For example, business people know how to bargain around price. And lawyers are often well trained in drafting and negotiating contract clauses to minimize risks for their organizations or clients. Architecting a deal means looking at deal points and legal clauses through a different lens where the parties seek to align interests and expectations around how they can best achieve the Shared Vision and Strategic Objectives, per the Guiding Principles.

This is an important distinction because often a WIIFMe approach sub-optimizes the overall potential of the relationship. Consider the 90-day payment term decision again. Using a conventional negotiation approach, it makes perfect sense for the buyer to pressure the supplier into taking a longer payment term. However, in the spirit of transparency agreed in Step 1 and the loyalty principle adopted in Step 3, the parties should review the costs of capital for each organization, which might reveal that the buyer has a far lower cost of capital than the supplier. The buyer ultimately decides it is less expensive for them to reduce the payment terms to ten days rather than paying the price premium that the supplier has integrated into the sales price. Having a 10-day payment term reduces the total cost of the exchange, creating value for both parties.

## Four Rules for Collaborative Contracting

This is a book about contracts and not so much about negotiations. Nevertheless, it is necessary to emphasize that a key component ensuring that the *What's In It For We?* mindset is kept in Step 4 is for the parties to follow the four rules for collaborative negotiations laid out in the book *Getting to We—Negotiating Agreements for Highly Collaborative Relationships*.[1]

---

**Rule 1: Sit Side-by-Side, Face the Issues Together** This means sitting side-by-side, not only mentally, but physically. The parties must not place themselves on opposite sides of the table. Once the parties have adopted a Shared Vision, Strategic Objectives, and Guiding Principles, they now ask how they can architect a deal to ensure their interests and expectations are aligned. This is *the* issue that the parties have to face together.

**Rule 2: Let the Principles Guide Behavior** The Guiding Principles adopted in Step 3 should be implemented in the actual contract. But they should guide the entire process also in Step 4. The principle of reciprocity is at the heart of all fair and value-creating deal-making. The parties must follow the principle of autonomy and refrain from using power when architecting the deal. They must be honest about facts and their intentions. And all representatives of the parties must act consistently, following the principle of integrity. There is no room for good cop/bad cop behavior when architecting a relational contract.

**Rule 3: Develop a Flexible Framework to Achieve a Shared Vision** A relational contract should by definition be a flexible framework where the outer framework consisting of the Shared Vision, Strategic Objectives, and Guiding Principles remains fairly firm but where the deal architected within this framework is flexible.

**Rule 4: Follow the Principles, Adapt the Goals** As discussed in Chapter 14, the ends do not justify the means. In some cases, short-term savings or margin targets that each party may have are not necessarily be possible to achieve without violating some of the Guiding Principles. The parties must keep this in mind and realize that it is quite likely that pursuing short-term wins at the other party's expense will most likely be commercially worse for *both parties* in the long run and will likely lead to shading.

Using a WIIFWe mindset requires the parties to have a holistic perspective of how the deal points come together, effectively supporting the Shared Vision and Strategic Objectives. Consider the example of building a house. The Guiding Principles are the foundation. The parties use the Guiding Principles as they work through every specific deal point in the contract. While there may be hundreds of deal-specific points in a contract, they can all be boiled down to three key pillars—value provided, compensation, and other terms (see Fig. 15.2).

This chapter focuses on how to craft the deal-specific points through the lens of each of the three pillars.

1. **Value Provided**: In the contract, the value provided is expressed by what the seller is providing (e.g., goods, services, overall solution, or other valuables). The contract will describe what is provided. For example, there

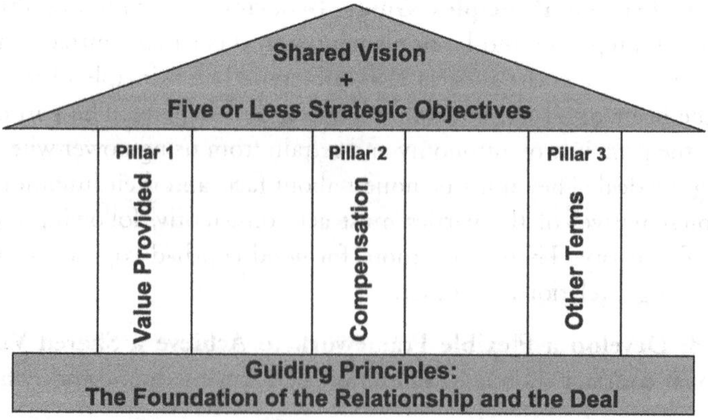

**Fig. 15.2** Pillars of the Shared Vision and Strategic Objectives

may be functional requirements, volumes, quality criteria, delivery times, service level agreements, and operational aspects.

2. **Compensation:** Compensation includes both economic and non-economic exchanges one party (i.e., the buyer) will give the other party (i.e., the supplier) for the value provided. In the contract, compensation is expressed in clauses about price, payment terms, set-off, contract duration, and incentives, and/or remedies.

3. **Other Terms:** Other terms include business or legal decisions that affect the relationship. In a contract, other terms can consist of elements such as rules for termination and exit, intellectual property rights, limitations of liability, jurisdiction of law, and a litany of other clauses typically classified as, "that's an issue for Legal."

Sadly, it is far too easy for contracting parties to have misaligned interests and expectations while negotiating the deal points. When this happens, one or more of the pillars get out of alignment, weakening the parties' ability to achieve their shared vision and strategic objectives. Consider the following typical example of how misalignment can happen in an outsourcing agreement.

A University elects to outsource its facilities management and food services functions. The University has developed a compelling business case and in doing so establishes a baseline of its current costs and service levels. It finds it currently spends $10 million on these facilities and food services and has an APPA Service Level Standard of three (3).[2] Based on the results of a competitive bid event, the University expects that it should be able to receive the same or better service with a cost savings of $1 million. The University also expects to increase efficiency in internal processes by 10%. Combined, the University's business case forecasts a $2 million savings.

After conducting due diligence and negotiations, the University selects a supplier who offered a contract price of $9 million. The price is based on a calculation of the supplier's direct and indirect costs for delivering the services at $8 million plus a profit of margin of 12.5%, or $1 million.

If one looks at the expected financial outcomes for the University and the supplier, the buyer will expect a value of $2 million and the seller a value of $9 million in revenue of which $1 million is profit. If it would be possible for the parties to completely anticipate the future, the deal could be made on these levels and all would be fine. This is a win-win deal, so the parties' economic interests are aligned. In a perfect world, everything can be anticipated, there will be no future surprises, and hence, there will be no disappointment leading to "shading" behavior as described by Oliver Hart.[3]

The problem is that the future is difficult to predict, especially in complex and high-risk deals. So, what can go wrong and push the parties out of alignment?

First is the well-known and ubiquitous problem of scope creep. To avoid scope creep, the University's procurement team shares the specifications for the services, including a detailed statement of work and estimated volumes. Also, the University's lawyers suggest the University includes a "scope sweeper" clause in the contract, stating that the supplier must carry the risk of scope increases, providing additional services at no additional cost for the University. The scope sweeper clause serves to protect the University's $2 million business case.

Let's look at how scope creep (and the scope sweeper clause) fails to work for the parties as intended. One of the services in the contract was cleaning, which states the frequency of cleaning for various situations. For example, elevators' button surfaces should be wiped clean each evening. Six months into the contract, the COVID-19 pandemic breaks out and cleaning frequencies are revised to hourly.

The problem is increased frequency would decrease the value obtained by the supplier, who would have to absorb the additional costs of providing these unplanned services. Let's say the added costs at the beginning of the pandemic would be estimated at $200,000. This would lower the obtained value for the supplier to $800,000. However, as the pandemic persisted the additional costs exceed $1 million, leading the supplier to incur an overall loss.

Several other examples could be given where conventional thinking regarding contract clauses falls short of optimal in a complex and highly dependent relationship. For example, the University's President fears poor food handling in the cafeteria might cause an E.coli breakout, which might lead to lawsuits. In response, the University's lawyer asks for a high liability cap, again to protect the University's business case of $2 million. But this liability cap may, again, jeopardize the entire business case for the supplier if things go bad. Or consider the fact this is the first time the University has outsourced services. Their standard contract template calls for a termination for convenience clause. The supplier reluctantly accepts the clause in order to close the deal, even though it has based its business case of $1 million in profit on an assumption of at least a two-year contract term.

As one can see, the third pillar of "other terms" is highly important in determining the ultimate value obtained by each party. In a transactional contract negotiation, the negotiation over legal terms is typically a zero-sum game in that what one party gains, the other party loses. The parties may still end up in a deal where both parties gain, but because of bargaining power, one party may enter the relationship at a lower value level than expected in advance.

The underlying problem is that the contract is incomplete, meaning that business factors and unplanned events can occur during the life of the agreement. When this happens, either party's business case can be significantly impacted by contractual clauses such as a scope sweeper, liability cap, and termination of convenience. But there are also factors which may be outside of the control of either party. For example, the state in which University is located may increase the state minimum wage which increases the supplier's labor costs by 15%, eroding value from the supplier's business case. Since the cost increase was outside of the control of the supplier, the supplier asks the University for a price increase. If the University says no, the supplier will likely be disappointed and start to "shade," withdrawing cooperation by being less proactive or decreasing service levels to a bare minimum—all without breaching the contract. The University will probably react negatively to this and start to "shade" in turn. And it goes in a vicious circle creating a negative tit-for-tat cycle that erodes trust and creates friction in the relationship.

Note that in the minimum wage example, the supplier is possibly still making some profit if the 15% wage increase does not fully erode the supplier's 12.5% profit margin. From this perspective, it will still be a win-win deal if the buyer refuses a price increase. Nevertheless, the supplier will be disappointed, since its expectation (contract reference point) is that it will make $1 million in profit and not just any number above $0. The Account Manager running the account may not get a bonus, or worse, may get fired because they are not meeting the minimum financials needed by the supplier's corporate headquarters.

While the example provided is for a service contract, the logic can easily be applied to a large number of other contract types.

This example underscores how it is easy for contracting parties to end up in a situation where they have conflicting interests and have not dealt with their expectations in a way to avoid disappointment and shading. Here are three lessons and key pieces of advice to prevent unintentional misalignment of interest or expectations:

1. Use win-win economics with a spirit of winning together and losing together. The economics should not just be win-win at the time of entry into the agreement, but also all throughout the term of the contract.
2. Ensure the parties contract with "realistic" expectations which consider unanticipated events. If events happen that decrease value, the parties

should lose together equitably—avoiding a win-lose scenario. This helps avoid or at least mitigate shading.
3. Ensure the Pillar 3 clauses in the contract are fit for purpose and aligned with the Guiding Principles (as referenced in Fig. 15.2).

Each lesson is explained below.

## Use Win-Win Economics

To deal with the first lesson, it is necessary to understand the various economic models and how each can change the nature of a relationship and the corresponding deal points.

First, it is important to understand that an economic model is more than the "price" or a "pricing model" representing payment to the supplier. The choice of the economic model is always tied to some exchange of value such as service delivered in an outsourcing relationship. For example, referring to Fig. 15.2, the first pillar describes what is being provided and the second pillar describes how the seller is to be compensated. Both pillars are affected by the choice of the economic model.

For sourcing contracts where there is a buyer-supplier relationship, there are three main types of economic models: transaction-based, output-based, and outcome-based models. The book *Strategic Sourcing in the New Economy* provides a comprehensive overview of each.[4] For our purposes, we will only briefly discuss them, with a particular focus on creating aligned interests and expectations between the parties. Also, we will view each through the lens of how each is different using the University outsourcing example.

*Transaction-based* economic model—here the seller is compensated for providing transactions (performing tasks or activities). Typically, this means that the seller is paid *per* something, be it per hour, per full-time-employee, per kilometer driven, per server installed, or per call. Pillar 1 will then contain a specification of the activities or the transactions to be provided, where Pillar 2 specifies the price per activity or transaction.[5] If the University above used a transaction-based economic model, they would pay the supplier a per-hour charge for custodial work.

*Output-based* economic model—here the parties change perspective. Rather than buying activities, they buy pre-defined supplier outputs. A performance-based agreement is a classic example of an output-based economic model. In the University example, the supplier agrees to perform the book of work for $9 million where the work is defined as achieving service levels equal or better than APPA Level 3 standards. In many cases, a performance-based agreement calls for the supplier to pay liquidated damages or receive incentives based on performance—or output. So if the supplier's performance does not meet the designated performance levels, they will make less money overall.

*Outcome-based* economic model—here the parties evolve their perspective even further, compensating the seller for achieving mutually agreed desired business outcomes. An outcome-based economic model is most appropriate for a Vested sourcing business model where the buyer and supplier agree to collaborate to achieve boundary-spanning business outcomes.[6] Using the same University example, an outcome-based economic model would be appropriate if the supplier agreed to invest in process improvements or innovations that would help the University transform their facilities management operations. Here, the supplier is rewarded for implementing creative solutions that drive value for the buyer. For example, assume the supplier invested in having vacuuming robots in every college dorm. While there was an initial investment, if the supplier lowered the totaled costs of cleaning and increased the APPA scores in the dorms, they would earn an incentive based on the value created.

It is important to note any of the three economic models (and similar ones) can be used in a relational contract. And while they are more focused on sourcing situations, the logic of each model can be used in other contracts, such as franchises, joint ventures, or public-private partnerships.

The contracting parties should understand how the choice of the economic model affects how much the parties can align interests and expectations and run the risk of disappointment and shading.

When using a *transactional* economic model, the parties easily integrate conflicts of interest into the heart of the deal. When the University's supplier is compensated for activities or transactions (e.g., $18 per hour for every custodial worker), the supplier will have a perverse incentive to use more custodial workers. Transaction-based pricing often creates a zero-sum game between the parties when negotiating. There can, however, still exist good reasons to use a transaction-based economic model. The important thing is that if the parties use a transaction-based economic model, they must be aware of the risk of building conflicting interests into their deal. And once they know the risk, they should agree to jointly monitor and manage the risk in the governance structure they establish in Step 5 of the relational contracting process.

When using an output-based economic model, the parties' interests are more aligned because the supplier's compensation is tied to the supplier's performance. For example, if the University uses an output-based economic model, as is common in a performance-based agreement, the supplier's payment would be closely linked to their performance. As such, the supplier is incentivized (or penalized) for staying within the quoted price and delivering on the APPA Level 3 commitments as measured by the APPA Standards. This creates more alignment of interests than if the buyer is simply getting paid to have custodial workers show up every day to clean without a formal link to performance.

When using an outcome-based economic model, the parties' interests are even more aligned since the supplier is directly incentivized to contribute to the actual business outcomes the buyer wants to obtain through the deal. As we saw above, if the University entered into a Vested outsourcing agreement with an outcome-based economic model, the supplier would receive an incentive for investing in creative ideas to drive down the cost to clean and increase APPA audit scores.

It is important to remember that no economic model is better than the other; they all work, even though they are a more or less good fit depending on the situation. However, parties wanting to use an output or outcome-based economic model should *always* use a relational contract because when they shift to outputs or outcomes because there is increased interdependency and collaboration is needed between parties to succeed. Combining an output or outcome-based economic model with a transactional contract will typically not work because the higher risk opens the door for increased shading—especially when unanticipated events occur.

For example, assume the University signs a performance-based agreement where the supplier's management fee is at risk based on achieving pre-defined service levels. The supplier achieves both penalties and incentives based on performance against service level agreements (APPA Level 3 scores). One of the service levels is the uptime of critical equipment such as HVAC equipment. This metric would be fine if the supplier was accountable for making decisions about the equipment. However, under the agreement, the University maintains control of capital expenditures. The supplier had been asking the University to replace one of its main HVAC systems that serve the majority of the dormitories, but the University claims they do not have a budget for such a large expense. Over time the supplier finds themself spending significantly more time on HVAC maintenance than expected, which erodes their profits. The inadequate HVAC equipment is susceptible to outages, and each time there is an outage, the supplier incurs a penalty. The supplier complains to the University claiming the outages are not their fault, pointing to the University for not modernizing the equipment and to the HVAC parts supplier for failing to keep stock of such old parts. In this discussion, one or both or one of the parties end up below their expectations (i.e., contractual reference points) and start to shade. Simply put, the interdependence and complexity make it easy to feel the "the other guy" is at fault when disappointed. There are no mechanisms to deal with this risk in a transactional contract, whereas there are such mechanisms in the relational contract.

## Ensure Realistic Expectations

The second lesson is that contracting parties should ensure they contract with realistic expectations to consider unforeseen events. Why? Once again consider Oliver Hart's work on shading in which one party reduces their collaboration, performance, or investment in a relationship when they perceive they are not being treated fairly. Taking unforeseen events into account when setting realistic expectations means the expectations are set at levels that are fair, i.e., which follow from the guiding principles. It also means that the parties accept that they cannot anticipate everything; therefore, their expectations may not be met due to circumstances which none of the parties could realistically have foreseen. What they instead should expect is both parties collaborate on the situation, using the guiding principles.

In the example with the University, this means that the University should not be too fixed on its $2 million savings target. Equally, the supplier should not be too fixed on its $1 million margins.

Unrealistic expectations or a rigid focus on the initial business case create risks. If, for example, the University refuses to accept a price increase associated with the new minimum wage law, the supplier will feel this is unfair because it is out of the supplier's control. The supplier is likely to shade, especially if the University has a pattern of making decisions that the supplier perceives as unfair. It could, however, be equally unfair to let the buyer carry all the risk of the new minimum wage law. In this case, the parties may decide to split the risk. Neither is happy, but both view this as a fair decision. Of course, this will vary from case to case. The critical point is to use a relational contracting *What's In It For We* mindset or the parties will risk losing more on shading than what they gain from aligned interests.

## Ensure Contracting Clauses Are Fit for Purpose

As demonstrated in the University example, it is also important to ensure the other contract clauses (Pillar 3) are fit for the purpose. A quick review of a conventional transactional contract shows that many typical clauses found in transactional contracts are in breach of the guiding principles. Some examples are:

- One-way audit rights, key personnel clauses, and liability clauses which are in breach of reciprocity
- Scope sweeper clauses obliging the supplier to provide services without a right to compensation which are in breach of the equity principle
- Termination for convenience clauses giving one of the parties' discretionary power in the relationship which are in breach of the autonomy principle
- Limitation of liability clauses that fail to keep the risks for the relationship as a whole as low as possible which breaches the loyalty principle

While the clauses as drafted are typically in breach of the guiding principles, the *concept* of the clauses themselves is *not* in breach of the guiding principles. For example, it is appropriate for contracting parties to exit the relationship if needed.

The challenge? *How does one write contract clauses which best support the partnership?* To do this, one must use the guiding principles as a lens for drafting clauses that are fair, balanced, and aligned with the intent of the partnership.

Think about this: *What would it mean to align all of the clauses in a contract to the guiding principles?* It requires a change of one's mindset. From a *transactional viewpoint*, Pillar 3 clauses are written with a *"What's In It For Me?"* mindset, with lawyers choosing contract language to *protect the business case* for their organization. To adopt a *relational view* means viewing contract clauses through the lens of the guiding principles—in particular the principles of loyalty and equity. The loyalty principle means that all parties' interests should be treated as equally important and forces the parties to think of their relationship as if it was one virtual entity. Applying the loyalty principle obliges the parties to maximize the benefits and opportunities and minimize or optimize the costs and risks *for the partnership*. The equity principle complements the loyalty principle by obliging the parties to ensure a proportionate allocation of risks and opportunities.

Shifting to relational contracting also forces the parties to ask new questions. The initial question is not "how" these clauses should be worded differently. Instead, the question becomes "why" Pillar 3 clauses exist in the first place. Once one answers this question, it becomes easier to recast common contract clauses into relational contracting clauses.

Below, we consider three common clauses to show how each differs when looking through a transactional contracting lens versus a relational contracting lens.

## Scope Sweeper Clause

As discussed with the University, the purpose of including a scope sweeper clause is to protect the buyer's business case since any increased scope would lead to additional payment to the supplier. Of course, the supplier wants to avoid having a scope sweeper clause to protect their business case by mitigating potential losses.

The right question to ask is not which party should carry the risk of unknown or changed need of scope. Instead, the relevant questions to ask are questions such as:

- How can we together ensure that the "scope of the unknown" is minimized?
- What is a fair process both parties should use when there is a need for additional volumes, services, etc., over what was anticipated when signing the contract?

### *Ensuring the Risk of Unknown Scope Is Minimized*

The risk of unknown scope often haunts contracting parties. This is especially true in large infrastructure projects such as building bridges, schools, roads, and hospitals. Progressive construction contracts are using concepts such as "partnering" or "early contractor involvement" to deal with this problem.[7] Here, the buyer and the supplier jointly gather as much information and data as possible before signing the contract to minimize the unknown factors. This allows the parties to make plans with much higher predictability and therefore lower the risk premiums in the price.[8]

A similar concept has evolved in large outsourcing contracts where the buyer and supplier go through a "joint baselining" effort. However, here, the baseline is most often defined after the supplier is selected and is one of the first initiatives the buyer and supplier complete. Microsoft and Accenture successfully applied this technique when Microsoft outsourced their back-office financial operations which involved transferring work from both internal operations and myriad suppliers operating in Microsoft subsidiaries.

After the contract was signed, Microsoft and Accenture established a transition team that jointly set a baseline of the work as the work transitioned to Accenture.[9] Taking time to inventory the work as it transferred—and doing it together—enabled both parties to actually align on the scope of work.

The transparent and collaborative approach of the above methods minimizes the risk of scope disconnections and is aligned to the loyalty principle of lowering costs and risks for the partnership as a whole.

### Developing a Process to Deal with Unknown Scope When It Arises

While partnering and joint baselining can help ensure unknown scope is minimized, it should be expected that large and complex contracts may still be haunted by scope creep. For this reason it is essential to agree on a joint process the parties can use when scope creep does occur. The process should include how the parties will address the concern of who should carry the risk of unknown scope when it does happen. It is then essential to distinguish between unknown scope, which reasonably could have been discovered before signing the contract, and needs for additional scope arising after contract signing. With regard to the first kind of scope creep, the loyalty principle provides a simple rule: The party should carry the risk that, before signing, could have discovered the unknown scope at the lowest cost.[10] In practice, this means ensuring the party that will carry the risk be allowed the necessary time and access to validate the scope—something that is often glossed over in a rush to get to a signed deal.

Which party should carry the risk of those factors which none of the parties reasonably could have predicted? This will vary from case to case. What is important is that in a relational contract, the principle of equity should apply. Applying the equity principle means the party carrying the risk should be given a proportionate compensation (i.e., a transparent risk premium or a price discount) for taking the risk. In any case, such scope creep should be dealt with using the change control procedures described in the next chapter.

## Limitation of Liability Clause

The conventional approach to liability is to shift risk. The buyer's best option is to have unlimited liability for the supplier—or at least to have a very high cap. If the supplier causes damage, the buyer will only have risk above the cap. Having a cap helps the buyer create a more compelling business case. Of course, the supplier will want to have a low liability cap, trying to protect their profit margins as much as possible. Typically, the party with the most market power "wins" during the negotiation.

When looking through a relational contracting lens, the optimal question becomes how to collaborate to minimize the risk of the partnership as a whole. The parties change their mindset from shifting risk to jointly determining a process for continuous risk management where the parties regularly identify, classify, and jointly decide how to mitigate risks. This is done both at the beginning of the contracting process and as part of the ongoing governance after the contract is signed. The general rule of thumb is the party in the best position to mitigate the risk should take the responsibility to mitigate the risk.

But what if the parties face a situation where damage has occurred and the question of risk allocation arises? Once again, the loyalty principle provides guidance; the parties having the cheapest insurance policy covering the potential liability should assume the risk because this reduces the cost of mitigating the risk. Of course, it is not possible to buy insurance for certain types of risk. Here, the parties must turn to the equity principle, making sure that the party carrying the uninsured risks is compensated with proportionate potential rewards and/or a risk premium.

## Termination for Convenience Clause

It is common sense that longer-term contracts have a greater risk of having factors and assumptions change after signing the contract. For example, an organization might want to change its sourcing strategy altogether. Or it may be acquired and the new owners already work with a different supplier they wish to use. Or perhaps the supplier fails to invest in needed technology and their product offering falls behind. For these reasons and many others, buyers typically want a termination for convenience as it provides the greatest flexibility.

On the other hand, a supplier will want to include safeguards such as early out payments that protect any investments they have made (i.e., unrecouped transition costs, reimbursement for asset-specific investments made that cannot be used by other customers, etc.).

Is it possible to align a termination clause with the guiding principles? The answer is yes, but it depends on how the clause is drafted. For example, a termination of convenience clause allowing a buyer to terminate the contract with a 60 day written notice, yet does not compensate the supplier for investments made, would be in breach of the equity principle. Also, a termination of convenience may easily be used to exercise power over the other party in breach of the autonomy principle.

If termination of convenience is not appropriate, then what is?

First, it is important to recognize there are situations where it is appropriate to terminate a contract early. Once again, consider the University example. The University contracted for outsourced facilities management and dining services and all was going well. However, the new state governor requested the state procurement team to look for ways to lower state-wide costs for the top five spend categories—one being facilities management. The state-wide procurement team developed a business case, showing if the state could create a state-wide contract spanning across the fifty-plus universities and community colleges, the cost savings would be significant. A competitive bid event reinforced the cost savings projections to be realistic. The state procurement agency asked each of the state's various university and community colleges to "opt-in" to the new state-wide contracting vehicle. Looking at a termination clause through the lens of transparency and using the loyalty principle, an analysis might reveal that it would cost the buyer more to remain in the contract than what the supplier would lose if the contract is terminated.

Situations like the above are real and should be contemplated. However, the parties should adopt a *termination for justified reason* clause instead of a conventional termination of convenience clause. The parties can then specify under what justified conditions the contract can be terminated early. Also, the exit provisions should align with the guiding principles. For example, the parties would turn to the reciprocity principle creating bilateral termination rights for both the buyer and the supplier. Using the loyalty principle, the parties would agree on an appropriate off-ramp period allowing ample time and support for the parties to unwind their relationships. This may or may not be symmetrical based on the dependency and ease of unwinding the relationship. Last, the termination provisions would turn to the equity principle and allow the supplier to recoup any asset-specific investments that had not yet received a full return on investment.

These examples provide an overview of how to rethink three clauses using a relational contracting perspective. Using the guiding principles forces the parties to adopt a fresh view on some common contractual clauses, shifting from using market or state power to working together to come up with more fair and balanced contract clauses that are more fit for purpose. A key benefit? Both parties align on more realistic expectations which ultimately reduce shading after the contract is signed.

It is important to understand that there is seldom one "right" answer or solution when it comes to clauses such as the ones discussed above. What would be an unfair liability clause in one contract could be compatible with the guiding principles in another. This is partly because it is necessary to always look at the total risk allocation in the contract when assessing its overall fairness. It is also because the *process* of agreeing on a particular clause—aided by using the guiding principles—is as important for a clause's fairness as its actual content.

## Why Should You Do It?

Having adopted the Guiding Principles in Step 3, it is tempting to ask more provocative questions such as

(1) Why even add more concrete contract language if the Statement of Intent with the Guiding Principles serves as the de facto constitution for the relationship? Why can't the Statement of Intent and Guiding Principles simply be all that is needed?
(2) Why must contract clauses align with the Guiding Principles?

Let's explore both questions.

## Why Have Concrete Contract Language?

The examples above show the guiding principles provide solutions to deal with the most difficult situations that the parties may face in the deal, such as unexpected scope increase, damaging events, a need to prematurely terminate the contract, and others. So why bother adding more clauses to the contract?

One might ask, "Why continue from there? Why add more contract language with specific clauses? Will there be sufficient understanding for the parties to simply use the guiding principles?"

The question may seem out of touch with reality since most organizations would not consider just applying the guiding principles without having at least some reference to mainstay contract clauses like termination and liability. Nevertheless, it is still an important question to ask. Answering this question requires going to the very reasons why contracts are entered into in the first place. As covered in Part II of the book, Professor Oliver Hart has provided two complementary answers to this question. First, contracts are written to avoid the hold-up problem, (i.e., a situation where the parties opportunistically abuse each other's dependency to extract or extort value from the other party after the contract has been signed). In theory, this problem could be avoided by applying the guiding principles. To (ab)use the other party's dependency to extract value would be in breach of the principle of autonomy and it would be possible to craft clear enough contract language to deal with the hold-up problem.

Being satisfied with only the guiding principles would, however, not completely address the second reason of why. According to Hart, contracts also fulfill the essential function of clarifying the parties' expectations of each other—getting them on the same page. In this respect, the contract becomes a reference point for their expected gains from the relationship (Chapter 1). If unexpected events occur causing expectations not to be met, the negatively-affected organization will likely shade (i.e., consciously or unconsciously withdraw cooperation) if the other party is unfair in how they solve the matter.

To apply only the guiding principles would be to write a contract open to a lot of interpretation. Simply put, it would be too flexible; significant ambiguity could lead to misaligned views and therefore shading. As such, it is important to write a contract with a balance between too rigid and too flexible a contract. This means having a formal relational contract that relies on both the guiding principles *and* written contract clauses.

Oliver Hart and his co-author John Moore pointed to the balancing act between rigidity and flexibility in the contract when setting expectations during the contracting process.[11] A flexible contract is ideally preferable since it gives the parties the freedom to find more mutually beneficial solutions within their contract. But unfortunately, humans suffer from the *self-serving bias*—meaning they interpret things and events to their advantage. Simply put, people interpret factors to favor their situation. What Hart and Moore predicted—which has proven to be accurate beyond their research—is that if an unexpected event occurs for a party in a flexible contract, the self-serving bias will tend to make people feel entitled, to and therefore expect a larger share of the pie, or if something bad has happened, a smaller share of the loss. But since *both* parties will suffer from the self-serving bias, their expectations will be misaligned, which may lead to shading.

Contrast this with a contract with minimal wording. Here, the parties have the greatest flexibility. However, Hart and Moore argue this creates a trap for one or both parties to be unfair (or at least perceived as being unfair). For example, if a contract does not provide for a specific response to a cost increase in the market but only states that the parties shall negotiate in good faith, the self-serving bias will easily lead to a situation where both parties will feel that *the other* party shall bear the cost increase or a least a larger part of it. The result is that one or both parties will typically not want to meet the other party's expectations. If the weaker party feels they are forced to bear the cost of the increase, they will perceive this to be unfair and, consequently, they will feel aggrieved and shade.

Simply put, a contract only based on the guiding principles may be *too flexible*, leaving too much room for different interpretations, failed expectations, and therefore risks of shading.

The dilemma is how does a contracting professional write a contract that strikes a good balance between flexibility and rigidity? Where should the line be drawn? If Goldilocks—from the children's fairy tale "Goldilocks and the Three Bears"—were a contracting professional which contracting approach would she select? When should the pen be laid down?

There is no clear answer. We use a rule of thumb for contracting professionals to be specific on matters which have the highest risk of leading to conflicts of interest. This typically calls for Pillar 3 clauses, as referenced in Fig. 15.2, to be very integrated with the deal. However, what these clauses are and how they are worded will vary from case to case. Typically, it is important to include formal contract language for clauses such as term, termination rights, contract breaches, and consequences of those and similar clauses. Also, the parties need to be clear in establishing the rules for governing the relationship (Step 5—discussed in the next chapter).

## Why Do Contract Clauses Need to Align with the Guiding Principles?

The second question is why must contract clauses always be aligned with the guiding principles. The answer to this question should be obvious but deserves discussion.

A leading reason to align contract clauses with the guiding principles is to avoid contradictions in the contract. If the parties on one hand say to each other that they shall follow the guiding principles but on the other hand, have rights and obligations in the written clauses not aligned with those principles, then which shall prevail? The guiding principles or the clauses?

This problem can rather easily be solved by simply stating in the contract that the more concrete clauses shall prevail. However, such a resolution could sub-optimize the contracted value. The primary reason for aligning contract clauses with the guiding principles is *to avoid shading*, and thereby to avoid losses and other risks. Let's revisit the University outsourcing contract. The parties adopted the autonomy principle, but the University's lawyer asked for a scope sweeper clause anyway. The supplier reluctantly agreed because they feared they would lose the contract if they did not agree. This very act of forcing a clause incongruent with the guiding principles into the contract will diminish the supplier's trust in the University's commitment to the guiding principles.[12]

Also, consider what can happen after the contract is signed. If a need for additional service is discovered after the contract is signed, the supplier has a choice to make. They can either accept the new scope which will reduce their profit or ask the University to discuss the situation in light of the guiding principles. If the University points to the black and white letter of the contract saying the clause prevails over the guiding principles, the supplier will be disappointed and is likely to shade.

Thus, a contractual solution stating the clauses prevail over the guiding principles will not prevent shading. And, where a relational contract is a good fit where there is medium to high dependency and risk between the parties, avoidance of shading is the main reason for having a written contract in the first place. Anyone thinking about using a contract not aligned to the guiding principles should therefore carefully think again.

## From Theory to Practice

As stated throughout this book, a relational contract should be written as a flexible framework. The foundation of the framework is the Shared Vision, Strategic Objectives, and Guiding Principles which should rarely change over the term of the agreement. Within the framework lies the specific deal points and other contractual clauses that best support the parties to achieve the Shared Vision and Strategic Objectives.

But how do organizations transition from traditional contract clauses to relational contract clauses? The answer is simple; it starts with getting the right people in the room having the right discussions. With Island Health and the Hospitalists, it meant creating a cross-functional Deal Architect Team challenged to rethink their contract.

Courtney Peereboom was chosen as the lead from the Administrators and Dr. Jean Maskey volunteered to take on the lead role from the Hospitalists. Peereboom and Maskey were joined by four more Administrators and four Hospitalists. Also, each organization brought in an outside counsel to assist the team in translating their intentions into the physical contract. With the team in place, they set out to have scheduled working group meetings where they would hammer out their Vested labor service agreement. The parties engaged a neutral Certified Deal Architect specializing in win-win contracting to facilitate key workshops.

Having a Deal Architect Team set the tone that the relationship would drive the contract. The team built on the relationship by establishing both formal and informal "two-in-a-box" buddy roles chartered to develop certain aspects of the deal. In addition to working on specific deal points, the two-in-a-box team members set out to further build stronger relationships between the Administrators and Hospitalists.

Dr. Ken Smith was buddied with Catherine Mackay, Executive Vice President & Chief Operating Officer. Mackay had a nursing background and was interested to learn more about clinical aspects of what the Hospitalists did so she asked Dr. Smith if she could shadow him for a shift. At first, Ken was apprehensive. But then thought to himself, "that is the old way of thinking." Dr. Smith recalls Mackay followed him around all day and had great questions. "She was intrigued, and we discussed how Hospitalists are positively affecting patient care." Kim Kerrone could sense the energy Mackay had after the day she shadowed Ken. "She became a big champion of the Hospitalists and helping them work through operational issues to be more effective became a priority."

Kim Kerrone's formal "two-in-a-box" partner in the Deal Architect Team was Dr. Spencer Cleave, MD, CCFP. The duo was chartered with what all felt was likely the greatest challenge—developing a new solution for how they would rethink the pricing model for the relationship. Historically, doctors are paid on a very transactional basis. Kerrone and Dr. Cleave addressed the elephant in the room early. "We only have so much money given the nature of our world, so we have to figure out ways to work with the money we've got. Spencer and I set out to develop the funding model – *together.*"

Peereboom reflected on how the Deal Architect Team had to approach the pricing model given the budgetary process and constraints of the British Columbia governmental environment. "We had to figure out a way to get to a place where we both win-win but where the funding model would still meet all of the government rules." She continued, "We really had to think outside the box and explain to the Hospitalists some of our realities related to needing to comply with regulations, along with some of the other funding pressures and difficult decisions we make as Administrators. I think the more we talked and they got to understand our environment and we got to understand their needs, we were able to get to a better place. Sometimes they were difficult conversations that required many meetings."

Dr. Maskey points to the Statement of Intent as a key success factor in helping them shift to relational contracting and putting the concept into the contract clauses. "Courtney and I realized many, many times as we worked on the details of the contract together that the real 'gold' spun out of all of the work and the words that we put together to form the contract was the process and the resulting relationships. During the workshops with the Deal Architect Team, we often referred to the Shared Vision, Guiding Principles, and Intended Behaviors that were developed at the first three-day workshop with the full team, especially during difficult conversations where people might fall back into their old 'us versus them' mindset."

With the Deal Architect Team in place and individual and enterprise relationships fostering, the team found themselves shifting away from the acrimonious "contract negotiations" stance and leaning into how they could draft a contract that would best support their Statement of Intent. Dr. Maskey shares it was refreshing. "There was a trusting atmosphere and conversation, as opposed to the experience with all other contract negotiations, which usually fell apart at this stage."

The Deal Architect Team ultimately created a pricing model with both a fixed and variable component that the Administrators and the Hospitalists manage together.

Having a fixed component sent a strong signal to the Hospitalists. First, the Hospitalists had job security and trusted that the goal was not to eliminate their jobs but to work within the budget. Second, it gave them the autonomy they desired to manage their schedule.

Kerrone explains: "The underlying premise is the Hospitalists are the experts, and they know the patient care required. As such, they figure out their own patient load and do their own schedule to manage within the money that we have. It is also based on an annual amount, so there is flexibility throughout the year to manage their total hours; they can 'save' some hours in the slower summer months and bank them for the busier winter season."

The contract also allowed the Hospitalists to earn incentives. The first incentive stemmed from the variable side of the compensation package. For example, Hospitalists can earn incentives if they can optimize scheduling and "save" variable hours through improved allocation of shifts or hours. Hospitalists can also earn incentives when they help improve billing.

The results were a win-win. Kim Kerrone shares her pride: "The Hospitalists have their allocation, they know what it is, they have a budget and they manage it. It just works. And last year they came in under budget. It was awesome!" That level of collaboration and innovation was unheard of and impossible in previous iterations of contracts and the relationship.

# Tips and Tools for Getting Started

A contract is commonly negotiated in two parallel negotiations—one with the businesspeople negotiating Pillars 1 and 2 and the lawyers negotiating the Pillar 3 clauses. But this is a flawed view, as seen in the example scope sweeper, liability, and termination for convenience clauses noted above. The way a clause is drafted can have a significant negative impact on the parties' ability to achieve their Statement of Intent. For this reason, we recommend having lawyers and businesspeople working together in an integrated fashion when architecting the contract such as with Island Heath and the Hospitalists. Doing so helps ensure that the lawyers understand the intent of the relationship and increases the likelihood contract clauses are effectively designed to support the parties' shared vision and strategic objectives in a fair and balanced manner.

As one begins to architect their contract clauses, the following four-step process will help in crafting the relational contracting clauses.

## Pre-work

- Get a copy of your existing contract (or one of your organization's standard contract templates).

## Step 1: Pick a Contract Clause You Want to Recast as a Relational Contracting Clause

For ilustrative purposes we have chosen the below clasue.

> *The supplier undertakes to perform all its obligations with personnel who are suitable, qualified, and competent for the required purposes, and with sufficient resources to fulfill its obligations under the Agreement and to treat the Customer as a prioritized customer.*

## Step 2: Complete an Analysis Asking the Following Questions, Writing Your Answers

Fig. 15.3 illustrates how the contract clause is analyzed.

| What is the overall purpose of the clause? | To regulate Supplier's obligations regarding the quality of personnel end to prioritize Customer. |
|---|---|
| What risks are addressed in the clause? | Too low quality because of insufficiently skilled or knowledgeable personnel. Poor performance because of under-prioritization by Supplier. |
| Alignment with Guiding Principles: | *Reciprocity*: The customer does not reciprocally commit to ensuring that the retained organization is skilled enough. |
| Is the clause aligned to the Guiding Principles | If the answer to 3. is *no*, how should it be written to ensure alignment? |

**Fig. 15.3** Example of a contract clause analysis

## Step 3: Discuss How You Should Re-Write This Clause for a Relational Contract

Below is an example of how this clause can be re-written to a relational contracting clause which aligns with the reciprocity guiding principle.

*The parties will undertake to perform all their obligations with personnel who are suitable, qualified, and competent for the required purposes, equipped with sufficient resources to fulfill their obligations under the Agreement.*

## Step 4: Repeat Steps 1–3 for Each Clause

### Contract Work

Once you have an agreement on key deal points, you will need to translate them into the actual contract clauses.

# A Look Ahead

Once the parties have successfully architected the deal points to align interests and expectations, it will be time to move on to Step 5—Stay Aligned.

# Notes

1. Jeanette Nyden, Kate Vitasek and David Frydlinger, *Getting to We: Negotiating Agreements for Highly Collaborative Relationships* (New York: Palgrave Macmillan, 2013), pp. 123–134.

2. The Association for Higher Education Facilities Officers (APPA Institute) has created standards for facilities management that are graded by a sliding scale from Level 1 to 5 where Level 1 is the highest standards of cleaning service and Level 5 is the lowest. Each level is defined by a range of tasks and their frequency. The cleaning levels are as follows: Level 1 Orderly Spotlessness, Level 2 Ordinary Tidiness, Level 3 Casual Inattention, Level 4 Moderate Dinginess, Level 5 Unkempt Neglect?

3. For more on shading, see Part I of this book.

4. B. Keith, K. Vitasek, K. Manrodt, J. Kling, *Strategic Sourcing in the New Economy: Harnessing the Potential of Sourcing Business Models for Modern Procurement* (New York: Palgrave Macmillan, 2016).

5. Ibid.

6. Ibid.

7. These approaches are helpful but fall short. A problem with these approaches is that after the discovery phase, which is often carried out collaboratively, the rest of the relationship is regulated by a transactional contract, which often results in the kinds of problems and shading behaviors predicted when a transactional contract is used when a relational contract is a good fit.

8. Kate Vitasek and Karl Manrodt, with Jeanne Kling, *Vested: How P&G, McDonald's, and Microsoft are Redefining Winning in Business Relationships* (New York: Palgrave Macmillan, 2012).

9. To be clear, the early contractor involvement process should not be mistaken for a relational contract. Unfortunately, the parties use a transactional contract in the building phase of the project and thus often have to face problems when the still always existing unknown factors appear.

10. Readers familiar with law and economics literature will recognize this as the principle of the cheapest cost avoider (see, for example, S. Gilles, "Negligence, Strict liability and the Cheapest Cost Avoider," *Virginia Law Review*, Vol. 78, No. 6 (September 1992), pp. 1291–1375).

11. Oliver Hart, John Moore, "Contracts as Reference Points," *NBER Working Paper No. 12706* November 2006, revised 2007.

12. Erlei, Mathias and Reinhold, Christian, 2016. "Contracts as Reference Points—The Role of Reciprocity Effects and signaling Effects," *Journal of Economic Behavior & Organization*, Elsevier, vol. 127(C) (2016), pp. 133–145.

# 16

## Step 5: Stay Aligned

Steps 1–4 in the relational contracting process get the parties to a fair and balanced contract. Step 5 helps the parties stay aligned. A key part of staying aligned is for contracting parties to openly accept that complete planning is impossible. Rather, they develop and follow a governance structure specifically designed to manage change and uncertainty to stay in continual alignment (Fig. 16.1).

This chapter goes into detail about how to put Step 5 into practice. We explain what it means and why it is essential. We then provide real examples of how to turn the theory into practice. The chapter ends with tips and tools for putting Step 5 into practice.

## What Does It Mean?

In a relational contract, the glue that binds the relationship and contract together is a governance framework which the parties use to jointly manage the relationship post-contract signing. Well-designed governance mechanisms enable the parties to address the dynamic nature of the business—both for today and the future. Implemented good governance keeps parties' interests and expectations aligned throughout the life of the agreement.

Unfortunately, many organizations—especially those representing "buy-side" organizations in buyer-supplier agreements—view contract governance more from the standpoint of "compliance" to the original contract. In this

© The Author(s), under exclusive license to Springer Nature Switzerland AG 2021
D. Frydlinger et al., *Contracting in the New Economy*,
https://doi.org/10.1007/978-3-030-65099-5_16

| DIMENSION | TRANSACTIONAL CONTRACT | | RELATIONAL CONTRACT |
|---|---|---|---|
| FOCUS | The commercial transactions | → | The commercial relationship |
| RELATIONSHIP | Arms-length relationship | → | Partnership |
| SOCIAL NORMS | Disconnected from social norms | → | Mutually discovered and agreed social norms are explicitly included as contractual obligations |
| PRIMARY RISK MITIGATION MECHANISMS | Risk mitigation by use of market power and state power | → | Risk mitigation and avoidance by creation of continuous alignment of interest |
| PLANNING | Aims for completeness, i.e. tries to have contract clauses covering all future events of the relationship | → | Accepts that complete planning is not possible and aims to create a fair and flexible framework for managing change and uncertainty |

**Fig. 16.1** Staying Aligned

regard, governance is approached from one party having oversight of control over the other.

Research by the European academics Florian Moslein, Humboldt University of Berlin, and Karl Riesenhuber, Ruhr University in Bochum, Germany, suggests that the time organizations spend on corporate and agreement governance is a critical component toward achieving its goals.[1] This is especially true when service providers play vital roles as key extensions of a firm's capabilities. Moslein and Riesenhuber's work points to a weakness in agreement governance: the lack of a generally accepted definition of the term *governance*. To make matters worse, Moslein and Riesenhuber note that governance structures typically are customized to the scale and scope of the work. This poses a dilemma: How can you define what a governance structure is when there is a moving target on what you are governing?

The question is one the University of Tennessee has been studying for almost twenty years. An excellent place to begin is to define *governance*. First, using the Webster Dictionary, let us look at the definitions of *govern* to help gain clarity around what governance means.[2]

*Govern (verb)*

(a) *to exercise continuous sovereign authority over, especially: to control and direct the making and administration of policy in*
(b) *to rule without sovereign power and usually without having the authority to determine basic policy*

(c)  *to prevail or have decisive influence*

The UT research into some of the world's most successful business partnerships shows organizations adopt an insight—versus oversight—governance philosophy. The governance structures studied were collaborative versus controlling in nature, which follows the guiding principle of autonomy. For example, in buyer-supplier relationships, the focus shifted from managing the supplier to managing the business with the supplier. UT's research uncovered many good governance practices designed to help business partners make proactive changes to reach the parties' shared vision and objectives.[3]

As a general rule, a good governance structure provides a framework and guidance on the necessary mechanisms for decision making, renegotiation, and modification as circumstances change. We propose the following eight governance design principles for formal relational contracts (Fig. 16.2).

Once the parties have designed their governance structure, they should incorporate governance into their actual agreement—referencing a contractual commitment to governance. Often this is a contractual schedule where the parties document the "playbook" which they will follow. This playbook should be underpinned by the parties' Statement of Intent, which includes their Shared Vision and Guiding Principles. When business circumstances create a situation that puts tension on the relations—whether large or small—the parties should use their governance structure and their Statement of Intent to help them through making the most appropriate decisions.

## Why Should You Do It?

There are several compelling and closely related reasons to embed a robust governance structure and supporting governance processes in the relational contract. Remember that one of the primary purposes of a relational contract is to keep the parties' interests and expectations *continuously* aligned. The problem is that it is impossible to write a contract that plans for all contingencies that can create misalignment during the term of the contract. As we have frequently repeated, a fundamental premise of all complex contracts is that they are incomplete. Things will be missed when architecting the contract and unexpected events will occur. Governance is a key mechanism to deal with the challenges of contractual incompleteness. Governance will assist the parties in ensuring that they frequently communicate, align their views, update their plans, check their progress toward the shared vision and objectives, and control that their interests do not start to diverge. In the end

| Design Principle | What this Design Principle Does |
|---|---|
| Separate "Key" Roles | The best organizations view their relationship through more than just the day-to-day operations by creating formal roles/job descriptions to focus on four key aspects of a relationship:<br>1) Relationship Manager(s) who manage the overall relationship,<br>2) Commercial Manager(s) who proactively work to keep the contract in alignment with the business needs,<br>3) Transformation Manager(s) (for relationships where there is a significant focus on transformation/innovation),<br>4) Operation Manager(s) who focus on day-to-day operations. |
| Tiers | A tiered structure provides a formal structure to manage the relationship at multiple levels. Larger deals typically use a three-tier governance structure (operations, management, and strategic levels) |
| Peer-to-Peer Communications (Two-in-a-Box) | "Two-in-a-Box" communications is a contemporary management technique that seeks to eliminate hierarchies and provide more streamlined communications. Individuals with similar roles at different organizations are teamed and encouraged to have direct communications. |
| Cadence | The cadence establishes the formal rhythm of the business. For example, in a three-tier governance structure the operations level may meet weekly, the management level meets monthly and the strategic level meets in a formal Quarterly Business Review. |
| Issue Resolution | Formal mechanisms the parties use to raise and solve issues. The best practice is to create an issue resolution process that leverages Two-in-a-Box problem-solving at the lowest level and the tiered structure. |
| Continuity of Resources/Key Personnel | Creates formal processes and mechanisms the parties agree to for replacing key personnel. Often this is done with a bi-lateral "key personnel" clause for the "key" personnel designated in the most senior separate roles noted above. |
| Onboarding | Creates formal processes and mechanisms for ramping up new team members working under the scope of the partnership. Onboarding is especially essential for Key Personnel. The level and onboarding details are typically tailored to the level/role. |
| Relationship Management Mechanisms | Creates formal processes and mechanisms which the parties deem as essential for managing the relationship. For example, in an outsourcing relationship creating the joint budgeting process, and other mechanism is how the parties will measure and monitor relationship health. |

**Fig. 16.2** Governance Design Principles

continuous communication is the only way to avoid misaligned expectations and the shading that may occur.

By having governance mechanisms in place, the parties will go far in preventing and dealing with misalignments. By meeting and communicating frequently, the parties will develop informal relationships and ties—i.e., *informal relational contracts*—as described, for example, in repeated game theory (refer to Chapter 5).

But often, this will not be enough to ensure alignment. This is another place where guiding principles come in. The governance structure and processes ensure that the guiding principles are kept alive in the relationship.

Legal scholar Ian Macneil taught that agreements could be "governed efficiently only if the parties adopt a consciously cooperative attitude."[4] Creating a governance structure based on the guiding principles takes the concept of Macneil's "consciously cooperative attitude" and puts it into practice. A leading practices is to start every governance meeting by reminding all participants of the guiding principles, and by referring back to them during discussions, so they are kept top of mind and re-activated. This ensures, which is critical, that the commercial deal is kept embedded in the parties' social relationship. Without governance in place, this would not be possible and the relationship will risk derailing.

Following the guiding principles when *changing* the contract is also an essential part of living into the guiding principles as part of the parties' governance of their relationship. As with the process of architecting the deal, the guiding principles will help the parties ensure their joint activities and decisions are aligned with the governance structure, e.g., when resolving issues and problems as well as managing change with stakeholders and mitigating risks.

We hope it is clear that skipping or short-cutting on governance would be a huge mistake, creating a severe risk that the relationship and the commercial deal will fail. It may be tempting to skip a governance meeting if everything is going smoothly in the relationship and business is good. Take, for example, Dell and FedEx, whose relational contract was profiled in *Harvard Business Review* and is part of a more extensive teaching case study by the University of Tennessee. Dell's Rob McIntosh referred to results attributed to restructuring the Dell-FedEx contract as a "fairy tale story" in a video with *SupplyChainBrain* magazine.[5] However, after the first few years, senior executives felt things were going so well; they stopped attending regular governance meetings. Quarterly business reviews slipped to biannual and then even less frequent. Robert McIntosh, now Dell's Senior Vice President, Dell Global Fulfillment, Logistics and Trade, explains, "Everything was going really well under the Vested agreement, and it was easy to take our eye off the ball. But this is a good lesson learned. Just because your car's running right doesn't mean it doesn't need maintenance."[6] In short, Dell and FedEx fell victim to the strategic drift ailment.

The Dell-FedEx example shows the importance of keeping up the discipline of good governance. But how do you get people to live into their intentions and follow the governance mechanisms you have carefully designed? A key part of motivating people to adhere to governance is helping team members understand *why* governance is essential.[7]

This means helping team members—especially executives—understand a key reason why things are going so smoothly, and *applying* the What's In It For We? mindset and governance mechanisms to ensure continued success. Simply put, a condition for success is through continual alignment using the parties' governance mechanisms—in essence living into the agreement.

## From Theory to Practice

As we have learned in this chapter, staying aligned requires the parties to agree to formal governance mechanisms embedded in the relationship. The parties will use these governance mechanisms well after the contract is signed to keep their interests and expectations aligned. This is backed by the parties' Statement of Intent, with the Guiding Principles helping the parties prevent falling into struggles based on relative bargaining strength when circumstances change. Combined, the governance structure and Statement of Intent ensure the parties stay true to the spirit of their relationship. More importantly, it ensures the parties' real deal is always in synch with the parties' paper deal.

Janet Grove, the legal counsel for Island Health, explained how the governance mechanisms differ from conventional agreements. "The contract sets the Shared Vision and the Guiding Principles upfront. As such, you see more decisions referred to that are trusted to the governance framework than in a normal contract. There is a recognition that things will evolve and how you manage the evolution is entrusted to a framework."

Let's take a closer look at how Island Health and the Hospitalists jointly developed the governance framework and mechanisms for their relationship, promoting transparency and joint governance mechanisms designed to propel the parties toward their shared vision and desired outcomes. For example, one of the key design principles is a tiered reporting structure that supports managing the agreement throughout its term (see Fig. 16.3).

The governance structure includes an Operations Team where the focus is on managing day-to-day operations. This team meets frequently, based on the business needs at hand. The Operations Team reports to the Governance Team. The Governance Team consists of four separate teams that focus on various aspects of the relationship.

Finally, the Governance Team reports to the Core Steering Team, which meets every six months. Specific project teams help implement improvement initiatives designed to help the parties achieve their joint desired outcomes. The teams are designed in a "Two-in-a-Box" fashion with Administrators and

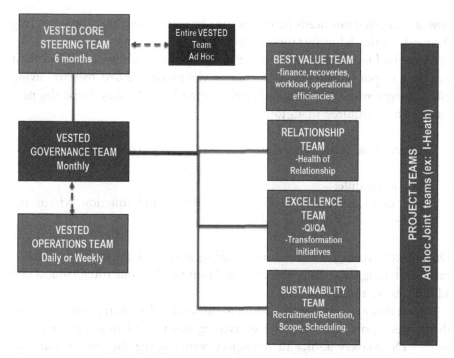

**Fig. 16.3** Three-Tier Governance Structure

Hospitalists sitting side-by-side on each team, with common objectives. Each of the four governance teams has two-in-a-box co-chairs and is augmented by subject matter experts from both the Administrators and Hospitalists to focus on how to best achieve the desired outcomes assigned to their team. For example, the Best Value Team is co-chaired by Dr. Tyler Cheek, and Courtney Peereboom and meets the first Wednesday of every month. Six subject matter experts from within the Administrator and Hospitalist groups join Dr. Cheek and Peereboom as they work through the budget and the data, and analyze the hours required by the Hospitalists.

While each governance tier and the team has a specific focus, all have a common focus to "live the intentions of the Vested Shared Vision." Also, the Island Health Hospitalists governance structure applies the design principle of having clear roles that separate relationship management, operations management, transformation management, and financial/contractual management aspects of governance.

Dr. Smith comments, "We now have a framework on how we're going to distribute the work of getting things done. We have timelines and teams who are responsible, and sometimes there are even smaller subcommittees to get certain projects worked on or done. And so it now is much more organized. It now is answering our needs better for the physician group and also answering the needs of the Administration far better."

Once the Deal Architect Team had designed the governance framework, it was time to put it into place. In essence, the parties needed to start "living into the agreement." Courtney Peereboom and Dr. Maskey faced the next hurdle which required them to:

- Populate these teams with equal numbers of Hospitalists and Administrators;
- Set up a schedule;
- Get a time and cadence of meetings that could function within the complex schedule of a hospital system.

Dr. Maskey recalls. "I remember thinking it seemed impossible we could manage staffing these committees in addition to all of our usual clinical and administrative responsibilities."

It took almost a year for the parties to institutionalize their governance, but the parties report "one year later everything was up and running like clockwork." Dr. Maskey adds, "In retrospect, working together to facilitate the quick development and stability of the governance teams allowed us to build on the momentum. This strengthened the resolve to make this new way of business' stick,' as the responsibilities of each team required this collaborative work."

Dr. Ken Smith appreciates the benefits of the new governance structure. "The positive thing about the Vested relational contract concept is that it's an ongoing work in progress that you have to manage every day. Most contracts get signed and then you talk to each other in two or three years. Misperceptions and animosity or whatever can grow with that in time. In this contract the two sides are constantly meeting and talking about things, which I think it's like any good marriage or relationship – it's essential."

Dr. Smith sits on two of the committees—the Governance Team and the Best Value Team. He notes that the initial six to eight months of living in the agreement were literally "just trying to get a handle on watching how we were doing." For example, he said one of the Best Value initiatives was finding better ways to monitor based on pay periods: "How many physician hours we were using, and what the patient census was doing. Were we under budget or over budget, so we had a real sense from our ongoing live perspective how we were doing based on the global budget that we have. Before, our statistics were poorly understood by the Hospitalists ourselves, and not understood or accepted from the administrative viewpoint. Now we have a mutual platform for data collection and how we interpret it and understand it; it continues to develop and morph to try and capture some of the things we were doing that weren't captured before like inpatient hospital consults for various specialist colleagues. It's given us a mutual understanding of how we're doing the scheduling and we've put in some new scheduling. It gives us all reassurance that we know if we follow that pattern we're good; it gives the Administrators the sense that the Hospitalists are following the very sort of regimented guidelines before we use more resources so that they're being used in the most efficient manner."

A crucial role of the teams is to help the parties transform their intentions into practice. This includes using the Guiding Principles to make sound decisions when they face misaligned interests. Dr. Maskey gives an example of how this works: "When we get stuck and find ourselves starting to slip into old negotiation behaviors, we pull out the Guiding Principles. When we start to look at problems through the broader lens of our intentions, it always helps us get unstuck." The Hospitalists realize there is a specific approach in discussing different aspects of the contractual relationship and fulfillment issues. Those involved in these teams have observed that everyone now knows each other; even difficult conversations can occur effectively and are productive. The documentation aspect of those conversations has also changed. This new culture and set of standard operating procedures embrace documentation as a means to generate further value for both parties, rather than as a potential weapon in the dispute resolution process.

Let's look at an example of how the parties worked through the significant changes resulting from COVID-19.

The pandemic hit the healthcare industry particularly hard and one could expect tensions to run high in the face of uncertainties and change. We interviewed the Island Health-Hospitalist team to see how they fared in the wake of the pandemic. Specifically, were they living into the intentions and guiding principles they put in place as part of their formal relational contract? And did the relational mechanisms they established in their contract help them fairly and flexibly work through the many issues raised by the pandemic?

Kim Kerrone (Island Health's Vice President for finance, legal, and risk) explains the situation. "When the pandemic hit we were suddenly faced with a 60% reduction in overall patient census on the one hand - yet on the other hand physicians needed to manage higher-risk COVID patients. The impact on budget and workload and was drastic: physicians treated far fewer, yet higher-risk patients. Questions such as who would get to work what hours and who would have to work in the new high-risk COVID ward were front and center."

Dr. Jean Maskey (SIHI Hospitalist) explains how the parties' formal relational contract helped them be ready to address the changes in a fair and flexible manner: "Our Vested relational contract uses Guiding Principles such as autonomy and equity. Using these Guiding Principles as the backdrop for decisions, we found an effective way to rethink schedule allocations to reduce Hospitalist hours while keeping all physicians employed. Part of the process also 'banked' hours which can be used for future surges. Without our Vested relational contract, this would have been arduous under the old contract."

## Tips and Tools for Getting Started

There is no singular or absolute "right" governance framework. Instead, contracting parties use the eight design principles (refer to Fig. 16.2 shown earlier) and create a best-fit governance framework to meet the complexity and unique factors of the relationship. For example, Microsoft and Accenture's governance structure for managing the OneFinance outsourcing relationship which now spans 116 subsidiaries around the world which differs vastly from Island Health and the Hospitalists who have team members that—while working in different buildings—are in the same city. Likewise, governance in a buyer-supplier relationship will differ vastly from an investment-based relationship, such as a joint venture, a public-private partnership, or an alliance partnership.

The good news is there are proven governance design principles for creating a sound governance framework. You can use the below tips and tools to help you create your governance structure.

### Pre-work

Research whether the industry or deal type has established governance best practices. For example, a simple Google search of "franchise governance best practices" reveals numerous resources. Also, use Fig. 16.2 shown earlier in this chapter, which points to eight proven governance design principles.[8]

### Step 1: Review the Definitions

As a group, review the purpose and high-level best practices associated with the governance design principles. Discuss which ones should apply in the relationship. If one should not apply, why? How should each design principle be customized for the relationship?

## Step 2: Design Your Governance

 Work through each design principle to design a governance framework. If the research reveals known best practices, the parties need to factor these into their decisions, ensuring the recommendation is in harmony with the Guiding Principles. For example, if research reveals power-based approaches that would violate the autonomy principle, these should be not be considered as a best practice.

### Separate Roles

- What roles are needed to support your Shared Vision and Strategic Objectives for your relationship? Common roles are:
  - Relationship management
  - Operations management
  - Commercial and contract management
  - Transformation management (for highly strategic relationships where transformation and innovation are an essential component to achieve the Shared Vision and Strategic Objectives)
  - Unique subject matter roles. For example, in a large pharmaceutical supply chain outsourcing relationship the parties had a Two-in-the-Box role for regulatory compliance management due to the unique need to manage significant government regulations associated with the distribution and storage of various pharmaceutical products
- Document the responsibilities for each of the roles

> **Tip!** *It is very common to understaff your governance structure. We highly recommend that large and complex relationships have at least three full-time individuals for each party that govern the relationship. For example, Microsoft and Accenture's OneFinance relationship has sixteen full-time people as part of the core governance team (eight from each company).*

### Tiered Structure

The governance structure should include "tiers," with each tier having specific responsibilities for managing different aspects of the business. The parties should determine what tiers they need. This structure creates vertical alignment among upper management, middle management, and day-to-day workforce—as well as alignment across the contracting parties.

Each layer is accountable for examining the relationship and business success from its viewpoint and ensuring that the relationship is focused on the strategic, transformational, and tactical elements of managing the business.

As one completes this exercise, think through how the governing bodies will interact and how the separate key roles for service delivery, transformation, commercial management, and relationship management "map" into the organization structure. As one works through this exercise consider the following:

- How will you support multiple regions, divisions, or business units?
- What leadership level, from both organizations, will be represented in each governing body?
- What functions require management positions to provide focus?

 *We suggest at least two tiers; most common is a three-tier model; some organizations have four tiers*

 *Many find it helpful to name the tiers. For example, a common three-tier naming convention is "Top-to-Top, Board of Advisors, and Operations Committee"*

### Peer-to-Peer (Two-in-a-Box) Relationships

Once the parties have identified the key roles and tiers, they can assign team members into the governance framework. Getting the right team members plugged into ongoing governance ensures the parties are fostering appropriate relationships and connections at the right levels. Creating Two-in-a-Box peer-to-peer relationships for each key role at each level ensures the parties are fostering the right connections at the right levels. For each tier, determine who will be Two-in-a-Box partners (Fig. 16.4).

 *Most teams find it helpful to put actual names in the boxes during this exercise. However, when you draft the actual contract schedule, we recommend using titles — not name. Using positions or titles will prevent you from having to update the contract schedule every time a new person rolls on/off the account.*

| Tier Level _____ Partner 1 Member | | Tier Level _____ Partner 2 Member |
|---|---|---|
| | peer to | |
| | peer to | |
| | peer to | |
| | peer to | |
| | peer to | |
| | peer to | |
| | peer to | |
| | peer to | |
| | peer to | |
| | peer to | |

Add or delete rows as appropriate

**Fig. 16.4**  Two-in-a-Box Partner Template

## Cadence

A key design principle is to designate a formal cadence for each governance tier. For example, in an outsourcing relationship, one may have Tier 2 governance meet face to face for a Quarterly Business Review. For each tier, determine the appropriate cadence (Fig. 16.5).

## Continuity of Resources/Key Personnel

Consider the decision you have already made to mutually identify a limited number of people designated as "Key Personnel" for both parties (Fig. 16.6).

*Ensure these people are truly key to the smooth functioning of the relationship, as the process of replacing them will be significant.*

| What | Cadence | Purpose/Agenda |
|---|---|---|
| Top-to-Top (Tier 1) | | |
| Board of Advisors (Tier 2) | | |
| Operations Committee (Tier 3) | | |
| Others? (Tier xx) | | |
| Other? | | |

Add or delete rows as necessary for your plan.

**Fig. 16.5** Determine Appropriate Cadence

| Partner 2 Key Resources | | Partner 2 Key Resources |
|---|---|---|
| | peer to | |
| | peer to | |
| | peer to | |
| | peer to | |
| | peer to | |

Add or delete rows as appropriate.

**Fig. 16.6** Continuity of Resources/Key Personnel

Once one has identified the Key Personnel are identified, the parties should agree on and document a contractual provision that prevents either party from unilaterally removing, replacing, or reassigning Key Personnel for a specified timeframe. This concept is often known as a Key Personnel clause. Consider the following when drafting these rules:

- What is the process for one party to propose a replacement resource?
  - What is the desired timeframe for notification?
  - What is the approval process for the new Key Personnel?
- What is the process for the buyer?
  - If different, why and is it fair?
- Develop and document a process for communicating Key Personnel changes.

## Onboarding

Onboarding is often an overlooked governance practice. Good governance should always include commitments on how the parties will ramp up new staffing in Key Personnel roles on the team. This includes determining the onboarding activities and other training most appropriate for the agreement and relationship. When you draft your governance schedule, it is helpful to write a description of the training and onboarding requirements to which the parties agree to hold each other accountable.

*Many organizations find it helpful to have one or more resources designated as "onboarding" resources, which are chartered to formally ramp up new team members on the Statement of Intent and contractual components essential to that person's job. This often includes a formal PowerPoint presentation delivered by the designated individual(s).*

*Some organizations create customized online learning modules (for example, a pre-recorded PowerPoint presentation/webinar) that outlines the key components of the parties' agreement and why and how it is different.*

*Some organizations require a "test" to ensure key governance roles understand the intent and contractual obligations they will need to "live into."*

## Issue Resolution

Good governance means having a formal process for managing issues. Start by creating a classification system for issues from least problematic to most problematic. These definitions should be included in the formal agreement. Figure 16.7 provides an excellent reference that can be leveraged or modified.

 *Many organizations find it helpful to link real examples to each classification to make it easy to gain consensus on what each means.*

 *We recommend at least three categories and a maximum of five.*

You will also need to define the steps of the formal issue-resolution process. Some organizations use a flow chart, others a bullet process, and still others a table. There is no "right" answer. Strive to create a sense of accountability, resolving issues promptly using an agreed-upon escalation and decision process. The issue resolution process should:

- Set time frames for resolution
- Establish clear responsibility from operational levels through executive leadership
- Verify that the breach of contract process follows the overarching master agreement

Last, determine how to track and report issues.

| Classification | Definition/Impact |
| --- | --- |
| Issue | Medium impact; low urgency |
| Concern | Medium impact; medium urgency |
| Problem | High impact; high urgency |
| Conflict | Unresolved problem |
| Breach of Contract | Unresolved conflict |

**Fig. 16.7** Issue Classification example

*Many teams incorporate a flow chart and even outline decision rights for each governance tiers. For example, Vancouver Coastal Health and Compass granted decision rights and authority at the lowest level employees to solve issues with a cost of less than $50. This meant even a custodial worker could spend up to $50 to resolve an issue without having to get a supervisor's approval.[10]*

## Relationship Management Mechanisms

Determine the mechanisms (methods and activities) that will measure the ongoing health of the relationship. For each mechanism, specify the intended purpose—what will be accomplished by each (employee satisfaction, customer satisfaction, a leading indicator of issues or problems, etc.).

 *Some organizations have several mechanisms for capturing performance and relationship management criteria. For example, P&G uses a mix of audits, a customer satisfaction survey, a Relationship Assessment Survey, and performance against key performance indicators.[11]*

 *The actual mechanisms do not have to be completed to complete your agreement. We have seen organizations take up to 3-6 months to finalize the mechanisms.*

 *Consider using a Compatibility and Trust Assessment overall health of the relationship such as how Island Health and the Hospitalist used the CaT assessment (as explained in Chapter 12).*

 *Factor in things that "bigger picture" or do not fall into a frequent cadence. For example — annual budgeting cycle, financial reviews, etc.*

## Contract Work

Once you have designed the governance framework, you will need to document the decisions and commitments to managing the relationship as part of the formal agreement. Most teams reference the governance framework in the actual master agreement but document the details of the governance framework in a Schedule. No matter how you technically approach incorporating your governance, it is essential to remember that contractually including governance commitments is a foundational element of any formal relational contract.

## A Look Ahead

Once the contracting parties complete the five steps in creating a relational contract, they and their team will be firmly on the path to establishing their playbook for a successful working relationship. The next step in the journey is taking the contract from a simple written document and transforming it into the way of working—creating mutual value, mitigating risk, and becoming an excellent commercial partner.

## Notes

1. Florian Mosleinand Karl Riesenhuber, "Contract Governance—A Draft Research Agenda," *European Review of Contract Law*, Vol. 5 (2009), p. 248.
2. See the Merriam-Webster definition of governance at https://www.merriam-web ster.com/dictionary/governance.
3. See Kate Vitasek, Mike Ledyard, and Karl Manrodt, *Vested Outsourcing: Five Rules That Will Transform Outsourcing*, 2nd ed. (New York: Palgrave Macmillan, 2013); Vitasek, K. et al., *The Vested Outsourcing Manual* (New York: Palgrave Macmillan, 2011). Also see "Unpacking Outsourcing Governance: How to Build a Sound Governance Structure to Drive Insight Versus Oversight, A UT, CEB IACCM white paper available from the Vested Library, https://www.ves tedway.com/vested-library/.
4. Ian R. Macneil, *Contracts: Instruments for Social Cooperation* (South Hackensack, NJ: F B Rothman, 1968).
5. "Dell Embraces Vested Outsourcing," *SupplyChainBrain*, (video) January 10, 2014. Available at https://www.supplychainbrain.com/articles/17881-dell-emb races-vested-outsourcing.
6. See Vitasek, K. et al., "How Dell and Fedex Supply Chain Reinvented Their Relationship to Achieve Record-setting Results" (Case Study) *University of Tennessee*, June 26, 2018 and David Frydlinger, Oliver Hart and Kate Vitasek, "A New Approach to Contracts," *Harvard Business Review*, September–October 2019. Available at https://hbr.org/2019/09/a-new-approach-to-contracts.
7. Moslein and Riesenhuber, Ibid.
8. Many books and courses are devoted to designing good governance. For example, the University of Tennessee offers 24 modules on governance as part of the *Creating a Vested Agreement* online course see https://www.vestedway.com/ courses/creating-vested-agreement-2020/. Chapter 7 of *The Vested Outsourcing Manual: The Guidebook for Creating Highly Collaborative Relationships* covers governance. The Sourcing Industry Group offers an entire course on the topic and consulting firms provide a plethora of consulting advice on the topic.
9. Kate Vitasek and Karl Manrodt, with Jeanne Kling, *Vested: How P&G, McDonald's, and Microsoft are Redefining Winning in Business Relationships*

(New York: Palgrave Macmillan, 2012). Also see Vitasek, K. et al., "Vested for Success Case Study: Microsoft/Accenture OneFinance," University of Tennessee, 2012. The case study is available for free download at https://www.vestedway.com/vested-library/.

10. Vitasek, K. et al., "From Competitive to Collaborative Bidding Approaches: How Vancouver Coast Health Harnessed the Potential of Supplier Collaboration for Environmental Services" (Case Study) University of Tennessee, March 6, 2016. The case study is available for free download at https://www.vested way.com/vested-library/.

11. See Vested, Ibid. and Vitasek, K. et al., "How P&G and JLL Transformed Corporate Real Estate" (Case Study) University of Tennessee. 2012. The case study is available for free download at https://www.vestedway.com/vested-lib rary/.

# Part V

## Are Relational Contracts Legally Enforceable?

The last question we are often asked is: *"Are relational contracts really binding? Would a court enforce them?"*

Answering the question of legal enforceability is significant for three reasons:

1. When one asks about the enforceability of the relational contract, we enter into the core of legal contract theory which raises the question of why *any* contract is enforceable. This is a question where legal scholars cannot agree even though numerous attempts have been made.
2. There is no unified contract law applicable in all jurisdictions over the world. The cost to conduct the research needed to answer the question of whether a formal relational contract as proposed in this book is globally enforceable would be daunting, if not impossible.
3. Much of the weight in the decision will depend on the express details of a specific contract and relationship. Enforceability of any contract may hinge on a specific paragraph, sentence, or even a comma.

With these three reasons in mind, we suggest it is folly to contend that all relational contracts are enforceable. Instead, we set out to provide an overview of why formal relational contracts, as outlined in this book, are legally enforceable—or at least should be.

Our ambition for this final chapter is both high and modest. High, because we intend to substantiate that relational contracts (as presented in this book) are indeed enforceable in a court of law. However, we are also modest because we cannot provide all the evidence needed to claim that every relational contract is enforceable in every jurisdiction around the world based on current laws at the time of publication.

Another question is whether it is necessary to make the relational contract enforceable, i.e., to make the relational contract into a formal, legally binding contract. As we have said earlier in this book, it is not mandatory; there will be many benefits of improved collaboration and stronger relationships even if the relational elements such as the guiding principles are not incorporated into the formal contract. However, in our view, the end-goal should be a formal relational contract unless there are good reasons not to.

The following chapter starts with an overview of contract in law, setting the stage for how to address the question of whether a formal relational contract is legally enforceable. The focus shifts to a deep dive on the principle of the good faith doctrine and how a formal relational contract seeks to uphold, enhance and help enforce the concept of the doctrine of good faith between contracting parties. Last, we review significant court rulings regarding relational contracts at the time of publication, which point to relational contracts being upheld in courts in the UK and Canada.

# 17

# Legal Considerations of Relational Contracts

This book has predominantly discussed contracts from a social or economic perspective that can be studied scientifically. In this chapter, we are entering the world of *contract law*, which requires another pair of glasses and a different set of questions.

## What Is Contract Law?

Generally speaking, the term "contract law" refers to a body of sources, which through history have become the accepted answers to legal questions about contracts. In most jurisdictions, contract law comprises a body of statutes, preparatory works to such statutes, court cases, and legal doctrines. Most countries have some form of legislation, such as the Uniform Commercial Code found in the United States. However, some countries rely more on judicial practice and case law. Regardless of the jurisdiction, there are three fundamental questions contract law aims to answer:

1. When are parties considered to have entered into a binding contract?
2. What rights and obligations do the contracting parties have?
3. What are the remedies for contract breaches?

These questions appear in, as an example, the United Nations Convention on Contracts for the International Sale of Goods (CISG).[1] The CISG applies to

© The Author(s), under exclusive license to Springer Nature                    **261**
Switzerland AG 2021
D. Frydlinger et al., *Contracting in the New Economy*,
https://doi.org/10.1007/978-3-030-65099-5_17

the sales of goods between contracting parties from different United Nations member states unless the parties have outlined other provisions in their contract. Part II of CISG deals with the first question above and sets out rules regarding offer and acceptance familiar to all law students. Part III of CISG is the main body of the convention and focuses upon the questions two and three (noted previously), including obligations on the seller to provide the agreed-upon goods on time and at a certain quality. The buyer's obligation to pay the agreed-upon price and remedies if the seller or the buyer breaches the contract, as well as numerous other aspects, are also covered.

Contract law statutes in most jurisdictions follow a similar structure and cover similar content as found in the CISG.

## Freedom of Contract

An underlying principle of contract law in most jurisdictions is *freedom of contract*. This principle simply means it is up to the parties to decide what rights and obligations they should have. Often, this principle is expressly set out in statutes. For example, the freedom of contract is set out in article 6 of CISG which states: "The parties may exclude the application of this Convention or, subject to article 12, derogate from or vary the effect of any of its provisions."[2] The general statutes under CISG come into play when the parties have not agreed upon a specific matter.

There is no jurisdiction where there is complete freedom of contract. For example, contracts to assassinate someone are either illegal or unenforceable. Contract laws in most countries often have legislation applicable to consumer contracts aimed at protecting consumers' interests. Employment contracts and lease contracts are other areas in which freedom of contract is often restricted.

## Interpretation of Contracts

Another important area in contract law is the *rules for contract interpretation*. If a court is asked to solve a dispute between two contracting parties, the court will typically start by confirming whether a binding contract exists. The fact that the parties do (or do not) have a contract may be at the center of a dispute between the parties. However, most contract disputes related to the second and third questions noted previously (what rights and obligations the parties have and what the remedies shall be for breaching them). For example, the parties may disagree whether a seller was obliged to deliver a good at a certain point of time and therefore whether the seller has delivered late or not. If a late delivery has occurred, it may be necessary for the court to determine what the remedies should be (e.g., damages, right to terminate the contract) if not stipulated in the contract.

When answering such questions, the court must review and consider the contract. For example, the written contract may include rules about delivery times, but the rules may be ambiguous. Or the contract may be silent about delivery times. In both cases—ambiguity and silence—the court must interpret the contract to establish what rights and obligations the parties have. In most jurisdictions, construing the contract is viewed as an exercise where the parties' intentions at the time of entering the contract are established.

The rules for contract interpretation vary between jurisdictions. For example, common law courts around the world such as the United States, UK, and Canada typically place more emphasis on the written wording of the contract. Civil law courts such as those in Germany and France look beyond the four corners of the written document. Nearly every jurisdiction has clearly defined rules and/or protocols for contract "gap-filling." Common law courts can, for example, apply a concept called "implied terms," which means there are some rights and obligations not explicitly set out in the contract that are considered part of the contract since the parties must be assumed to have "implied" them when entering into the contract. Civil law courts also use similar methods but do not use the concept of implied terms.

It is important to note the basic principle of freedom of contract also applies to the rules of contract interpretation. For example, contracting parties often include a clause that states if there is a conflict between the main body of a contract and the appendices, the wording in the main contract document shall prevail. In an instance of ambiguity or error, this "rule" guides the court on how to interpret the intentions of the agreement.

The fact that there is freedom to contract regarding the rules for contract interpretation is highly relevant to relational contracts and is discussed in more detail below.

## The Good Faith Doctrine

In answering the question of whether a relational contract as described in this book is enforceable, it is essential to combine the basics of contract law with a concept known as the *doctrine of good faith*. The main reason why we argue that the formal relational contracts as we describe in this book are indeed enforceable is there exists, in most if not all jurisdictions, a doctrine of good faith. Courts use the good faith doctrine to interpret and enforce contracts on more moral grounds. When one writes a relational contract based on the six guiding principles as we recommend, the parties are in essence tying into the existing doctrine and duty of good faith. The parties use freedom of contract to say: "This is what good faith means to us." As such, the courts will be obliged to listen to what the parties have expressed in their contract.

Samuel Martin writes in "The Evolution of Good Faith in Western Contract Law"[3] that the concept of good faith has existed since the Roman Republic, when preeminent Roman legal scholar Cicero wrote: "Ut inter benos bene agier oportet et sine fraudatione." This is interpreted as "one must act well, as among good men without fraudulence." Roman law recognized the concept of "bona fide" and most Western civilizations have developed legal systems that require "good faith" between contracting parties. For most jurisdictions, the concept of good faith or bona fide means fidelity to promise.

In US law, the legal concept of the implied covenant of good faith and fair dealing arose in the mid-nineteenth century because "the express contract language, interpreted strictly, appeared to grant unbridled discretion to one of the parties."[4] In 1933, with *Kirke La Shelle Company v. The Paul Armstrong Company et al.*, the New York Court of Appeals said:

> In every contract there is an implied covenant that neither party shall do anything, which will have the effect of destroying or injuring the right of the other party, to receive the fruits of the contract. In other words, every contract has an implied covenant of good faith and fair dealing.[5]

While there is no single definition of what good faith in contracting is, common law jurisdictions typically equate good faith as asking what "the average reasonable person" would have understood the parties to have meant at the time of their agreement.[6]

## A Frustrating Concept

The concept of good faith is frustrating to many because as the exact legal function and definition is vague.[7] To make matters worse, the function and meaning vary across jurisdictions and philosophy of use. Civil law nations such as Germany and France have codified the obligation of good faith into law. Other jurisdictions—especially those that fall under common law, such as the US, UK, Australia and Canada—are much more vague about the concept of duty to apply good faith in contracts.

The concept of good faith falls into what legal and moral philosopher Ronald Dworkin calls an "interpretive concept."[8] The concept of good faith is not like a physical object such as a chair. A chair has agreed on criteria which, when fulfilled, make people agree that a certain thing is a chair. Rather, the concept of good faith is similar to concepts such as decency, politeness, or evil. While people universally understand these concepts, they do not necessarily agree on the criteria needed to be in place to call a certain behavior decent, polite, or evil. Instead, it is necessary to look at the social practice regarding the application. This means that the concept has to be interpreted, often in a back-and-forth movement. The social practice in which the concept is used is analyzed to interpret the meaning of the concept; likewise, the social practice itself is interpreted by applying the concept. In essence, social norms emerge which help people understand what behaviors are decent, polite, or evil. What is "good faith" in contracts? Below is a summary of how various jurisdictions "see it."

## Good Faith in the United States, Germany, and France

The *United States* is relatively straightforward when it comes to the duty of good faith. The United States Uniform Commercial Code (UCC) Section 1-203 states: "Every contract or duty within this Act imposes an obligation of good faith in its performance or enforcement." §205 of the US contract law text, "Restatement of Contracts Second" adds: "Every contract imposes upon each party a duty of good faith and fair dealing in its performance and its enforcement." Last, UCC Section 2-103(1)(b) contains a definition of good faith saying, "good faith in the case of a merchant means honesty in fact and the observance of reasonable commercial standards of fair dealing in the trade."

The direction is clear; if a contract dispute occurs, the parties can refer to these rules, claiming that the other party has breached an obligation to act in good faith.[9]

In *Germany*, the concept of good faith appears in the concept of "Treu und Glauben". §242 of the German Civil Code provides (in translation): "The debtor is bound to perform according to the requirements of good faith, ordinary usage being taken into consideration." §157 of the same act adds: "contracts shall be interpreted according to the requirements of good faith, ordinary usage being taken into consideration." The *Treu und Glauben* norm has been described as an open norm, suggesting "a standard of honest, loyal and considerate behavior of acting with due regard for the interests of the other party, and it implies and comprises the protection of reasonable reliance."[10]

In *France*, good faith is addressed in the concept of "Bonne foi." Article 1134 of the French Civil Code provides that contracts should be performed in good faith. Article 1135 (in translation) states: "Agreements oblige a party not only to what is there expressed but also to all the consequences of equity, custom and the law to give to the obligation according to its nature." The concept of "bonne foi" at least includes an obligation of loyalty and cooperation.[11]

Similar rules regarding good faith exist in most jurisdictions including Belgium, Italy, Spain, the Netherlands, Russia, Japan, China, Brazil, and India. While the exact meaning and function vary slightly between jurisdictions, the core message remains the same; the good faith doctrine is used to construe contracts and oblige contracting parties to act under basic principles such as honesty, loyalty, and integrity—all principles discussed in this book.

## Good Faith and Relational Contracts in UK and Canadian Court Practice

When asked whether relational contracts are enforceable, the most ardent skeptics are typically lawyers from common law countries, not least from England. It is commonly known among lawyers that the UK courts have not historically recognized the general duty of good faith in contracts. However, the concept of good faith entered into UK contract law when the High Courts of the United Kingdom ruled on the *Yam Seng Pte Ltd. v International Trade Corporation Ltd.* case in February 2013.[12] Interestingly, the UK High Court directly coupled the concept of good faith with the concept of relational contracts.

On January 23, 2009, Mr. Presswell (representing the company International Trade Corporation Limited) emailed Mr. Tuli, who represented the company Yam Seng Pte Limited. Mr. Presswell had been selling fragrances for forty years and he wanted to offer Yam Seng the right to sell the Manchester United fragrances in duty-free shops in several geographic territories in the Middle East, Asia, Africa, and Australasia.

Mr. Tuli agreed to do business. A short-term contract was signed, initially with a term from May 2009 until April 2010; it was later extended until December 31, 2011. The contract itself contained only eight clauses. According to the final clause, the agreement was to be governed by English law.

On July 29, 2010, Mr. Tuli emailed Mr. Presswell terminating the agreement for breach of contract. The case ended up in the UK High Court in front of the Honorable Mr. Justice Leggatt. In its claim for damages, Yam Seng claimed that ICT had breached the contract by:

- failing to ensure that orders placed were shipped promptly;
- failing to provide products when promised or, in some cases, at all;
- undercutting the duty-free price agreed with Yam Seng to offering the same products for sale at a lower price in the domestic market in the same territory in which Yam Seng was operating; and by,
- providing false information to Yam Seng on which ICT knew that Yam Seng was likely to rely on when dealing with its customers.

The Yam Seng-ICT contract was a typical example of an incomplete contract. The contract itself contained only eight clauses and was written by Mr. Tuli and Mr. Presswell, who were not trained lawyers.

Justice Leggatt could deal with Yam Seng's first and second claims by interpreting the wording of the contract. But this was not possible regarding the third and the fourth claim. However, Justice Leggatt found the facts were clear: ICT had allowed competing resellers to undercut the duty-free prices in countries such as Singapore. And ICT had provided Yam Seng with false information on which Yam Seng had relied.

The dilemma for Yam Seng? There were no obligations in the contract preventing ICT from acting in this way. Since English laws applied, this was highly problematic for Yam Seng. Yam Seng claimed that ICT had a duty to act with loyalty and thus *not* undercut the duty-free prices and to act with honesty by *not* providing false information—even if those duties were stated nowhere in the eight clauses representing the relationship. Yam Seng argued that ICT had an implied duty to act in good faith when dealing with Yam Seng and those duties of loyalty and honesty are part of this good faith duty.

The dilemma for Justice Leggatt? At the time of the case, Leggatt noted, "the general view ... appears to be that in English contract law there is no legal principle of good faith of general application."[13]

"What to do?" Leggatt must have asked himself. Well, he took a bold step. A *duty of good faith* could, according to Leggatt, be *implied* in "any ordinary commercial contract based on the presumed intention of the parties."[14] What this duty of good faith requires is, however, sensitive to context.[15] For example, in contracts that only involve a simple exchange, Leggatt found it hard to imply a duty to disclose information. However, the contract between

ICT and Yam Seng was not about a simple exchange, but rather a longer-term business relationship with interdependencies. Leggatt concluded the ICT-Yam Seng contract was a *relational contract*:

> 'Relational' contracts, as they are sometimes called, may require a high degree of communication, cooperation and predictable performance based on mutual trust and confidence and involve expectations of loyalty which are not legislated for in the express terms of the contract but are implicit in the parties' understanding and necessary to give business efficacy to the arrangements.[16]

With this as the backdrop, Justice Leggatt set a precedent and the ensuing trend for UK courts to imply good faith for relational contracts. This precedent has become persuasive in other jurisdictions, including courts following either common law or civil law jurisprudence.

For example, a similar step was taken by the Supreme Court of Canada with the *Bhasin vs. Hrynew* case.[17] Before *Bhasin vs. Hrynew*, the Canadian courts were divided on whether Canadian common law recognized a duty of good faith or not. With *Bhasin vs. Hrynew*, the Supreme Court of Canada firmly established that such a duty does exist. And again, the term "relational contract" appeared:

> Commercial parties reasonably expect a basic level of honesty and good faith in contractual dealings. While they remain at arm's length and are not subject to the duties of a fiduciary, a basic level of honest conduct is necessary to the proper functioning of commerce. The growth of longer-term, relational contracts that depend on an element of trust and cooperation clearly call for a basic element of honesty in performance, but, even in transactional exchanges, misleading or deceitful conduct will fly in the face of the expectations of the parties.[18]

The evolution in the UK and other common law countries has continued with other cases. The most significant (at time of publication) is *Alan Bates and Others vs. Post Office Limited*.[19] On March 31, 1998, Mr. Alan Bates entered into a contract with the British Post Office granting Bates the right to become a sub-postmaster and run a post office branch in his store. A few years later, the Post Office implemented a new computer system named Horizon. As part of the Horizon initiative, Mr. Bates and all other sub-postmasters were required to use the new Horizon system. The Horizon system became the foundational basis of operations between the Post Office and the sub-postmasters, which included how the Post Office and sub-postmasters managed accounting practices. But, Mr. Bates and hundreds of other sub-postmasters ran into problems when the Horizon system showed accounting shortfalls from the sub-postmasters. The Post Office called for payment of the deficits and, in many cases, terminated sub-postmasters for failure to pay. Mr. Bates and the other claimants held that they were not in breach of contract nor had failed to pay; rather, there were errors and bugs in the Horizon system, showing incorrect accounting figures.

Nearly twenty years later, the case ended up in the UK High Court as a group litigation with over 500 claimants. The case landed in front of the Honorable Mr. Justice Fraser.

The court needed to construe the contract as previously discussed. This would mean analyzing the implicit terms of the written contract and determining the implied obligations of the parties. Mr. Bates and the claimants argued a large number of contractual terms should be implied including:

- To provide a system which was reasonably fit for purpose, including any adequate error repellency;
- To cooperate in seeing to identify the possible or likely cases of any apparent or alleged shortfalls and/or whether or not there was indeed any shortfall at all;
- To communicate, alternatively, not to conceal known problems, bugs, or errors in or generated by Horizon that might have financial (and other resulting) implications for the claimants; and
- Not to suspend the claimants (i) arbitrarily, irrationally, or capriciously, (ii) without reasonable and proper cause and/or (iii) in circumstances where the Post Office was in itself in material breach of duty.

This brought up the main legal issue of the case; was the contract a relational contract? For *if* the contract were relational, the parties would fall under the duty of good faith the UK put into practice with the *Yam Seng Pte Ltd. v International Trade Corporation Ltd.* case in 2013. As such, many of the implied terms stated by the claimants would prevail.

Having reviewed the *Yam Seng* case and several subsequent similar cases, the High Court concluded that under UK law, there is no *general* duty of good faith....

> ...but that such a duty could be implied in some contracts, where it was in accordance with the presumed intentions of the parties. Whether any contract is relational is heavily dependent upon context, as well as the terms. The circumstances of the relationship, defined by the terms of the agreement, set in its commercial contact, is what decided whether a contract is relational.[20]

A key outcome of the *Bates* opinion was the High Court—for the first time—defined a litany of characteristics describing the attributes of a relational contract. It was now easy to "see" what was meant by a relational contract. These characteristics included:

- There must be no specific express terms in the contract that prevents a duty of good faith being implied into the contract.
- The contract will be a long-term one, with the mutual intention of the parties being there will be a long-term relationship.
- The parties must intend that their respective roles be performed with integrity, and with fidelity to their bargain.
- The parties will be committed to collaborating with one another in performing the contract.
- The spirits and objectives of their venture may not be capable of being expressed exhaustively in a written contract.
- They will each repose trust and confidence in one another, but of a different kind to that involved in fiduciary relationships.
- The contract in question will involve a high degree of communication, cooperation, and predictable performance based on mutual trust and confidence and expectations of loyalty.
- There may be a degree of significant investment by one party (or both) in the venture. This significant investment may be, in some cases, more accurately described as substantial financial commitment.
- Exclusivity of the relationship may also be present.

The High Court also analyzed the more specific meaning of the duty of good faith being applicable for relational contracts. Justice Fraser held that "both the parties must refrain from conduct which in the relevant context would be regarded as commercially unacceptable by reasonable and honest people. Transparency, cooperation, and trust and confidence are, in my judgement, implicit within the implied obligation of good faith."[21]

The case ended in December 2019 when the Post Office settled out of court for £57.75 million after the Post Office lost an additional appeal in the UK court system.

## The Use of Good Faith in Contract Interpretation

So, while a good faith doctrine seems to exist universally, there is no universal standard approach for determining how to apply it. The methodology for interpreting the contract used by the UK High Court is insightful, but not compulsory outside its jurisdiction. To establish whether the contracting parties are under a duty of good faith, the court first looks at the relationship, asking whether the contract can be defined as a relational contract. If it is a relational contract, obligations not explicitly set out in the contract are considered and the parties' behaviors (good faith) are considered. This method of applying the doctrine of good faith differs from how the duty is used in the United States, Germany, or France, where a *general* duty of good faith exists.

The UK court's approach to classifying contract types (simple/transactional vs. relational contracts) makes sense in a world more and more characterized by commercial arrangements where relational contracts are a good fit (refer to Chapter 9). The UK's approach also aligns with the views of Ian Macneil, Oliver Williamson, and the University of Tennessee researchers, which all state there is a continuum of types of relationships/contracts between buyers and suppliers.[22] If one uses the continuum logic, it is sensible that the scope of the duty of good faith should vary depending on the nature of the commercial relationship.

Regardless of the jurisdiction, one point is clear and compelling. The concept of good faith serves a function in the practice of contract interpretation, both when contracts are ambiguous and where they are silent. Other tools also serve this function, such as the doctrine of implied terms, as used in the common law cases described above. While there is overlap between these "tools," a distinctive characteristic of the good faith doctrine is its connection to moral and ethical principles such as honesty and loyalty. Courts use the concept of good faith to interpret contractual language and to fill in gaps where the contract is silent by using such principles. For example, in the Bates case, Justice Fraser found the Post Office's behaviors to be "oppressive" and the Post Office liable for their lack of transparency and cooperation in resolving the issues raised by the sub-postmasters.

It is safe to contend there will likely never be a universal definition of good faith across all jurisdictions—or perhaps even a common definition across all types of contracts in a single jurisdiction, such as in the UK evolution. However, one thing is common regardless of which jurisdiction one studies; the concept of good faith is used as a moral lens, imposing obligations regarding honesty, loyalty, and integrity not explicitly set out in the contract. Even though this may be contested, it can be argued the good faith doctrine serves as a switching point between law and morality when it comes to contracting.

## So Just What Is Good Faith? And Who Gets to Decide?

A key question, however, remains: *what does good faith mean since there is no common definition?* And *who gets to decide?* From one perspective, it is not very important to have a universal definition of good faith. Why? The basic principle of freedom of contract gives contracting parties the ability to define what good faith means *for them* in their unique contract. This is indeed what we recommend contracting parties do when adopting the six guiding principles of reciprocity, autonomy, honesty, loyalty, equity, and integrity. In doing so, the parties simply add clarity to what is now a very vague and generic good faith concept. A court or arbitration tribunal would then, when construing the contract, be obliged to follow the parties' definition to eliminating ambiguities and filling contractual gaps.

One can easily argue that the meaning of good faith can be found in the six guiding principles. They already underlay many of the contract laws in various jurisdictions. Specifically, each guiding principle is a social norm acting in the broader societal system of norms. A goal is to prevent the contracting parties from harming one another when doing business. Seldom has the good faith doctrine been used where one or more of these guiding principles was not used.

Some skeptics have argued the inclusion of the guiding principles in a formal relational contract is redundant. Why include them if they already apply as generalities lumped together as "good faith"? The logic maintains that they are already included in contract law and how courts interpret cases. There are several reasons for this.

First, the good faith concept is vague. By formally detailing the general rules of conduct between the parties, the parties provide more clarity to themselves and the courts on how they want the contract to be interpreted. Formally drafting and explicitly integrating the guiding principles overcome a flawed assumption that all users know what good faith is. Take for example the *Bates* case. Justice Fraser's judgment stated the Post Office's behavior was oppressive.

Should the Post Office assume all of its employees consistently know what good faith is and how to act? From the court ruling, it is obvious many of the Post Office employees and management in the *Bates* case did not hold a consistent definition of "acting in good faith." Taking the time first to agree, then write down, and finally include the guiding principles in the actual contract document helps the parties understand the nuanced meaning of the duty of good faith—something the courts already apply—but at their discretion. Simply put, it is risky to assume that all employees working under a complex contract share a common definition of the nuanced concept of good faith. Why not help them "get it" by including simple, plain language in the contract around the guiding principles which set behavioral expectations?

Second, while a formal relational contract can guide the court on the parties' intentions over how they want to apply the duty of good faith, perhaps the most valuable feature of a formal relational contract is that it is written and used *by the parties*. As we saw with the Island Health-Hospitalists, a formal relational contract (as outlined in this book) becomes a rulebook or owner's manual for the contracting organizations—especially the users of the contract. Thinking of the contract as a living playbook instead of some legalese document stuck in one's desk drawer helps the contract users "live into" the intention of the broader organizations who write the contract. One of the most significant benefits of the five-step relational contracting process outlined in Part IV is it helps the parties think through and document their intentions for the softer side of the contract. How should the parties act (Step 3—Guiding Principles)? And how can they sustain the relationship (Step 5—live into the agreement using governance mechanisms)? In essence, when business happens, the contract users will have an understandable, valuable, and viable rulebook to fall back on, rather than an overly prescriptive, rigid, and irrelevant document, written by lawyers, for lawyers, in a way only lawyers can understand.

Third, like the contracting parties, courts do make mistakes. If the parties know what they want, why take the risk of having a dispute in front of a judge that may interpret the contract against the parties' expectations and intent? For example, the UK Post Office was unhappy with Justice Fraser's ruling and appealed (which was denied). Consider for a minute the possibility that Justice Fraser was wrong. What if the Post Office had initially drafted what they felt were their intentions regarding good faith? Why assume Justice Fraser would just "know" what is best? Why would the contracting parties forego guiding the court on their intentions and expectations, instead of leaving the analysis and resolution to chance?

## Why Relational Contracts Are Enforceable

As we have seen in this chapter, most jurisdictions now include some aspect of the duty of good faith in contracting ties moral obligations to legal situations. When a contract is incomplete or silent on a matter, the court will construe the contract to best understand the contracting parties' intentions at the time of writing the contract. Contract law provides for freedom of contract. As such, the contracting parties can document how they would like the court to interpret their intentions if the parties litigate. We argue an excellent way to have the parties provide clarity on their intentions of what good faith is via the guiding principles, and how they advocate the contract be interpreted. And the court would be bound to follow the parties' intentions.

Therefore, we see little doubt that the relational contracts, as described in this book, will be enforceable in nearly all jurisdictions across the world. As noted in the Part V introduction, it is not mandatory to take this step and convert the relationship into a legally binding contract. Organizations not wanting to take this step should, however, think carefully. Let's say two organizations adopt a one-page relational charter similar to what the Royal Australian Navy did with the FFG program where the charter is not part of the actual contract, but which the parties still intend to live by. Depending on the context and not least jurisdiction, such a charter could be seen as having legal effects. For example, let's say that the doctrine established by the UK High Court in *Alan Bates and Others vs. Post Office Limited* would apply. If the parties adopt a relational charter, it is quite likely that they are entering into a contract considered a relational contract according to that doctrine. And they would then have to explicitly state that they intend that the contract is *not* a relational contract to avoid this, which may appear strange if the parties simultaneously are agreeing on establishing a relationship of trust and transparency.

Our point is that even those organizations that do not want to take the step to convert their relationship into a formal relational contract may still be doing this, depending on how the courts in their relevant jurisdiction interpret contracts.

## Notes

1. See the "United Nations Convention on Contracts for the International Sale of Goods (Vienna, 1980) (CISG)," *UN Commission on International Trade Law*, available at https://uncitral.un.org/en/texts/salegoods/conventions/sale_of_goods/cisg.
2. Ibid.
3. Samuel Martin, "The Evolution of Good Faith in Western Contract Law," Posted 25 May 2018. Last revised: 13 Jun 2018, *Yeshiva University, Benjamin N. Cardozo School of Law, Students.* https://papers.ssrn.com/sol3/papers.cfm?abstract_id=3177520.

4. Harold Dubroff, "The Implied Covenant of Good Faith in Contract Interpretation and Gap-Filling: Reviling a Revered Relic," *St. John's Law Review*, Vol. 80, No. 2 (2006), pp. 559–619.

5. Kirke La Shelle Co. v. Paul Armstrong Co., *Court of Appeals of the State of New York*, November 21, 1933.

6. Martin, Ibid. See also Peter M. Gerhart, Contract Law and Social Morality, Chapter 11 (Cambridge University Press 2021) where the author shows how the good faith requirement simply requires the parties to reasonably account for the interests of the other party to a relationship, given the relationships terms and history. That allows courts to determine enforceable obligations not expressly covered by the contract.

7. Peter M. Gerhart, *Contract Law and Social Morality*, Cambridge University Press, 2021.

8. Ronald Dworkin, *Law's Empire* (Cambridge, MA: Harvard University Press, 1986), p 45.

9. The US Supreme Court has not directly defined "good faith" in contracts, but some guidance can be drawn from Justice Potter Stewart's often-cited opinion in Jacobellis v. Ohio, 378 U.S. 184 (1964), which wrestled with the definition of pornography: "I shall not today attempt further to define the kinds of material I understand to be embraced within that shorthand description [of "hard-core pornography"], and perhaps I could never succeed in intelligibly doing so. But I know it when I see it."

10. See Simon Whitaker and Reinhard Zimmermann, "Good Faith in European Contract Law: Surveying the Legal Landscape," in Zimmermann and Whitaker, *Good Faith in European Contract Law* (Cambridge, UK: Cambridge University Press, 2000), p. 31.

11. Ibid., p. 37.

12. Yam Seng PTE Ltd v International Trade Corporation Ltd [2013] EWHC 111 (QB) (1 February 2013). Available at: http://www.bailii.org/ew/cases/EWHC/QB/2013/111.html.

13. Ibid., p. 121.

14. Ibid., p. 131.

15. Ibid., p. 141.

16. Ibid., p. 142.

17. Bhasin *v.* Hrynew, 2014 SCC 71, [2014] 3 S.C.R. 494 [Docket 35380]. Available at https://scc-csc.lexum.com/scc-csc/scc-csc/en/item/14438/index.do.

18. Ibid., p. 60

19. Bates & Ors v Post Office Ltd (No 3) [2019] EWHC 606 (QB) (15 March 2019). Available at http://www.bailii.org/ew/cases/EWHC/QB/2019/606.html.

20. Ibid. Section 721.

21. Ibid. Section 738.

22. See Chapters 1 and 2.

# Conclusion

Contracting practitioners are encouraged to consider Albert Einstein's often cited words, "To raise new questions, new possibilities, to regard old problems from a new angle, requires creative imagination and marks real advance in science."

Our goal in writing this book is to encourage commercial managers and contracting professionals—those within for-profit companies, public institutions, and outside law firms—to take Albert Einstein's advice and think beyond conventional transactional contracting in search of a better way to build long-term strategic relationships.

Remember, relational contracting itself is not new; it has been debated and discussed since the 1960s. However, we have offered a fresh perspective for a better way—*formal relational contracting*. Throughout this book, we have shown how the power of turning proven relational contracting practices into a formal relational contract can increase trust not just between individuals—but also between organizations. Ultimately formal relational contracts help prevent backsliding and shading that frequently slips into today's complex business relationships post-contract signing. Simply put, aligning informal relational contracting practices with the formal aspects of a contract can create a proven and powerful way to overcome the contracting paradox.

It is essential to understand that simply incorporating the relational aspects within an existing contract is not enough. Sadly, we have seen organizations try to cut and paste relational aspects in a contract and have hopes they will reap the rewards from relational contracting. For example, in one case, a contracting professional at a high-tech company cut-and-paste the Shared

© The Editor(s) (if applicable) and The Author(s), under exclusive licence to Springer Nature Switzerland AG 2021
D. Frydlinger et al., *Contracting in the New Economy*,
https://doi.org/10.1007/978-3-030-65099-5

Vision and Guiding Principles from a successful relational contract for logistics services in the Netherlands into a contract with a service provider offering similar services in Asia. The logic was simple; why take the time to go through the five-step relational contracting process we share in Part IV of this book if you can just leverage something from another contract. On the surface, it sounded like a quick way to create a formal relational contract. The results? While the high-tech company had a contract that expressed they would have a strategic relationship based on a Shared Vision and Guiding Principles, there was nothing *shared* about the vision at all. And the Guiding Principles were simply words on a page with empty actions behind them. The service provider quickly realized the relational aspects were lip service and something that was stuck in a drawer never to be looked at until the expiration date one year later.

Our experience in relational contracting requires three critical ingredients for success:

1. A mutual belief and commitment to the principles of relational contracting.
2. The investment of time working together through a formal relational contracting process to embed the principles as operational standards. We have provided a proven relational contracting process in Part IV (How) of this book.
3. The investment of time to maintain the relational contracting principles of your relationship, especially the adoption of an effective method for issue resolution and, as necessary, enforcement. Ideally, your formal relational contract will include relational aspects as outlined in Step 4 (Stay Aligned).

Simply put, the high-tech company had none of the three essential elements of a relational contract despite claiming that they had a formal relational contract.

## But What If...

You might be thinking, "What if my organization is not ready to make the shift to a formal relational contract?" While we strongly advocate for a formal and enforceable relational contract, we recognize it may not be possible for some organizations. The three reasons most often cited are:

1. Businesspeople often see limited use for contracts because they don't trust them or understand them. Large-scale uptake of relational contracts may therefore depend on simplification and fundamental changes in contract design, so they start to be practical operational tools. This is one reason why we are advocates of using plain language and visualization in contracts.[1]
2. There is limited case law for relational contracts, which creates uncertainty over their enforceability (especially under common law). As a result, many corporate lawyers remain nervous about the use of relational contracts. In addition, few have direct experience in either drafting or negotiating such agreements.
3. The size and value of your relationship do not warrant the necessary time spent.

If you find yourself in a situation that prevents you from creating a formal relational contract, we recommend you shift along the contracting continuum as far as you can.

One of the best ways to do this is to follow the lead of the Royal Australian Navy who used a formal relational contracting process to get to an informal relational contract. Following the five steps outlined in Part IV (How) is a proven relational contracting process that can be used for both informal and formal relational contracts. We just ask that you go into the process eyes wide open or you might find yourself in the same situation as Chrysler which backslid and shaded when the New Sheriffs rode in after the Daimler Chrysler merger.

Captain Greg Laxton, Executive Director Fleet Support Unit for the Royal Australian Navy, provides sage advice:

> The Royal Australian Navy had great success with relational contracting in the Navy's FFG Guided Missile Frigate program. However, it has been hard to replicate this success more widely because the relational success factors reside outside of the contract. While it is great to have a relational 'Charter' and associated governance processes – the Navy found that often the performance-based contract itself was not aligned with the intent of the relationship.
>
> As key leadership moves on there is a risk that the relational intent is lost and people revert to asking 'what does the contract say?' I believe that the 'formal' aspect is the missing magic sauce in achieving wider success with relational contracting across more programs. Integrating the relational constructs with the formal contract is a brilliant concept. I consider it a 'must do' for any large, complex contract.

RelianceCM offers another great example of how an organization can shift along the contracting continuum without a formal relational contract.[2] RelianceCM is a small outsourced contract manufacturing business in Corvallis, Oregon. Scott Schroeder (RelianceCM's third owner) learned quickly how cut-throat the contract manufacturing world can be. "We dealt with corporate buyers that used a hammer in negotiations. All our customers thought about was cost, costs, and costs. Every day we had to fight for customers because we'd hear things like 'Yeah, we love that you are local, but we can go to a manufacturer in China for a third of the price.'"

Schroeder was looking for a better way when he enrolled in the University of Tennessee's Vested Outsourcing executive education course on relational contracting for outsourced deals. Schroeder was invigorated as he left the course, but quickly became deflated once back in the office.

> I quickly realized getting customers to create a formal relational contract was like the tail wagging the dog. We were a small company dealing with mostly large businesses. We couldn't force our customers to change their contracts. So I went back to my notes. A key takeaway for me coming out of the UT course was that the heart of Vested is trust, transparency and compatibility between a buyer and supplier. I realized I could apply many fundamental Vested concepts to the way we did business, even if our clients didn't want to change their way. And if RelianceCM was willing to make the first move to change, we could perhaps change the way our customers saw us and eventually work with us.

Schroeder took the first step in the relational contracting process by laying the foundation by focusing on trust, transparency, and compatibility. One of RelianceCM's first moves was to be more transparent with their customers. Schroeder was surprised at how quickly transparency fostered trust. "Transparency is one of the key things we have found really buys us credibility and trust in the relationship as we begin a relationship with our customers. And the more transparent we are, the more transparent and open our customers became with us. What happened was we could have fact-based discussions about how RelianceCM was adding value for the money they were paying."

Of course, some clients did not respond or took advantage of transparency. Here, Schroeder realized their clients' values simply were not aligned with RelianceCM and he slowly shifted RelianceCM's efforts away from supporting these clients to those where the relational principles were paying off. In fact, the benefits of relational contracts were paying off in a big way and Schroeder admitted the early results even surprised him. In the first year, RelianceCM doubled its revenue and significantly improved its profit margin. Schroeder explains why. "Our conscious effort to be transparent and drive trust helped two key customers feel comfortable in significantly increasing business with us. And our increased trust means RelianceCM feels comfortable entering into shared risk/shared reward economics with their clients."

RelianceCM shows the power of relational contracting. "While RelianceCM has never created a formal Vested contract, we've learned first-hand the benefits of adopting Vested's WIIFWe foundation of trust, transparency, and compatibility. We understand what clients need and they understand what we're capable of, so there's limited wasted motion. If a client is not a good cultural or capability fit, we know when to say no. And for those that are a good fit, we are not afraid to pull out all the stops to make them successful."

## Variations of Relational Contracting

Over the years, we have seen more companies explore relational contracting well beyond one-to-one strategic business relationships, using the concepts to create a collaborative supply ecosystem. Relational contracting in multi-party environments is most effective when the various players in the ecosystem acknowledge their co-dependent relationships in terms of delivering products or services.

McDonald's offers one of the most impressive examples of this in practice.[3] McDonald's has come to learn the potential for successful innovation and risk management is exponentially increased through strategies that institutionalize collaboration not only between McDonald's and the suppliers, *but also between suppliers.*

In fact, McDonald's creates a virtual playground for suppliers to openly share breakthrough advancements, feeding off each other to drive improvements that not only benefit McDonald's, but the suppliers. John Burke, Executive VP, and CEO of Armada Supply Chain Solutions, puts it this way. "Suppliers have come to realize they really can't gain anything by not working with another supplier – but they can gain a lot if they can devise ways to improve overall System performance such as reducing costs or increasing sales."

People who are new to the System share their astonishment that McDonald'ssuppliers like working together. Eric Johnson, CEO of Baldwin-Richardson Foods, explains his reactions when he first came to the McDonald's System in 1997 after acquiring Richardson Foods. "Outside of McDonald's most of the suppliers are typically in a short-term win-lose environment that is typically cut-throat trying to win the next big RFP or purchase order. At McDonald's, I found myself sitting at the same table and engaging in discussions about how we could all partner to make real impacts for the System. No other customer I had ever dealt with was even close to this kind of collaboration." Johnson continues, "At McDonald's, I quickly learned that it is much better (and fun) to grow the pie than worry about how big your slice is today. There is plenty for all."

McDonald's and suppliers also benefit from risk management. Suppliers collaborate to create comprehensive, specific blueprints to meet any emergency condition that could develop, whether it's a quality or safety issue, or loss of assured supply due to disaster. OSI Group's Vice President, McDonald North American Business Team Lead Michael Boccio explains the value of working closely with his competitors. "There was a time when a competitor built a new facility in southern China. To their surprise, it turned out the Chinese military had an old munitions dump located directly under the neighborhood where the building was located. The supplier only became aware of this fact after a huge explosion happened underneath their plant one afternoon while the plant was closed. It took out about 20 square blocks and sent a cloud plume 2-1/2 miles into the sky that required diversion of air traffic at nearby Hong Kong International Airport. The contingency plan was in place. The OSI Group immediately trucked product the 1,500 miles to ensure McDonald's restaurants had assured supply and quality until the other supplier was able to recover. Things happen all the time...and all we have to do is pick up the phone."

When there is a contingency situation, the supply community "circles the wagons" to make sure McDonald's assured supply to the restaurants is not in jeopardy. Jose-Louis Bretones-Lopez works with McDonald's strategic sourcing and credits suppliers with amazing success stories. "Because of our suppliers, we find the supplies we need. For example – the floods in Australia and how horrible they were. We were able to get supplies to the restaurants against all odds. It's a very typical thing that everyone is scrambling. Distribution Centers are completely ruined. Roads are impassable. Cows are floating. But because of that strong commitment, we get food to restaurants."

But can the McDonald's System be replicated? While we have not seen another organization be as successful as McDonald's, we are starting to see others make attempts. Most recently, there are segments in the oil and gas and construction industries seeing benefits from developed *relational codes* across a group of companies. An example is the UKNorth Sea oilfields, where demanding geographic conditions combined with price volatility combine to drive a need for more dynamic approaches to contract and performance management.

Another example of a variation of relational contracting is when entire industries establish collaborative *industry codes of practice*. Industry codes of practice reduce disagreements and disputes and reduce or eliminate the cost and time associated with a resolution between trading partners in the industry. Legal scholar Lisa Bernstein was one of the first to shed light on this type of relational contracting in her article titled *Opting Out of the Legal System: Extralegal Contractual Relations in the Diamond Industry*.[4] More recently, industries such as the insurance and aerospace sectors are exploring the development of voluntary codes that would establish principles of governance to improve supply chain resilience, to increase efficiency, and, potentially, to streamline issue resolution.

We predict organizations and industries will significantly increase the desire to explore industry codes of practice to restore more balanced trading practices. Why? Industries today might be facing a pandemic, but next time it will be something else.

## Good Luck on Your Journey

We hope we have inspired you to add your organization's name to the growing list of organizations—the Canadian government, AstraZeneca, Discovery HealthMedical Scheme, EY, Stedin, and the Swedish telecommunications firm Telia—who are proactively using formal relational contracts to help build better strategic partnerships. Or perhaps you will be inspired by the story of Island Health and South Island Hospitalists, Inc. (SIHI) to get unstuck from what seems an impossible contracting situation. Whatever your motive, remember that formal relational contracts are not meant for every type of contract. However, they are especially powerful for highly complex relationships in which it is impossible to predict every what-if scenario. These include complex outsourcing and purchasing arrangements, strategic alliances, joint ventures, franchises, public-private partnerships, major construction projects, and collective bargaining agreements—such as the one between Island Health and SIHI. However, if you find yourself stuck remember the start of the journey can be as easy as how Scott Schroeder started: lay the foundation with Step 1 by changing the discussion to one of how to build a more trusting relationship by improving transparency and compatibility.

For many (and maybe most!), creating formal relational contracts will require a significant change in mindset. It will mean not only accepting that formal relational contracts are real, but they are a smart solution for strategic relationships where there is a high level of dependency, risk, and complexity. For those of you taking the challenge, we hope our research, insights, and the five-step relational contracting process help you challenge the status quo in your organizations. And for those wishing to continue their learning journey, we have outlined several resources in Appendix 2.

## Notes

1. Shawn Burton, "The Case for Plain-Language Contracts," *Harvard Business Review* (January–February 2018). Available at https://hbr.org/2018/01/the-case-for-plain-language-contracts. See also, Stefania Passera and Helena Haapio, "The Quest for Clarity—How Visualization improves the Usability and User Experience of Contracts," in Huang W & Huang M (eds.) *DVVA 2013: Innovative Approaches of Data Visualization and Visual Analytics* (Hershey, PA, USA), pp. 191–217.
2. Kate Vitasek and William DiBenedetto, "How One Small Business Competes with China Building Circuit Boards *and* Building Relationships," (Case Study) *University of Tennessee*, 2019. Free download available from the UT library at https://www.vestedway.com/vested-library/.
3. Kate Vitasek and Karl Manrodt, with Jeanne Kling, *Vested: How P&G, McDonald's, and Microsoft are Redefining Winning in Business Relationships* (New York: Palgrave Macmillan, 2012).
4. Lisa Bernstein, "Opting out of the Legal System: Extralegal Contractual Relations in the Diamond Industry," *The Journal of Legal Studies*, Vol. 21, No. 1 (January 1992), pp. 115–157 (The University of Chicago Press). Available at https://www.jstor.org/stable/724403.

# Appendix 1: Statement of Intent Examples

A Statement of Intent (SOI) is the foundational pillar of your relational contract. A formal relational contract should *formally* reference your Statement of Intent, because the Statement of Intent is one of the foundational components of a relational contract. At a minimum includes the parties Shared Vision and Guiding Principles. Many companies also choose to include Intended Behaviors Fig. A.1).

To develop your SOI, you will need to combine each of the work products you completed in Step 2 and 3 into a formal Statement of Intent (SOI). This

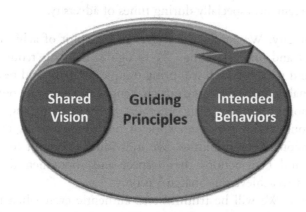

**Fig. A.1** Statement of Intent

© The Editor(s) (if applicable) and The Author(s), under exclusive licence to Springer Nature Switzerland AG 2021
D. Frydlinger et al., *Contracting in the New Economy*,
https://doi.org/10.1007/978-3-030-65099-5

appendix provides two real examples showing how a SOI can be formally embedded in your contract.

**Example 1**

The first example is a public example from Vancouver Island Health (Island Health) and SIHI (South Island Hospitalists, Inc). The Statement of Intent began on the bottom of page 1 of their contract and was the fourth item mentioned in their contract (preceding information was part of general background information):

4. Island Health, SIHI and SIHI Members have the following "**Shared Vision**":

   (a) Together, we are a team that celebrates and advances excellence in care for our patients and ourselves through shared responsibility, collaborative innovation, mutual understanding, and the courage to act, in a safe and supportive environment.
   (b) We will be recognized leaders in healthcare.
   (c) We will achieve this vision by building relationships grounded in trust and respect, and anchored in the following Guiding Principles and Intended Behaviors.

5. Island Health, SIHI, and SIHI Members have the following "**Guiding Principles**" that will guide us in our actions and decision making related to this Agreement, especially during times of adversity.

   (a) Reciprocity: We conduct ourselves in the spirit of achieving mutual benefit and understanding. We recognize that this requires ongoing give and take. We each will bring unique strengths and resources that will enable us to overcome our challenges and celebrate our successes.
   (b) Autonomy: We give each other the freedom to manage and make decisions within the framework of our unique skills, training and professional responsibilities. We individually commit to make decisions and take actions that respect and strengthen the collective interest to achieve our Shared Vision.
   (c) Honesty: We will be truthful and authentic even when that makes us vulnerable or uncomfortable. This includes honesty about facts, unknowns, feelings, intentions, perceptions, and preferred outcomes.
   (d) Loyalty: We are committed to our relationship. We will value each other's interests as we value our own. Standing together through adversity, we will achieve our Shared Vision.

(e) Equity: We are committed to fairness, which does not always mean equality. We will make decisions based on a balanced assessment of needs, risks and available resources.

(f) Integrity: Our actions will be intentionally consistent with our words and agreements. Decisions will not be made arbitrarily but will align with our Shared Vision and Guiding Principles. Our collective words and actions will be for the greater good of the relationship and the provision of patient-centered care.

6. With the **Guiding Principles** as our foundation, Island Health, SIHI and SIHI Members will actively promote the following "**Intended Behaviours**" to build a positive culture that will enable us to achieve our Shared Vision and extraordinary results.

(a) Patient-Centered: This is our true north. We will, in collaboration with patients and families, strive to identify opportunities to include them as members of the team. We will be guided by the patients' values, beliefs and interests in designing and delivering health care services within the context of our evolving system.

(b) Honesty: We will communicate the truth and we will trust in an open and honest dialogue that has congruence between words and actions. We will commit to transparent decision making.

(c) Collaboration: We will take a team approach to identify challenges, generate ideas, and together achieve desired outcomes.

(d) Empathy: We will continually build and maintain good relations through careful consideration, forgiveness and mutual understanding of one another's work, perspectives, emotions, and experiences, without judgment, to achieve our Shared Vision.

(e) Forward Focus: Together, we acknowledge and commit to learn from our past and move forward. We will pursue our Shared Vision as the primary focus of achievement and jointly champion changes that add value for our patients, families, communities, colleagues and ultimately ourselves.

(f) Communication: We will engage in proactive dialogue and transparency in a safe, collaborative environment to support our Shared Vision. In this pursuit, we commit to:
    i. Listen actively
    ii. Encourage participation
    iii. Seek clarity and be curious
    iv. Say what we mean
    v. Be kind

  vi. Hold good intentions
  vii. Be hard on the problem, not the person
  viii. Have courage for difficult conversations
  ix. Share information and discuss interpretation.
(g) Accountability: We will acknowledge and assume collective responsibility for our words, behaviors and decisions as evidenced by:
  i. Closing loops on communications
  ii. Making realistic commitments and follow-through
  iii. Circling back when we can't follow through and suggesting options
  iv. Being consistent
  v. Balancing bedside thinking with system thinking
  vi. The degree we conduct ourselves in accordance with the Intended Behaviors described above.

7. In the event that unfortunate differences arise between SIHI and Island Health or SIHI Members and Island Health, those differences will be resolved in accordance with the terms of the Agreement and the Dispute Resolution Process described in this Agreement.

## Example 2

The second example is from a global real estate and facilities management outsourcing agreement. The Statement of Intent starts as the third clause in the master agreement. In the agreement, clause 1 contained general background information and clause 2 was a list of schedules and the appendix.

## 3. Statement of Intent

### 3.1 Shared Vision and High-Level Desired Outcomes

For this Agreement, the Parties have committed to a Vested sourcing business model combining a formal relational contract with an outcome-based economic model. The Parties have mutually established the following "One Team" Shared Vision and the following high-level Desired Outcomes.

**Shared Vision**

*One Team, collaborating and innovating to optimize facilities and workplace services solutions, ensuring mission success while achieving all business objectives.*

- Be recognized by leadership and employees as a **critical strategic partner** who ensures mission success.
- Provide an **optimal workplace environment** to enable employees to achieve enterprise objectives and mission success.
- Sustain a **high-performing, fully integrated team**, and a winning culture.
- Be **outstanding stewards** of all corporate real estate resources.

## 3.2 Guiding Principles

To achieve their mutual Shared Vision and high-level Desired Outcomes, the Parties agree to a highly collaborative relational contract founded on the following Guiding Principles. These Guiding Principles are the shared set of critical social norms and values that will guide the Parties in all dealings during the Term of the Agreement.

**Guiding Principles**

- **Reciprocity.** Each organization will make fair and balanced exchanges that are mutually beneficial. We will place no expectation upon the other that we ourselves are not willing to bear.
- **Autonomy.** Each organization is empowered and expected to make objective business decisions that support achieving our Shared Vision.
- **Honesty.** Each organization will act in a sincere, forthcoming and truthful manner.
- **Loyalty.** Each organization is committed to this partnership, regardless of business changes.
- **Equity.** Each organization will act in an equitable manner to fairly balance risk and reward.
- **Integrity.** Each organization will act in a transparent and ethical manner.

## 3.3 Intended Behaviors

The following are the Intended Behaviors that both Parties will strive to follow day-to-day to foster an environment of trust, transparency, and compatibility. They represent the expected behaviors that will support the culture of the relationship and guide the One Team in its daily interactions. Buyer and Supplier each agree to proactively promote the Intended Behaviors with all One Team members within their respective organizations.

---

**Intended Behaviors**

**Empowered.** Each One Team member will act with confidence and the knowledge that they are authorized to perform their individual missions in support of the Shared Vision.

**Transparency.** Each One Team member will operate in a spirit of transparency to achieve our Desired Outcomes, which includes sharing our intentions, key data and information, and opportunities for improvement.

**Accountability.** Each One Team member will take ownership of their actions in every respect, in pursuit of our Desired Outcomes.

**Collaboration.** Teamwork is valued and necessary to achieve the full potential and success of the One Team. Each One Team member will actively engage others to achieve the Desired Outcomes.

**Communication/Openness.** Each One Team member will communicate in a truthful and respectful manner consistent with our Guiding Principles.

---

# Appendix 2: Resources to Support Continued Learning

This Appendix is for those wanting to continue their learning journey. Here we highlight resources—many of which are free.

## Case Studies and White Papers

Visit the University of Tennessee's dedicated research website where you can access dozens of case studies, including a complete case study of Island Health and South Island Hospitalists, Inc. The research library, in addition to dozens of case studies, contains white papers that are all open source—meaning they are free to access, and you can share with colleagues, clients, customers, or suppliers. Access at: www.vestedway.com.

## Courses

### The University of Tennessee Getting to We Online Course

The *Getting to We*® online course's unique format is designed for contracting parties (e.g., customer, supplier, a non-profit alliance, or joint venture partner) to complete together as a team. The course is designed to help you and your partner jointly develop a relational contract. You will be....

© The Editor(s) (if applicable) and The Author(s), under exclusive licence to Springer Nature Switzerland AG 2021
D. Frydlinger et al., *Contracting in the New Economy*,
https://doi.org/10.1007/978-3-030-65099-5

### The Relational Contracting Roadmap

| Online Course | Getting to We Toolkit | Workshops | Deliverables | Relational Contract |
|---|---|---|---|---|
|  |  |  |  |  |

- Team members review bite-size video-based topics on demand "just-in-time learning"
- Topics are aligned to where you are in the process, keeping you on track
- Includes a license to the *Getting to We* Toolkit®

- Practical resources and guides support you in "doing" – turning decades of relational contracting theory into practice!
- A Playbook provides the overall direction for each *Getting to We* step
- Individual Toolkits are used for completing Deliverables

- Your joint team (e.g. buyer and supplier) comes together in a series of workshops to collaboratively make decisions using the Playbook and Toolkits

- Team members complete Deliverables as they work their way through the course/workshops one Step at a time
- Core Team Leads ensure all Deliverables are complete

- Deliverables and decisions become the foundation of your relational contract
- Use the easy to follow Deliverables checklist to ensure you are not missing anything essential

*Frame your relational contract as you go!*

**Fig. A.2** The Roadmap to Getting to We—Relational Contracting

- Given a step-by-step roadmap for creating key components of your agreement
- Provided with a **RealPlay® Playbook** and *Getting to We* Toolkits that when completed properly will serve as the foundation for your relational contract (Fig. A.2). Access at: www.vestedway.com.

## University of Tennessee Collaborative Contracting Executive Education Course

The University of Tennessee offers a Collaborative Contracting Executive Education course (offered onsite in a two-day format and virtually in five mini-sessions). This intensive Executive Education course is ideal for individuals who want to take their negotiations and contracting skills to the next level. The highly interactive course provides an intimate Executive Education setting where participants learn cutting-edge relational contracting principles that "flips" conventional negotiations on their head, turning any negotiation into a more collaborative contracting exercise. Attendees learn how to complete the five-step process outlined in this book by getting hands-on experience applying their learnings to a case study where they negotiate and collaboratively construct a formal relational contract—including writing seven common contract terms such as liability and termination clauses which often pit business partners against each other. Access at: www.vestedway.com.

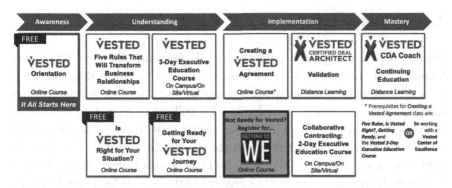

**Fig. A.3** University of Tennessee Relational Contracting Course Offerings

## University of Tennessee Certified Deal Architect Program

The University of Tennessee offers ten Executive Education courses as part of their Certified Deal Architect Program. While the overarching program is designed to help organizations create Vested agreements (a formal relational contract with outcome-based economics), courses can be taken as a standalone offering. For example, the Collaborative Contracting and Getting to We courses are popular courses for those wishing to focus only on relational contracting (and not on making a shift to outcome-based deal). Three of the courses are free (Fig. A.3). Access at: www.vestedway.com.

## Commercial Officers Group's Commercial Project Management Certification Program

Commercial Officers Group (COG) offers free webinars on Commercial Project Management, in which relational contracting is a central and recurring theme. The sessions emphasize the importance of applying the concepts, such as relational contracting and its tenets, to real-life situations through case studies and exercises. Access at www.commercialofficers.com.

# Plain Language Contracting and Contract Visualization

We highly encourage organizations to make the shift to formal relational contracts, while simultaneously adopting "plain language" and contract visualization techniques.

## Harvard Business Review

Shawn Burton, the general counsel for GE Aviation's Business & General Aviation and Integrated Systems businesses, offers a compelling reason to make the shift to plain language contracts. His *Harvard Business Review* article tells the journey of how he and his colleagues set out to replace the unit's seven excruciatingly complicated contracts with one that even a high school student could understand. In the article, Burton describes how the team went about achieving that goal and the lessons learned along the way. He shares the results at: https://hbr.org/2018/01/the-case-for-plain-language-contracts.

## Stefania Passera

Stefania Passera is one of the leading thinkers (and doers) behind the contract visualization movement. She has been pioneering legal design for almost a decade, bringing design thinking and doing to in-house legal departments, law firms, legal tech startups, and public organizations. She wrote her Ph.D. dissertation (and several other publications) on how visualization can enhance the usability and user experience of contracts. Visit her website to find an extensive library and resources on contract visualization at: www.stefaniapass era.com.

## WCC Contract Design Pattern Library

The World Commerce & Contracting (WCC, formerly IACCM) Contract Design Pattern Library is an ongoing collection of contract design patterns—effective, repeatable solutions to commonly occurring usability, and understandability problems in contracts. Contract design patterns can help one organize and communicate contracts more clearly, so that they are effectively read, understood, and acted upon. Access at: https://contract-design.worldcc.com.

# General Contracting Resources

## WCC General Library

The World Commerce & Contracting website is an excellent place to delve deeper into the art, science, and practice of contracting. The Resource Center and Library are some of the many resources on the WCC website. Browse the library as a visitor or join as a member. With over 60,000 members across over 180 countries and over 25,000 corporations, WCC is leading the way in responding to the demands of global networked markets. Access at: www.worldcc.com.

## The Commercial Officers Group Library

The Commercial Officers Group (COG) website is an additional excellent source of practical tools and resources for commercial contracting and relationship management practitioners. COG also provides weekly gratis webinars related to relational contracting, collaborative commercial relationships and commercial project management, and stores the recordings of past webinars in their Library. Access at: www.commercialofficers.com.

# Index

© The Editor(s) (if applicable) and The Author(s), under exclusive licence to Springer Nature Switzerland AG 2021
D. Frydlinger et al., *Contracting in the New Economy*,
https://doi.org/10.1007/978-3-030-65099-5

9783030650988